POWER - REAL POWER

DRAMAS OF THE EARLY CHURCH

James E. Kifer

New Harbor Press
RAPID CITY, SD

Kifer/New Harbor Press
1601 Mt. Rushmore Rd., Ste 3288
Rapid City, SD 57701
www.NewHarborPress.com

Ordering Information:
Quantity sales. Special discounts are available on quantity purchases by corporations, associations, and others. For details, contact the "Special Sales Department" at the address above.

Power - Real Power / James E. Kifer. -- 1st ed.
ISBN 978-1-63357-427-4

Contents

INTRODUCTION 1

CHAPTER ONE: IN THE BEGINNING 15

CHAPTER TWO: THE FIRST PERSECUTIONS 29

CHAPTER THREE: THE INFANT CHURCH.......................... 43

CHAPTER FOUR: THE FACE OF AN ANGEL 57

CHAPTER FIVE: NEW REALMS: NEW CHRISTIANS 71

CHAPTER SIX: BORN OUT OF DUE SEASON....................... 87

CHAPTER SEVEN: ROMAN ADVENTURE 101

CHAPTER EIGHT: HEROD AGRIPPA BECOMES A GOD ... 113

CHAPTER NINE: THE JOURNEY BEGINS 127

CHAPTER TEN: THE FIRST CHURCH TROUBLES............. 141

CHAPTER ELEVEN: THE INVASION OF EUROPE 155

CHAPTER TWELVE: A TALE OF THREE CITIES 167

CHAPTER THIRTEEN: ETHEREAL AND VANISHING
POWERS 181

CHAPTER FOURTEEN: I MUST GO TO JERUSALEM 195

CHAPTER FIFTEEN: CHAOS IN JERUSALEM..................... 209

CHAPTER SIXTEEN: POLITICS, RELIGION
AND CHRIST 225

CHAPTER SEVENTEEN: JERUSALEM OR ROME 237

CHAPTER EIGHTEEN: COLOSSUS ON THE TIBER............ 251

CHAPTER NINETEEN: HELP OF THE HELPLESS 263

CHAPTER TWENTY: DEATH AND LIFE.............................. 275

INTRODUCTION

In the highly popular 1959 cinematic classic "Ben Hur" an early scene sets the tone and much of the plot for the remainder of the story. Two close friends, the Jew Ben Hur and the new Roman military commander in Judea, Messala, have reunited after many years absence. As young boys they had been as close and even closer than most brothers, but life and the ensuing years had separated them. Here in early first century Jerusalem Judah had become a wealthy man of great influence while Messala was well established as a rising star in the Roman Army. In the prime of early manhood each veritably radiates strength, and especially in the case of Messala an almost maniacal lust for more power. Still friends but in a scene that reveals the rising tension between the two Messala beseeches his Jewish friend to join him in his ambitiously planned climb to the top, to the side of the emperor himself, in Rome. His face and countenance reveal naked ambition and do more than hint at a ruthlessness which will brook no opposition. With a gesture of his hand, he simultaneously dismisses the fanciful Jewish belief in God and exalts his one true god, the Roman emperor. This, avers the grotesquely ambitious Messala is "...

power, real power." The growing chasm between the two boyhood friends has now become unbridgeable, and they bitterly part as enemies. The movie, among other things, becomes a story of the lust for real power and revenge.

It is all quite famous and though from the realm of pop culture "Ben Hur" and this scene, among many, have long been part of the fabric of our shared culture. It is fiction, but it is a fiction that with an uncannily remarkable similarity of imagery mirrors the real culture of the ancient world and its preeminent power, Rome. Few subjects have matched Rome in the veritable mountains of study and scholarship that have been historically produced. This small work is not meant to add to that scholarship but rather to the backdrop of the times that will be discussed.

The traditional lore is that in the depths and mists of antiquity, perhaps in the 750's B.C., settlers began to establish a small village on the Tiber River in the central Italian peninsula. Their home was called Rome after its traditional founder, Romulus, and then and there its history, in large measure a history of growth and expansion began. The centuries passed, Roman and Italian culture grew and developed so that by 100 B.C. there was on the banks of the Tiber a substantial city which dominated the Mediterranean world. Rome did not yet rule an empire for it remained a republic, with at least a portion of its citizenry having a say in public affairs through elections. It had grown militarily powerful with a highly organized army, which generally responded well and with ferocity to competent leadership. A factual scenario had developed, one which is immediately recognizable and familiar to any modern observer. The Romans had begun to divide themselves into factions and even into political parties which represented the competing classes, economic and personal interests within the state. Immediately understandable to a citizen of the modern, English-speaking world the Romans had divided into two political parties, representing oft competing interests. At this time of circa 100 B.C. the two most noteworthy leaders and aspirants to power were two military figures, Gaius Marius (157-86 BC) and Lucius Cornelius Sulla (138-78 BC). Marius, the definite senior of the two, was a major military reformer, a champion of the common people and the true authors of a factor which would change Rome from a republic to an empire, i.e., the ability to inspire an army in its primary loyalty to him, as a general, rather than to the state.

The man who opposed Marius, Sulla, was a competent general, twice a Roman consul (the highest office of the state) and a man of a highly refined brutality both professional and personal. His name itself, "Sulla," hints at a certain force of destruction, and historically Sulla did not disappoint. Eventually Marius, Sulla, followers, and armies squared off in the first of the great Roman civil wars of the first century B.C., a bloody conflict known as the Social War. Sulla, more representative of some of the older, more traditional Roman interests, but mainly most accurately described as a vehicle for his own ambitions, was the victor. No magnanimity can be found in Sulla's victory. In mankind's long and sordid political and military history the number of rampaging and bloody tyrants and despots is legion, yet Sulla is still one who deserves mention. He was the first man in Roman history to achieve power (and it was absolute power) solely by force. Laws, ancient traditions, the rights of the citizens and the most basic of civil norms meant nothing to Sulla. Effectively this one man, whose reach and influence, has been underplayed by history, effectively destabilized the entire Roman political and power structure. Elected consul, in 82 BC he revived the ancient office of dictator, and from thence his rule was absolute.

Sulla heartily endorsed and utilized the institution of proscription, whereby as dictator evidence of his desire on a piece of paper was enough to condemn any man or woman to a cruel death. The Roman historian Plutarch remarked that "... Sulla filled the city with deaths without number or limits," and added that eventually some nine thousand Romans were proscribed and murdered. Sulla celebrated his victory over Marius and ascension to power not with mercy (laughable to him) but a period which may be described as a sort of dessert of blood pudding after the main course of victory in the Social War. Like all men and women, though, Sulla passed from the scenes of this life. The historians relate that he submerged his appetites in caverns of debauchery and alcoholism and died in extreme pain with cirrhosis of the liver. Like all, though, good or bad, Sulla left behind a legacy, perhaps many legacies. For our interests, though, the legacy of Sulla most noteworthy was that he left in his wake the taste for rule by absolute power, a taste which always adhered to the Roman palate. Henceforth, the high and mighty, strived not for office, for responsibility or for mere authority but for raw, unrefined, absolute power.

With Marius and Sulla having joined the roster of deceased Roman notables, other men, ever more famous, entered from the wings and dominated the Roman stage. At various points, a trio of Roman aristocrats began to rise to the fore. As with all persons universally they had their similarities but also their differences. The first to make an entrance onto the Roman stage was Gnaeus Pompeius Magnus (106-48 BC), or more commonly to both his contemporaries and to history as Pompey the Great, or just Pompey. He was a soldier of great skill and had been a protégé of Sulla. He must have learned well for he soon acquired the moniker of "the Young Butcher," the name alone being adequate definition and description of the man to whom it is attached. Even to the many hardened veterans of the wars in which Rome always was involved young Pompey caught the eye of so many with his self-assurance, vanity, ambition, and undoubted skills on the field of arms. Pompey's early and mid-career days may best be described by the single phrase of "wars, wars and wars." He rose to high office and acceptance and favor of the upper classes which ruled Rome by his skill at arms. By 70 BC he had been named one of the two consuls of Rome so his entry and acceptance into the political, as well as the military arenas had been made. Still, for this power he remained a decidedly young man, and his days of greatest accomplishment and laurels remained. In the 60's BC Rome was beset with problems in its eastern regions, namely the eastern Mediterranean Sea where pirates had become so prevalent and well organized that they began to choke the eastern supply routes to Rome, a lifeline that was essential to the burgeoning power in Italy. So, Pompey, a brilliantly successful military commander on land but certainly no naval admiral was dispatched eastward. Unsurprisingly, though, for a man with whom success had become synonymous, under Pompey's command Roman forces defeated the pirates and reopened the eastern trade routes to Rome's tremendous advantage and relief. Pompey, though, was not the sort of man to be satisfied with minimal success. Under his authority now were large, experienced military forces with seemingly nothing more to accomplish. The eastern fringes of Rome's sovereignty held many appealingly delightful lands, all ripe for Pompey's conquest and the extension of Roman pre-imperial conquest. Into the countries now known as Syria and Jordan the Roman legions marched, and these ancient Biblical lands annexed to Rome. Even more interesting, though, did

Pompey find the land south of these two ancient kingdoms, a country different than any other. It was known to Rome as Judea, or "land of the Jews." Into Jerusalem itself came these strange Roman warriors from the west, representing a power so great that their leader, Pompey himself, entered the Great Temple, even the Holy of Holies itself and saw sights that baffled him. He was accustomed to religion, gods and goddesses created in statutory form or in the images of animals, birds or even insects. Now, though, this powerful general saw none of this in the most holy of places to the now subject Jews. Pompey did nothing though, no damage, no executions and off he went, eventually back to Rome. Yet this Roman conqueror had come to a physical scene that would be the stage for the greatest power struggle the world would ever witness.

Not only did Pompey return to Rome in triumph but he, in point of fact, received a "triumph," that special Roman celebration wherein the hero of the day is lauded and feted to a degree that he was sometimes declared to be a god. In his life this was already the third triumph which Pompey had received. For now, he was the darling of the masses and of much of the most influential classes and persons in Rome. He was made a consul, and his very name and presence radiated power. But Pompey was not alone.

Marcus Lucinius Crassus (115-53 BC), like Pompey, had been a commander of troops under Sulla, yet it was not for military glory alone that Crassus was to become known. This highly successful figure may likewise be described as the first successful businessman in politics, today a particularly American phenomenon. Crassus had large real estate holdings, was a highly active real estate trader and a construction contractor specializing in shoddy, overpriced housing. His historical reputation seems firmly affixed as ruthless and unscrupulous and one of grasping for wealth and power. To this we offer no contradiction. He was also wealthy from the ever-lucrative Roman slave trade, a wretchedly detestable business, which gave Crassus a special interest in this common Roman institution. So great was his interest that today, Crassus, to the extent that he is remembered outside history books and academic journals, is most associated with the actor Laurence Olivier who portrayed him in the 1961 movie "Spartacus", the great leader of a slave revolt in the 70's BC. With Pompey he brutally crushed the revolt, and the stage was set, at least to the hopes of Crassus, for his further advancement to the pinnacle of Roman power.

The third member of the First Triumvirate was a man who began with no particular reputation. He was, as were all these men a member of the Roman aristocracy, though of a minor branch. He was the youngest of the three, having been born in 100 BC, and from his youth was active in Roman politics, although his youth provided no military glory. A protégé of Crassus he was, though Crassus never really trusted him. From the least prepossessing background of the three triumvirs, his name was Gaius Julius Caesar. No author short of Shakespeare could adequately describe the character and accomplishments of this colossus in just a page or two, and certainly we shall make no such effort. His great opportunity came in 56 BC with a revolt of the Gauls, and he secured an appointment as army commander and with a few legions was dispatched to Gaul to suppress the rebels. In the space of seven years his troops suppressed and pacified Gaul (modern France), conquered modern Belgium, parts of Spain and for a period the southern half of Britain. He even marched his troops into the German lands as far east as the River Rhine. Even today this multi-talented genius is recognized as one of the great masters of Latin prose (though most was self-laudatory and self-glorifying). He was a military genius and administrator with few, if any, equals and could easily master men and situations virtually at will. Yet all this time he was away from Rome, the epicenter of power, to which he needed to return. The ultimate prize of sole and absolute power awaited in this onetime village on the Tiber River.

It was now 49 BC and as they always must, times had changed. Crassus was long dead, having been murdered in 53 BC at a Parthian wedding feast. Pompey remained a great power in Rome, still only fifty-seven, but perhaps more advanced by his years of sedentary lifestyle. Syria, Jordan, Judea, and the pirates were long in the past.

Caesar and his army had halted at the Rubicon River, north of Rome, and the Roman Senate had sent him directives that he was to disband his army, all in accordance with ancient Roman law and tradition. To Julius Caesar, though, laws were for other people to obey. With the power afforded by his own well-honed military skills and several powerful, experienced legions Julius Caesar entered Rome with his army. Rome would never be the same. All these events are well and thoroughly chronicled by many great historians, both ancient and modern. Suffice to say, though, a Second Civil War broke out between Caesar and Pompey, and its outcome was to be anyone's guess. The climactic moment of the war came at a place called Pharsalus in Thessaly. Caesar triumphed, Pompey himself became a fugitive and was finally run to ground in Egypt. There, he was murdered, and his severed head presented as a trophy to Caesar.

The great triumvirate of 60 BC, formed in the exigency of an equilibrium of power among three graspingly ambitious men was now reduced to one singular ruler, Gaius Julius Caesar. Crassus and Pompey died wretched deaths, their heads severed, and bodies mutilated and abased. Still, what a one remained, a man so talented in so many ways, so revered that in the immortal words of the great poet:

> "He doth bestrode the narrow world Like a Colossus, and we petty men Walk under his huge legs and peep about To find ourselves dishonorable graves."

No man in Rome's storied history, not even Sulla, had gathered to himself such power as had Caesar. The Senate proclaimed him dictator, later dictator for life, only because Caesar knew that the word "king" was anathema to the once proud Roman citizenry. So great was the power entrusted to this one mortal that the very word "Caesar" became translated as absolute ruler in the yet to be born languages of German and Russian, i.e., "Kaiser" and "tsar." Even today, with the presumed Biblical blessing of the Savior himself "Caesar" is synonymous with "state." This man's power was inexplicably great and grand, unchallengeable, and never to diminish except by perhaps his own death, the time and place doubtless reserved for his own magisterial selection. Or so, at least, everyone thought.

On the morning of March 15, 44 BC Caesar came to the Roman Senate chambers, an action generally of no particular significance. On this day, forever immortalized as the Ides of March, over twenty senators, armed with hidden knives and daggers, awaited him. All had their reasons for wanting him dead, and led by a true believer in the republic, Marcus Junius Brutus, over two dozen wounds were inflicted upon the surprisingly mortal man. As the blood drained from the butchered body of Julius Caesar so did all his power. The most noteworthy assassination in political history had claimed its victim. The First Triumvirate of 60 BC had been extinguished irrevocably.

The greatest plum of political power from antiquity was now ripe for the picking, and the question to be answered was the identity of the man who would first reach the tree to harvest the fruit. Brutus and his fellow assassin, Gaius Longinus Cassius, both experienced generals, organized armed forces in the ultimate hope of reestablishing the old republic. In a great clash at Philippi in Macedonia in 42 BC the republican forces met those under Mark Antony and a newcomer to the fray, the quite young Gaius Octavian (63 BC-AD 14), grandnephew and adopted son of Julius Caesar himself. The battle went to Octavian and Antony, Caesar's right-hand man, the republican forces dispersed, and Brutus and Cassius dispatched at their own hands. This put a finish to the republican past of Rome, and for the foreseeable future the nation would be ruled by the whims, edicts, and decrees of men alone. The only real question which remained was which men?

Its history had long accustomed Rome to joint rule by two or three men, none of whom at the onset of their power had the strength to overwhelm their co-regnants. So, it was again. Antony and Octavian (as he was commonly known) established a dual rule, but likely for the sake of appearances they included a third man, a general named Marcus Aernilius Lepidus (89 BC – 13 BC), an otherwise obscure figure who provided the third member of this new triumvirate.

In some ways Octavian provided a somewhat refreshing uplift to the sordid tale of Roman politics. It was a militarized century, with great armies, striving generals and important battles. While Octavian was not averse to military glory, he had the wisdom to know his limitations and relied upon a trusted friend Marcus Vipsanius Agrippa (64 – 12 BC) as his military general and advisor. Throughout the 30's BC both Octavian and

Agrippa matured, grew in stature among the Roman people and generally acted with wisdom and care.

As for Mark Antony even those of scant interest in history know something of the man, chiefly because of his long tryst with the Queen of Egypt, Cleopatra, formerly consort and mistress to Caesar himself. Antony, a man of undeniable military talents, long had maintained a reputation for harshness, crudity, and moral debauchery. His elevation to shared power did nothing to enhance or improve his character.

After the formation of this triumvirate Lepidus was soon dispatched by the other triumvirs, especially more powerful than he, and died in obscurity. A sharing of power between two men as ambitious as Antony and Octavian could not last, and ultimately a chasm was opened between the two. Like much of human history this was a period seemingly when all questions were settled by force of arms. In the naval battle of Actium in 31 BC Antony and Cleopatra's forces were routed by Agrippa. With the two lovers defeated their lives played out in what later generations have construed to be an almost farce of soap operatic stature. Each committed suicide, and at last Rome was ruled by one man, and one man only, Gaius Octavian. For better or worse, the power of Rome now lay in his youthful hands.

Octavian had more wisdom than almost any other Roman ruler and generally knew the proper methods and limitations of wielding the power of the state. History would demonstrate that he could wield power as ruthlessly and amorally as any man, yet his natural proclivities were towards peace. Formally and ostensibly, he recommitted many powers to the Senate, while firmly holding the state's greatest powers in his own hands. Proclaimed Augustus or "reverend" in 27 BC he was set above the entire state as the First Princeps ("first citizen"), but in point of fact the Roman Empire had been born with Augustus Caesar its first emperor.

Augustus's reign commenced the Pax Romana ("Roman Peace"), a two-hundred-year period not of absolute, but of relative peace. Augustus personally had few pretensions to military glory, and the Empire, except for very minor additions, had reached its geographical limits. A time of peace between nations, but not among contenders for power, for the jockeying of position to replace Augustus began many years before his death on AD 14.

Before this chapter is closed it seems to be a good point to review the fates of the main aspirants for power our essay has noted. Before Augustus arrived, our brief survey has noted eight historically famous men who contended for the sweet prize of power. Marius died a broken man, defeated by Sulla, yet Sulla himself died a miserable death in moral and alcoholic degradation. Of the Great Triumvirate of Pompey, Crassus, and Caesar two were murdered and one the centerpiece of the most infamous of all history's assassins. As for the latter, Brutus and Cassius, committed suicide after suffering a crushing defeat. This was likewise the fate of Mark Antony, leaving Augustus Caesar as the only man who obtained, maintained, and enjoyed power into an old age. He died as age seventy-seven and was succeeded by his stepson, Tiberius Claudius Nero Caesar (42 BC – AD 37), a man of no special talents or attainments and increasingly cruel and arbitrary towards the end of his reign.

The time, effort, strain, treasure, and blood expended upon man's insatiable desire for the temporary chimera of worldly power is evident. Its acquisition was only temporary, and its attainment made its holder the target for the next murder. Was power only for a short spell of earthly gratification and glory, for self-aggrandizement or for bullying and intimidating people and entire nations? Perhaps if the mighty Romans could not really come to terms with the proper usages of power no one could. Our cinematic fictional character, Messala, may have seen clearly the route to "power, real power," but was all this real power? On a day circa AD 30 outside Jerusalem in the obscure Roman province of Judea another man, not a Roman, had another answer. Before leaving a group of non-descript men whom he nonetheless loved with a desperate intensity he instructed them to return to Jerusalem where "... ye shall receive power." What ensued is the story of His and their living definition of "... power, real power."

CHAPTER ONE

IN THE BEGINNING

Here, somewhere close but nonetheless beyond the gates and walls of the great holy city of Israel, Jerusalem, stood eleven men on a pleasant late spring day. In this land of climatic extremes such days were gifts to be savored, but this one was different. After a three-year span, unlike any other lived before or since their Master was gone. He had been so many things to them, and He had repeatedly demonstrated gifts and powers denied to other men. Literally, He had loved them even to His own death, and they, as has the world for two thousand years, were trying to absorb the obvious facts of His death and resurrection. Yet fact it was, and as He had parted from them this man, who nobody had ever really known, had left them with the most enigmatic of all His words:

> "You shall receive power, after that the Holy Spirit is come down upon you: and you shall be witnesses unto Me both to Jerusalem, and to Judea, and in Samaria, and unto the uttermost part of the earth."

At this juncture perhaps the only word whose full meaning was truly grasped was "Jerusalem," where just a few weeks earlier history's most intensive and important drama had been staged. Yet even Jerusalem was not quite normal, for the Feast of the Passover was still in session. Jerusalem, a city of moderate proportions was intensely crowded with Jews from all nations and regions of the Diaspora. For a few weeks it became as packed and crowded as the most impacted zones of a modern megalopolis.

The Holy Spirit was, and even to many today His character, purposes and operations remain veiled in mystery. Still to them and to multitudes thriving yet today it was the word "power" which glowed but only through layers of ignorance, misunderstanding and bewilderment. What did these eleven men (soon to be twelve as a replacement for the fallen Judas Iscariot was selected) know of power? They were Galileans, a northern backwater region known for shepherds, farmers, and fishermen, who spoke in thick, crude accents immediately noticeable to the sophisticates from Jerusalem. The majority had been fishermen, and they were accustomed to being on the receiving end of the world's exercise of power. Most (but not all) were not brimming with formal education, but contrary to the thinking of pseudo-sophisticates that did not make them ignorant or stupid. Doubtlessly when they thought of power and its possessors, they, like all of us, immediately thought of the world in which they lived. To a Jew in the first century the two great sources of power with which he had to reckon were Rome and the Jewish religious establishment, in particular the priesthood.

All these disciples were observant, religious Jews, and they had been inured to the dictates of the Pharisees, Sadducees, scribes, the Great Council, the Sanhedrin and ultimately the high priest himself. They had aggregated to themselves power and formed the criminal conspiracy which had seemingly crushed the "new" religion taught by a non-descript Nazarene carpenter. This powerful Jewish religious hierarchy had relegated to itself the power to put any man or woman "outride the synagogue" if the poor miscreant ran afoul of the teaching of the establishment. In plain speech, they had the power to effectively wreck and even destroy the life of any man or woman.

The disciples were not historians, but they knew the world in which they lived. That world was Rome, where real power resided and was jealously guarded. Rome's presence was a daily reality of life with the tax collectors, the ubiquitous soldiers and the ever present, insufferably proud officials, the real and ultimate wielders of life and death power. Since 63 BC Judea had been a conquered land, and names such as Pompey, Julius Caesar, Mark Antony, and Augustus Caesars were more than historical identities, but had become daily reminders of the Jewish subservience to real power. This, the power to order thousands of soldiers to fight and die or to bend untold numbers of men and women to one's will is power, real power instinctively recognized in the time of the apostles and yet today. Was this the power they were to receive? They simply did not know, but after over three years with the great, now departed Master, they were somewhat expectant of being puzzled by statements He made. This was just the latest, but this one seemed to portend epochal changes even they had yet to experience. They obeyed their Master's voice, and into Jerusalem they came and assembled in an "upper room." With them were a few others, namely the brothers and sisters of Jesus of Nazareth, His mother Mary and Mary Magdalene. They were a perfect little congregation of the great unknowns of the world, but gradually this would change. Since these twelve men, the chosen apostles of Christ, will now become central to our story their names and identities need to be provided. They were Peter, his brother Andrew, the brothers James and John, whose father was Zebedee, Thomas, Nathanael (a/k/a Bartholomew), Philip, Matthew, James, son of Alpheus, Simon, and Jude (a/k/a Thaddeus), his brother, and the new man Matthias. The first six and apparently two more were Galilean fishermen, Matthew the occupational outsider as a publican and the others of undesignated occupations. An imposing group to be sure, and with but one substitution, the same men who had met not long before for the Last Supper.

It was but a few days hence that the apostles reassembled on the Day of Pentecost, the holy Jewish feast day, and in a twinkling of an eye the power structure of the world began to change:

> "And suddenly there came a sound from heaven as if a rushing mighty wind, and it filled all the house where they were sitting. And there appeared unto them cloven tongues like as of fire, and it sat upon each of them. And they were all filled with the Holy Spirit, and began to speak with other tongues as the Spirit gave them utterance."

The subsequent explanations of the meaning of these verses has been confusing, mischievous and at times even diabolical, but events described in detail will provide a reasonable, yet miraculous explanation. The first language for these men was Hebrew (or likely even Aramaic, an ancient dialect). Some likely spoke Greek as well since this was the lingua franca of the ancient Mediterranean world. The twelve, though, had been commissioned to "go into all the world and teach." "All the world" spoke a multiplicity of languages, and the miraculous gift of the Holy Spirit allowed all to understand the apostles in the language of each man and woman. It was a miracle, it was from God, and it was powerful, but it was just a modicum of the real power granted the apostles. Even miracles, though, come in different measures and degrees, and as astonishing as was this gift it was still simply a method for understanding the message. Certainly, it was not the message itself.

It was Peter, the outspoken, somewhat erratic, and un-predictable young fisherman, who stood up in the midst of a great assembly of Jews from many nations and began to speak. Neither he nor his fellow apostles commanded immediate re-spect for they endured the mockery of such as this:

"These men are full of new wine."

In that thick Galilean accent Peter began to speak, but though the voice may have been so familiar this was not the Peter of the denial. Neither was it the worldly exuberant Peter who believed he could walk on water as did his Savior, nor was it the supremely self-confident, even arrogant Peter of the Last Supper, who was so certain that his faith was far more advanced than the others. This was a humble man, but a man who now spoke with more power, real power than any man ever, oth-er than Christ Himself. To employ a Biblical phrase this was a man imbued with the Holy Spirit of God, and Peter recog-nized the historical and spiritual importance of the words he now spoke. To an audience of literally thousands of Jews, in Jerusalem for Pentecost, from "every nation under heaven" he wisely grounded his sermon in the Old Testament by proclaim-ing that at long last "... this is that which was spoken by the prophet Joel." Briefly (or at least briefly as recounted by Luke in the Acts of the Apostles) Peter gave a simple history of God's plan of redemption for humanity, a plan that pointed to and then culminated in God's own Son, Jesus Christ. Previously, the good apostle Peter seemingly had always acted and spoke with great self-assurance, but now his assurance was in the truth of which he spoke. His words began to crescendo upward and with power He spoke what remains the truth yet today:

> "Therefore, let all the house of Israel know assur-
> edly, that God hath made that same Jesus whom
> ye have crucified, both Lord and Christ."

To an assembly of Jews from widespread nations Peter spoke but no man nor woman who ever drew breath in this life could be excluded from the phrase "... ye have crucified." Many who heard the message "... were pricked in their heart, and said unto Peter and the rest of the apostles, Men and brethren, what shall we do?" These praiseworthy Jews identified a central (perhaps the central) problem of all humanity from Creation to the present and into the future, which is "what shall I do with my guilt?" Any thinking, sentient person is aware of his/her faults, short-comings and even abominable sins, and that person is aware of them until their cumulative weight becomes so overbearing that they break the sinner. That person who has no sense of self-insufficiency, of moral shortcomings and of true spiritual "self-helplessness" is in the scriptural phrase, truly a "brute beast." Yet, from the time of Adam their numbers are legion. Through Peter and the other apostles, though, God touched the hearts of these listeners, but He did so much more than provide a moment of self-reflection and guilt, a moment which easily slips away.

Thousands of years of Divine intentions and planning, of prophecies, of men and women of faithful deeds and of the ultimate offering of the only truly Lamb of God had lain the foundation for the words Peter spoke in answer to that simple question of "what shall we do":

> "Repent and be baptized every one of you in the name of Jesus Christ for the remission of your sins, and ye shall receive the gift of the Holy Spirit."

Remarkably it may be successfully asserted that more theological ink has dried on the phrase "gift of the Holy Spirit" through the ages than on the first simple declarative phrase, upon which our text will comment. On that late spring morning some two thousand years ago, humanity was offered the key to its redemption and salvation, and it has moved not an iota in two subsequent millennia. The key to salvation is Christ, and through him all doors are unlocked. The "keys to the kingdom," to power, real power, open not the locks to public office, to throne rooms, to armories of weapons, but rather they open the heart of the obedient disciple. Christ also provides an unlimited power that no earthly source dare offer. It is the key to Heaven and eternal life, and by any measuring rod that is power, real power.

Few, if any, organizations, have enjoyed such a successful and auspicious debut as did this Church established by Christ Himself. Over three thousand answered the apostolic call and were baptized, and the Church was born. Even by judging just the veneer of facts offered by the outward story, as observers we may discern the wisdom of God's commencing His Church at this place and at this hour in history. So many Jews from so many regions were gathered together at the most central location for all Jews, the city of Jerusalem. Though many of the first Christians lingered together in the city for a while eventually they went back to their homes, north, south, east, and west. By natural processes yet doubtless ordained by the wisdom of God the Church then had its first dispersion to many locales. Yet, many of the thousands of new disciples had come for only a short stay, and all provisions, especially food and water, were in limited supply. Not for the last time did many of these early Christians lack any sort of a dwelling place, yet the true love of God and the true Spirit of Christ already reigned supreme in the hearts of many:

> "And all that believed were together, and had all things common; And sold their possessions and goods, and parted them to all men, as every man had need."

Much pernicious nonsense has been written on this passage that the early Christians formed a socialist or communist society. Rather it seems a temporary expedient in answer to temporary circumstances. More than goods what these new Christians shared was the Spirit of Christ, which should ever be prepared to make sacrifices. Certainly, there were acquaintances, friendships, brothers, sisters, and the like, but many, perhaps most of this first church were strangers one to another. Likely the thought of power never passed the minds of any, yet all had been given a copious amount through their common indwelling of the Spirit of Christ:

> "They continued steadfastly in the apostles' doctrine and in breaking of bread, and in prayers."

Throughout the centuries which followed the Christian spirit has ever been manifest, but those first few days of the

Church's existence offer us an example of love, and care one for another that has never lost its golden hue. Even in Jerusalem it did not last to that widespread extent, but it is still a model to contemplate and emulate in the Christian walk. How did such a spirit of care and yes, love, of fellow human beings manifest itself from a movement that appeared to be dead and soon to be forgotten just two months before?

A reminder of the apparent weakness and dearth of power attached to Jesus of Nazareth and his followers must ever be contemplated. For three years a previously unknown Galilean carpenter had caused such an uproar that the rival factions of the Jewish religious establishment, many of whom bore copious amounts of ill will one to another, coalesced into a hard knot of conspirators who carried through the most masterful criminal conspiracy in history. Ordinarily, a man with the background of Jesus would have captured little or no attention from these self-anointed keepers of the flame of the Law of Moses and God's directives from heaven. Yet they were so successful that but a few weeks before they were reduced to a tiny clique of Jesus Himself and eleven loyal, but scared, disciples. Even that did not last for the Savior was gone. Any rational observer would grasp readily that this handful of well-meaning but apparently weak men would fade into the old tried and true fabric of the world, never to be heard from again. They lacked all those elements by which the world to this day measures real power. None had any fame other than perhaps a couple who had unwittingly drawn unwanted attention to themselves on that horrible night of the Savior's arrest and trial. As for money or lands all seemingly had made an adequate living, nothing more, nothing less. Save perhaps for Matthew, the successful publican, none had much acquaintance with wealth. Likely they came from good families, but families with neither wealth nor great influence. The concept possessing political power would have been laughable to any of them. That sort of power was greedily and violently guarded by the mighty Romans. Any that spilled or seeped from their grasp was clasped tightly by the ruling clique of the Jewish religious hierarchy and structure. Power, real power was foreign to humble fishermen and tradesmen from Galilee.

The real historical power was of the type and nature held by these Romans, many of whom had become legendary if not almost mythical. It was the power of a Pompey, a Julius Caesar or an Augustus, a power to direct huge armies of well-trained soldiers which could crush anyone or anything in their paths. It was the power to strip away the independence of any country coveted by Rome's voracious appetite. The power of the Jewish religious establishment was an endless series of mandates dictating the daily schedules, movements and even beliefs of its victims. Yes, it was power, real power, but power to what purpose and ends? Ultimately it was the power of the sword, and its ultimate extension was death and earthly oblivion. It, like all governments and states, was to be feared, certainly not loved, for an unwillingness or inability to accede to this power meant death and earthly oblivion. In our technocratic hyper innovative society of the twenty-first century nothing has really changed.

Peter and the other apostles who stood and spoke to the throng of listeners on that Day of Pentecost so long ago certainly had not that sort of power. Nor would they have wanted it. Their message was the one of true empowerment, and not limited to a few politicians, generals, and kings. It was (and is) the power of the answer to humanity's oldest question, perhaps never expressed better than by Job countless centuries before Peter and Pentecost:

"If a man dies, shall he live again?"

A marching Roman legion, fiercely armed and trained, often answered any question with death, and a word from Caesar or any of his henchman could be the terminal point for the earthly existence of any man or woman. The world's answer to this question then, now and until the planet's last gasping breath is a resounding no. Not only is there no life awaiting after this short terrestrial span but this temporal few years' residence on earth is not itself enviable. As a political philosopher once famously remarked:

"This life is short, nasty and brutish."

Most decidedly this was not the message borne by the apostles on Pentecost. Not only was the answer they gave to Job's question a resounding yes, but it was a positive response backed by incontrovertible proof. The founder of this religion and of His Church had died at the apparent power of the Romans and the Jewish establishment but had conquered death on that first Easter morning. Peter preached this to be sure, but even more wonderfully, he proclaimed that this same eternal life, neither nasty, brutish, or short, beckoned all the obedient disciples of the Savior. This was, and so remains, power, real power.

Almost all our knowledge of the early, "primitive" first century Church is given us in the New Testament, most particularly the book of the Acts of the Apostles, written by the beloved physician, Luke. It is an almost inexhaustible gold mine of stories, persons, and other treasured information. Most of all, though, it is a chronicle of an almost endless series of victories wrought by Christ and His apostles. It may just as easily be entitled the "Book of Victories." Yet to be victorious the victor of necessity needs a foe, a rival, an enemy, and who could have been opposed to the message brought by the apostles. It was not a victory over the Jewish officials who engineered the crucifixion of Christ, and neither was it a triumph over the Roman soldiers, who in the forgiving words of the Savior, "... knew not what they had done." It was no exercise of power overt the multitudes who taunted Him and shouted for His death. The victory, the first of many, the establishment of the Church on Pentecost, was a crushing blow for the only real adversary, Satan. Christ always had power over Satan, yet even the Son of God and the Son of Man was tempted by the deceiver and in the words of Genesis, he was able to "... bruise (the Savior's) heel." The victories of Jesus over Satan during the Savior's brief lifetime were numerous, but now He was gone. Only these men, no-account to Satan, of demonstrated weakness during the Passion, remained on earth. Yet these men, led by Peter, delivered a brutal blow on Pentecost, when now not so weak, inbued with God's Spirit, began in earnest the Church which Christ had died to establish. This was only the beginning of the victories over Satan and the world and only the onset of God's demonstration of His real power through the lives of the apostles.

The wonder of it all is still a marvel to contemplate. Some fifty days after their Rabbi, the Master, the Messiah Himself had been savagely seized, scourged, crucified and His body veritably hidden in a borrowed sepulcher, a dozen men, who when last studied and examined appeared like frightened children had now returned to the heart of the city where all these events had occurred. Not only in Jerusalem but they had gained the rapt attention of thousands and established the institution which the Savior Himself had promised would live forever.

By almost all standards to which the world, then and now, adheres, these twelve men expanded the boundaries of the definition for the word "ordinary." Ordinarily dressed, ordi-narily attired, of ordinary backgrounds, heritage, and families, of ordinary means and occupations, and of ordinary present worldly fame and notoriety (which meant none) to them were entrusted the keys of the kingdom. Their success was phenom-enal. Removed but one day from non-existence entity had be-come a burgeoning organization of several thousand of which these apostles were the very foundation. It is difficult to the point of impossibility to think of any organization, political, re-ligious social or otherwise which ever grew so large so quickly from such an unlikely beginning. To paraphrase a famous twen-tieth century figure "never in the field of human endeavor have so many owed not much, but everything, to so few." The Church continued to expand rapidly there in Jerusalem. Ethnically it was still a Jewish phenomenon, and a wise question would have centered on whether it would engulf the entire Jewish people. Surely even those bitter opponents of Christ, the conspirators in his death, could now comprehend the futility of opposition and perhaps even the grim reality of their previous sins. The power of this movement and its message was so great that sure-ly, they would now step aside. Or, at least, that is what an ob-server might have thought.

CHAPTER TWO

THE FIRST PERSECUTIONS

The apostles had shown themselves to be serious men, who accepted serious instructions in a serious way. Christ had directed them to go into all the world to teach the truth, but first the "world" was Jerusalem. The birth of the Church on Pentecost was a spectacular success and gave portentous promise that Jerusalem remained a fertile ground for even more success. One day at about three in the afternoon, a traditional time of prayer, Peter and John went to the Great Temple where multitudes consistently gathered. The Temple, aside from its great religious significance, had become a type of community center for the Jews, where thronging crowds gathered for a miscellany of purposes. Among other reasons these included a steady stream of the infirm, beggars, outcasts and other detritus of society who depended upon the temporary good graces and good will of just a few individuals from the steady stream of crowds to obtain just enough substance to eke their way through another miserable day. A prime example was a man, hopelessly crippled from birth, who was carried every day at placed at the gate Beautiful, to beg for alms.

It was just another dreary day, and as the crowds streamed by, he continually begged for just a little, anything which would help him sustain the bare sustenance of life. His success was rare, but this day he asked alms of two young men, Peter and John. Their eyes, perhaps with an intensity second only to that of the Savior Himself looked upon the pitiable man, and it was Peter who exclaimed:

> "Silver and gold have I none; but such as I have give thee; In the name of Jesus Christ of Nazareth rise up and walk."

This was not the fraudulent chimera of "faith healing," for the man's religious beliefs are not even mentioned. Neither is it a business transaction, a commercial transaction, for no party received any money. It was a Divine act of mercy, properly ascribed to Christ, and Peter took the man by the hand and lifted him up in preparation for the first steps he would ever take in his life. Actually, the previous sentence contains an imprecision, for instead of steps "... he leaping up stood" and walked with the apostles into the temple "... walking and leaping and praising God." This nameless man, with a new life, had learned what countless others Biblically and forevermore that Christ always delivers more than expected or even imagined. He had hoped for a coin, and he was given a new world. Such a manifestation of real power was hardly unnoticed and:

> "All the people saw him walking and praising God."

For three years such miracles had been frequently displayed and had even become the common coin of the unique Nazarene Rabbi, but He was gone now, crucified by His adversaries. So, who were these two non-descript Galileans, Peter and John, and how was any of this even remotely possible?

While all wondered about this and other matters, Peter, ever the evangelist, employed the opportunity to engage the rapt attention of the Temple worshippers to his brief history of Jesus and His rejection by them, his own people, the Jews. Peter and John had utilized the power of God to heal a man with an awesomely miraculous wonder, but he was more committed to the even greater message of the redeeming power of Christ's blood, a real power which made the guilty into the innocent. Yet before we modern observers leave the sermons of Peter and John, we are compelled to delineate a difference between the powers of governments, kings, governors and assorted rulers and the power here displayed by two seemingly ordinary fisherman. The power of the state is the power of the sword, for the state arranges and even takes life, sometimes legitimately. Never once, though, from antiquity to our more modern electoral dictatorships have the power brokers or the power-hungry given life. The real power demonstrated every day, but here most dramatically was and remains in giving life.

It is not known whether the common phrase "history repeats itself" had yet been coined in the early first century AD, but surely the concept was on the minds of certain who now enter, or perhaps more accurately reenter the picture. Christianity is not a secret religion performed under any veil or darkness. It is the religion of Light and openness, and the apostles' teaching was at the zenith of openness in first century Judea, openly teaching multitudes in the Temple itself.

Luke with his unfailing succinctness and thoroughness so writes this description:

> "And as they spoke unto the people, the priests, and the captain of the temple, and the Sadducees came upon them. Being grieved that they taught the people, and preached through Jesus the resurrection from the dead. And they laid hands on them, and put them in hold unto the next day: for it was now eventide."

So, they were jailed for the night, and the next day they were placed before this entire group, now joined by their leaders, the high priests Caiaphas and Annas and an assembly of the Sanhedrin. Marvelously they had reunited and reassembled substantially the entirety of the conspiracy which had crucified Jesus. Always it is dangerous to attempt to penetrate the thoughts of another person when those thoughts have not been revealed. Yet here an exception seems permissible. It had been a mere two or three months since the upstart Jesus of Nazareth had been confronted, crucified, and placed in a borrowed tomb, never to be heard from again. Certainly, those days to which his followers were already giving reference as the Passion were emotional and stressful, but they were past. Rumors of the Nazarene's return from the dead were as pathetic as these two rough, ignorant men which now stood before the Sanhedrin in all its majesty. Certainly, such a sight and scene was the last thing Caiaphas and his cohorts ever expected to behold. Further, they remembered that Jesus was practically bereft of any supporters on Calvary. His closet followers were cowards. Yet here they were, worsened by a night in jail, crude of speech in those thick Galilean accents and hardly plausible representatives of any sort of power.

This religious establishment had seen miracles, fulfilment of centuries of prophecy, the Son of God in the flesh, irrefutable evidence of His resurrection and now His once cowed followers as bold as Christ Himself. Yet still they admitted in belief, nor did they admit fear. The fear, though, was integral to their reaction, for why else would they call an assembly of the Sanhedrin for the matter of a couple of scruffy street preachers. Judea was always full of religious eccentrics, teaching this or that. These two men were different, though, because from their word flowed real power.

Power was the issue on the Sanhedrin court docket this day, for when Peter and John were placed before them Caiaphas inquired:

> "By what power, or what name, have ye done this?"

Peter, not the man of the night of his denial but filled with strength gave the only conceivable answer:

> "By the name of Jesus Christ of Nazareth, whom ye crucified whom God raised from the dead, even by Him doth this man stand here before you whole."

These two young fishermen plainly clad in the ordinary garb of a Jewish working man now stood before the assembled lords, the high and mighty, a veritable who's who of the good and the great in the day's Jewish society. Their physical contrast between the two was itself arresting. So young they were and further bedraggled by a rough night spent in jail, rough but robust and darkened by a life spent working in the sun Peter and John were easily marked from the accusing assembly. Likely the two were the youngest by far and easily the most simply and ill dressed. Many, especially the chief and high priesthood, were draped in black robes of their offices, all trimmed and accoutered with various regalia and paraphernalia calculated to impress and awe any who were witness to their splendor. The top men, Caiaphas, Annas and perhaps others were attended by a retinue of servants.

Many, if not most of these men, were intelligent and well read, highly educated in the history and ways of a highly educated people. They spoke well, some even glibly, and had a polish which life had denied Peter and John, who they recognized as "ignorant and unlearned men," fishermen and Galileans to boot. Outwardly it was a scene eerily a replica of that night months earlier when another Galilean stood before them. Such were the contrasts that their inventory may be made endless, yet the two most essential contrasts have yet to be extracted from the scene. Initially, in terms of power the apparent reins of that prized commodity still lay in the hands of Caiaphas and his cohorts. What power do prisoners possess, yet the ensuing exchange will focus on the meaning of power, real power. The second contrast between the two is the most important of all, not just in an ancient Jewish building of two thousand years ago, but now and for all times hence. Peter and John were saved and were the bearers of the message of the saving power of Christ, while their captors, accusers, and inquisitors, even with all the pomp, prestige, and glitz which their offices held were doomed. Ultimately that is the only real contrast with humanity, as the scene unfolds to so demonstrate.

The priests get to the core issue as they open:

"By what power, or by what name, have ye done this?'

Or, stated otherwise "How can you perform these wonderful miracles when we, the self-proclaimed religious elite are bereft of such power?" Peter, filled with the true power of God's Spirit replies by both fact and accusation, fact that Jesus Christ is the source of the only true power and accusation that they are the ones who crucified Him. Of course, the religious leaders already knew the answer to their own question, and even more so Peter and John were so aware that they knew.

Right then and there the best and the brightest of the Jewish establishment could have begun the physical destruction of Peter and John, but they were wise enough to refrain. They were not so wise, though, that after a caucus among themselves wherein they admitted defeat they arrived at a judgment which heralded the weakness of their own cause:

> "And they called (Peter and John) and commanded them, that they speak henceforth to no man in the name of Jesus Christ."

Taken all in all neither the Bible nor any historical source ever records so puny an effort, especially by supposedly "powerful" men to silence Christianity. Immediately, both Peter and John showcased the ineffectuality of the rulers' decrees and threats when they offered their rejoinder:

> "Whether it be right in the sight of God to hearken unto you more than unto God, judge ye."

So off they went the two apostles returning to the rapidly growing assembly of the disciples of Christ, and the Jewish religious establishment, with all its pomp and power, ingloriously defeated. Their fellows in faith praised God and "lifted up their voice to Him in one accord." This first persecution, the feeble attempt at a display of intimidating power was such an abject failure that there in Jerusalem, the disciples, now numbering in the thousands, drew even closer together and shared each other's properties under the auspices of the apostles. The Church, the weak little Church, had captured a great victory. In the affairs of this world, though, no such prize as a permanent victory exists, as the next round with the same opponents demonstrated.

The power to perform the miraculous signs and wonders which so illuminated Christ's ministry was given freely by the Savior to the apostles. The Church, energized, electrified by its humble yet powerful leadership was a burgeoning dynamo of growth:

"And believers were the more added to the Lord
such as should be saved."

To the Jewish religious hierarchy and their complicit conspirators such as King Herod Antipas and the Roman governor Pontius Pilate this was anathema. The Galilean carpenter had been nailed to a cross and died months earlier, yet it did not appear to matter. This Christ was proving literally to be more powerful "dead" than alive. The sick, the handicapped, the tortured of any sort were coming to the apostles, and "... they were healed everyone."

The very core of the criminal conspiracy against Christ and His early Church exploded in rage:

> "Then the high priest rose up, and all that were
> with him (which is the sect of the Sadducees)
> and were filled with indignation."

They hurled the apostles into the common prison and doubtless planned their demise. Power, though, was not confined to either the priesthood or the apostles, and that night an angel opened the prison doors and so exited the apostles. Early next morning all the apostles returned to the Temple and began once again teaching the simple doctrines of Jesus Christ. At the same time the high priest and Council summoned their officers to remove the apostles from prison and once again face charges. Obediently the officers journeyed to the prison, but quickly returned to the high priest and gave a message which must have dropped the heart and spirit of the priest to some strata below the soil of Judea when one witness spoke:

> "Behold, the men which ye put in prison are
> standing in the temple and teaching the people."

Insistent upon continuing one of the longest spiritual losing streaks in history the captain of the guard received orders from the high priest to re-apprehend the offending apostles and bring the alleged miscreants to him for judgment.

Not just the duo of Peter and John were now brought before the priestly powers but rather all the apostles. Caiaphas, with the mad zealotry he had demonstrated against Christ Himself called them to justice for continuing to speak and teach about this man and "... to bring (Christ's) blood upon us. Peter, the most prominent of the apostles and a rock of strength replied with words that remain foundational to Christian morality:

"We ought to obey God rather than men."

Power so often loves to preen itself and, in some manner, strut its very existence upon a stage where its audience and especially its subjects are bedazzled by its glories. The thoughts are compelled to visit thousands of years of history, where even, perhaps especially, the religious authorities engaged in almost orgiastic self-glorification by their dress in beautifully tailored and colored gowns and robes, mitres, scepters, conical hats, jewelry all seemingly without end to awe and humble the "laity" with their spectacular displays of superior dress and finery. Alas in its ways, the Great Council, the Sanhedrin, was little, if any different. Berobed in black gowns these seventy learned men, supposedly Judea's finest arrayed themselves in a semi-circular manner, and in the midst of them was placed the wretched figure of the accused, already presumed guilty of heinous acts, and most often trembling with fear before the mighty.

In modern times a definition of insanity has arisen and been placed and circulated into common speech. It is a sort of strange hybrid between popular and folk cultures, but in one common form its expression is that "insanity" is the repeated performance of the same act expecting a different result than before. Although no member of the Sanhedrin is recorded as having evinced any signs of insanity, as a collective body the Sanhedrin seems to have gone mad. Their attempted intimidation of two prominent apostles, Peter and John, having failed, the council seeks to replicate the same scene with the entirety of the apostolic group, all the while hoping for and anticipating a different result. This second attempt at intimidation with the forces of power and persecution is poised to fail for numerous reasons. The Sanhedrin's attempt is mistimed. Only a few weeks earlier these same men, including and especially their most prominent, Peter, were huddled surreptitiously in a dark upper room, frightfully awaiting their personal doom after witnessing the death of their Master. This was the same Peter who on that dark night was in such an emotional and moral whirlpool of turmoil and fear that upon being recognized by a young servant girl went into a profanity laden tirade denying three times that he did not even know Jesus of Nazareth.

These twelve men, all weak in the world's substance and indicia of power now stood before the powerful Sanhedrin, with an outward display not of bravado but of peace, courage, and acceptance. They were not afraid of any blows which the powerful Sanhedrin led by the ferocious high priest Caiaphas might strike. Our present study of power compels the inquiries of "how?" and "why?"

The first two persecutions of the Church, the arraigning of the apostles before the Sanhedrin, was a contest, but a match of a strange character. The Sanhedrin had a great power, although it still lacked the power to condemn a man to death, which resided and firmly remained in the hands of the Romans. It did, though, have the power to imprison, to physically punish an offender and most terribly ominous of all, the power to put a Jew "out of the synagogue," effectively to excommunicate him from his own people, his own religion, and his own God. The Council's power was real, to be repeated and somewhat terrifying to the average Jew. The apostles, though, law abiding to a man, seemed without awe and in fact, unafraid of the terrors of Caiaphas and the Sanhedrin. The simple apostles, though, possessed the plenary power of the Holy Spirit and were enabled to perform miracles, signs, and wonders in the manner and with the Spirit of Christ. Such powers certainly did not make the apostles either morally or physically invincible, but their possession in the rights hands (such as the apostles) served as a marvelous antidote to the strutting power of men who seek not life but destruction.

It is the second power which the apostles cherished and motivated them, impelling them always forward through all persecutions, of which this was only the beginning. It was the Savior Himself that pronounced:

> "God is not the God of the dead, but of the living!"

These were the men, almost literally scared to death earlier who saw unequivocally the death of their Master and who had hurried away for fear of their own deaths. Yet three days more they, led by this same Peter and John, had all seen and touched the resurrected Savior. Theirs was more than faith, for it was sight as well. To them, as to all Christians in all the centuries now and forever, death was still a certainty, but it was no longer a defeat. It would be the momentary "twinkling" of passage from this life to the real life of eternity. The apostles always had that knowledge. They faced Jewish priests, Roman governors, kings, soldiers, both Jew and Gentile and possessed a real power, the power of the knowledge of the defeat of death. Though they would suffer harshness, hardships, and endless persecutions they already shared in Christ's victory over death. Questions may have remained, as yet they do for all disciples, but the overriding fear that this brief sojourn on earth is all anyone is allotted was banished. The fear of death yet dominates the minds of the multitudes, but not the hearts of Christians, and certainly not the apostles. This is a power, a real power, a disbelieving world, including all the Sadducees sitting on the Great Council is forever denied.

But for the moment at center stage stood a dozen non-descript young men, and it was time for the Sanhedrin to make the next move. Some members, already sick to death of the Nazarene's followers wished to kill them now and likely obtain the retroactive permission of the Romans later. Even in an assemblage of notables and greats such as the Sanhedrin, though, all are not equal. Its most illustrious member now rose to speak, with his person and words commanding rapt attention. His name was Gamaliel.

The name alone commanded authority and veneration among the Jews, even the members of the intelligentsia, the priesthood, and the Sanhedrin. Most remarkable, too, because while the overwhelming majority of these men were Sadducees, Gamaliel was of the opposing political religious party, the Pharisees. He was the grandson of Hillel, among many Jews still two thousand years later venerated as Judaism's greatest scholar. When Gamaliel spoke, others might not necessarily obey, but they would listen. Into this fiery furnace of hatred and vindictiveness trod Gamaliel speaking the language of compromise. The Sanhedrin, since the trial of Christ, had done nothing but spew venom and seek the destruction of the Nazarene and his deluded followers. As for this disreputable dozen unlearned blue collar figures arrayed before the great men of Israel, they showed not a scintilla's evidence of moderating of their "fanatical" beliefs. They must be either destroyed or freed.

Now Gamaliel sought to break the impasse, and when he rose to speak his words as ever commanded the rapt attention of the audience. Judea was the land of false Messiahs, and especially in those days preceding Christ they seemed to teem in super abundant numbers. Gamaliel reminded them of two in particular, men named Theudas and Judas of Galilee, both of whom came to naught, with they and their followers either killed or dispersed. Gamaliel asked that they examine this Nazarene cult in the same light, and let events themselves make the judgment:

> "And now I say unto you, refrain from these men, and let them alone: for if this counsel or this work be of men, it will come to nought. But if it be of God, ye cannot overthrow it; lest haply be found even to fight against God."

In the vernacular then, "Wait and see." Although Gamaliel's words are of great wisdom one is entitled to inquire of him, supposedly the single greatest authority on Jewish law and history, how much more evidence he required. A three-year ministry of Christ, open and in precise fulfillment of thousands of years of Old Testament prophecy, miracles, His own resurrection from the dead and now His followers performing the same signs and wonders. We know not whether Gamaliel himself ever became a believer, but the skeptical observer votes unlikely.

Meanwhile, the Sanhedrin agreed with the great scholar and released the apostles but not before "beating them" and commanding that they "... should not speak in the name of Jesus." What abysmal malice and folly for the apostles departed "... rejoicing that they were counted worthy to suffer shame for His name."

No organization ever began more triumphantly than this Church built upon the Rock of Christ Himself and led by men gloriously worthy to be its foundation. Thousands had become believers, and no threats of death, neither sword nor lash, seemed to injure it. Could anything or anybody halt its growth? The early disciples themselves contributed answers to this question.

CHAPTER THREE

THE INFANT CHURCH

With the exception of that original company of progenitors, both human and animal, all living organisms enter this world in a state of infancy. This includes that Church founded by Christ in the first third of the first century. After millennia of prophecy and years of gestation this institution was in many ways "born grown" on the Day of Pentecost. It was a "big" baby, three thousand members in day one and from the Biblical records as many as five thousand and more joining its roles with an astonishing speed. Like most healthy infants it sparkled with an initial allure of innocence, of non- and even other – worldliness that attracted observers, who even if they did not become a part of the Church themselves were fascinated by such a quickly born and risen institution. Again, like all infants it was extremely vulnerable to outside dangers, for its newness and seeming innocence made it easy prey for predators. Even its founder warned against wolves "in sheep's clothing" who would prey upon it, yet so certain was Christ of its strength and permanence that He pledged that "...the gates of hell should not prevail" against it.

The first Church was not a delicate or dainty infant. She (Christ always referred to His Church as His Bride) had grown so quickly and with little or no organization in the beginning. Save for the twelve apostles the first Church in Jerusalem had no array of officers, no elders, deacons, priests, bishops, prelates, or clergy of any sort. In one sense its diversity would have please even the most fanatical of modern diversity fanatics, for it was composed of persons from many, many different lands in the ancient world. In another sense, though, it was an affront to a modern diversity zealot, for all its members were Jews, Jews from many nations.

All the earlier Christians seemed to be gathered in one place, Jerusalem, inasmuch as so many had originally come to the capital for Passover and Pentecost. Already it was a massive organization, and the initial spirit of all disciples, later to be called Christians, was exemplary. That spirit, a true spirit of Christ, still a beckoning beacon for all Christians was described immediately after the Church's founding:

> "All that believed were together, and had all things common; And sold their possessions and goods, and parted them to all men, as every man had need."

The believer is thrilled by reading of such a Christian spirit, but honesty compels the informed observer to note the similarity to a Marxist foundation doctrine:

> "From each according to his ability; to each according to his need."

Was the founding Church red, a communist organization, what has always been deemed to be the very antithesis of Christianity? Wisdom and caution compels the inquirer to refrain from a quick answer to the question but instead rely on the historical and Biblical records to provide a more definitive answer.

For the moment we return to the early form of this bright new institution. Its organization was minimal, and in fact, practically nonexistent. The Jerusalem Church was blessed with the greatest leadership ever known by a religious body, the twelve apostles personally chosen by Christ Himself. The observer is permitted, even encouraged, to compare the primitive simplicity of the initial Church with the two millennia of churches, be they Catholic, Protestant, Orthodox, or other, which have followed in its wake. Christendom has become accustomed and inured to top-down organizations of multitudes of office holders, many sincere men and women of God with the true Spirit of Christ but too many careerists and bureaucrats who have found their comfortable niche in the religious realm. Sadly, this observation is reality's recognition, be it ancient, medieval, or modern.

So, the first Church was large, burgeoning, Spirit-filled and loving. All marvelous qualities but just as the serpent appeared in Eden so also did he appear in these early days of the saved. In many fashions the early days of the saved. In many fashions the early Church was made to be eternally sustainable, with its qualities emulated and even expanded. The Church at Jerusalem, though, in certain very real manners could not be perpetuated. All Christians were its members, but not all members, however pure their intentions, could sustain themselves indefinitely away from homes and jobs. Just as they had all things in common many had an extreme generosity of spirit and converted their possession by selling them for cash, money that went into a common treasury overseen by the apostles.

True religion, sincere persons and genuine Christians from the outset have had to endure the taunts and calumny of the world, perhaps the most common being that all religion is a sham, and that Christians are really hypocrites. The believer and even a fair-minded non-believer recognizes this as a fallacy. Yet, the Bible is never remiss, nor God embarrassed to admit that some who follow His name merit one of the vilest of all title, hypocrite. The Church's first two hypocrites, one by one, now make their entrance. Anaias and Sapphira were a married couple that had generously made a contribution to the common fund, so aptly described:

> "(They) sold a possession, And kept back part of
> the price, Sapphira being privy to it, and brought
> a certain part, and laid it at the apostles' feet."

From the comfortable removal of two thousand years at first this appears innocuous and even commendable. It was Peter himself, though, who confronted Anaias with the whole truth:

> "Why has Satan filled thine heart to lie to the
> Holy Spirit, and to keep back part of the price
> of the land? Whiles it remained, was it not thine
> own? And after it was sold, was it not in thine
> own power? Why hast thou conceived this thing
> in thine heart? Thou hast not lied unto men, but
> unto God."

With this apostolic benediction Ananias fell dead. Three hours later, an unsuspecting Sapphira, came into Peter, and Ananias's death scene repeated itself with her.

Let us be honest and assert that the modern mind, even the modern Christian mind, almost instinctively recoils at the harshness of this punishment. Perhaps, we may muse, a public reprimand and censure of Ananias and Sapphira. The entire scene, though, demands a viewing from both sides, but not the two sides who are the apparent antagonists, Peter and the other apostles, and Ananias and Sapphira. The two litigants of this issue, an issue of surpassing importance, were God and Satan. For as Peter asked of Sapphira:

> "How is it that ye have agreed together to tempt
> the Spirit of the Lord."

Religion, including Christianity, has always had the serpent of hypocrisy gnawing at its vital core. One of the oldest canards of the skeptic is the accusation that "religious people are hypocrites" or more especially to our situation, "all Christians are hypocrites." With this accusation alone many scornful cynics seemingly expect the Christian, the Church, and all Christendom to react in abject horror, that they have been "found out." Of course, hypocrites and various religious and parasitical detritus have always attached itself to religion. The story began quite early, too, and its narrative record may boast of many dubious firsts, the first sin, the first lie, the first truth, and the first false usage of religion. In the Garden the serpent's temptation of Eve contained elements of truth built upon the foundation of falsehood, as he told Eve that:

"Ye shall not surely die: For God doth know that
in the day ye eat thereof, then your eyes shall be
opened, and ye shall be as gods, knowing good
and evil."

The first temptation was an appeal to humanity's pride, for
a woman and a man to seem more than they actually were, to
"... be as gods." The Bible then follows with a multi-millennial
story of endless false utilization of religion for personal pride
and glory, for private advancement and to appear more than ordinarily human, effectively to "be as gods." The Old Testament,
among other matters, is a running narration of man's self-eleva-
tion religiously in the form of outright false gods and religions,
of priestly castes and of the worship of God as a golden path to
self-glorification. Ananias and Sapphira wanted to appear more
than they seemed by receiving the plaudits of the crowd while
actually still hoarding much of the money from their presumed
sacrifice.

God's actions are subject to review, an abyss and instruction,
but God's unrevealed thoughts and motives are often merely
speculative to us. It seems, though, that God was laying down
an early marker in the history of His Church to unequivocally
state that the beloved institution for which His Son died was
not to be employed as a means of self-advancement and fraudulent moral preening. The Church's past, present and likely future indicate that even God's efforts have never been fully successful. Still, for this moment in those early days:

"Great fear came upon all the Church, and upon
as many as heard these things."

This infant Church truly was an apostolic Church, for the leadership, character and work of these men were all essential for its proper functioning. Soon, though, the inevitability of many aspects of human nature would converge, even in the very Church of Christ, and many would be the alterations in the Church's physical location and even in its administrative structure but not in the simple and eternal truths and teachings of Jesus of Nazareth. An attractive feature of the infant Church was a commitment, seemingly deep and widespread, for its members to take care of each other, to love each other and "... so fulfill the law of Christ."

THE WIDOWS

Widowhood in any age, culture or circumstances is fraught with a basic sadness, a woman's having lost her life's partner, love, and confidante. It may be recognized, defined, explained, and even analyzed, but it remains a status in life that likely must be experienced and lived to be truly understood. Widows and widowhood maintain an enormous Biblical presence, especially in the teachings of the New Testament, and particularly the gospels. Yet the Old Testament, and especially the Law of Moses, is hardly bereft of teachings and directives regarding widows.

In ancient society and the realities of a primitive pre-modern world the specific difficulties of widows were recognized, especially among the Jews. In a day when most labor and employment was overwhelmingly demanding in its physical element men were much better suited to the basic task of making a living. When a man died his surviving widow presumably was saddened and grief stricken but her troubles had to be borne under the inescapable blanket of reality. That reality was that her means of making even a living of bare sustenance were severely restricted. Even among the mass of the Jews, the Chosen People, the fate of a widow could be abysmal. It was not uncommon for people to view her husband's death as a judgment upon her for a presumably sinful life she had led. Effectively she was scorned by the most basic element of society, married men and women. Her lot could enter realms beyond "hard" and unless she had independent wealth, means of support or caring relatives widowhood could become synonymous with destitution. This was the way of society, though, and not the path which God intended. The widow's most commonly avoidable solution was remarriage, but a status easily acquired by a vibrant twenty-five-year-old was desperately beyond the reach of widows as they entered old age. A common and divinely ordained institution among the Jews, then, was the Levirate marriage, whereby men were responsible for their brother's widow. All were stop-gap measures, though, for a widow's life remained excessively difficult.

As with any life, though, the real change in the attitude towards and treatment of widows was heralded and prompted by the advent of Jesus Christ. Jesus not only spoke of widows, but He honored and even exalted them. The impoverished widow's giving of her last two coins and the woman who shoved and fought her path through a crowd to merely "... touch the hem of His garment" are cornerstones of an image of Christ and His teachings. On the reverse of the coin Jesus excoriated with scorching rhetoric the Pharisees and scribes for their neglect and even outright fraudulent and oppressive conduct towards widows. Decades later it was the Savior's brother, James, who gave us a definition of religion commonly forgotten but just as succinct and elevating now as it was when first written:

"Pure religion and undefiled before God and the
Father is this, To visit the fatherless and widows
in their affliction."

It is still inspiring to acknowledge that the first Christians
there at Jerusalem heartily and adamantly saw their commitment to widows as a commitment to Christ Himself. Yet herein
lay the nascent Church's first real problem, a problem that ultimately would lead to Church and world changing consequences.

Ethnically the first Church in Jerusalem was entirely Jewish,
all Jews who had accepted and obeyed Christ. Yet, just as any
nation and almost every organization may have a veneer of ho-
mogeneity, so too did these early Jewish Christians, for even
they were divided into two basic camps. Jerusalem was the capital and largest city in the Roman province of Judea, which for
Roman administrative purposes included Samaria and Galilee.
These were the "native" Jews and included, among others, all
the present twelve apostles. The Jewish people, though, had
long been scattered throughout the Roman world and lived and
prospered in many places. Still Jews, ethnically and religiously,
culturally they lived in the Hellenistic (Greek) world, spoke
Greek, and had adopted many Greek (or Gentile) way of life.
Temporarily they were merely sojourners in Jerusalem, having
come there for Passover. The native and Hellenistic Jews shared
the same ethnology, had shared the same Jewish religion and
were now brothers and sisters in Christ. Yet each group undoubtedly was more comfortable with its own kind. This has
been, is and ever will be a factor in human relations. Each nation may maintain a common citizenry, but it is a citizenry often as divided as united.

Likely, each group appeared somewhat alien to the other,
perhaps by speech, dress, or just certain ways of performing

basic tasks. The salient point is that they were different, and the Grecian widows began to surmise that they were seriously disadvantaged "... because their widows were neglected in the daily ministrations." From the comfortable vista of two thousand years removal, we are not compelled to take sides in an ancient dispute. Likely, neither group was deliberately wrong or in error. As frail, faultful humans (just as is the twenty-first century variety of this species) their natural inclination was to first look after their own. The Hebraic Jews are not necessarily to be commended but they are to be understood as first seeing to those widows who they personally knew. The Hellenistic widows likely were neglected to some extent. But if Christ's own disciples cannot resolve such an internal disciples cannot resolve such an internal dispute, then the question is begged, "who can?"

Like all matters in the opening chapters of the Church this dispute was submitted to the apostles for resolution. Fortunately, for both God and man, these twelve men understood their true role and the concept of proportionality. They were the vessels, the instruments handpicked by the Son of God to fulfill the Great Commission to teach the Truth to all nations, and so they realized. The benevolence to widows is always and ever extant in God's desires, but the apostles were entrusted with the greatest of all tasks, so:

> "Then the twelve called the multitude of the disciples unto them, and said, It is not reason that we should leave the word of God and serve tables."

This is the wisest decision the apostles could have made, but their wisdom had not become exhausted by one simple decision, for they continued:

> "Wherefore, look ye out among you seven men of honest report, full of the Holy Spirit and wisdom, whom we may appoint over this wisdom."

Rarely is the Book of Acts designated as a handbook for management principles, but this one stated decision of the apostles bulged with them. In addition to a quick recognition that simply they had no personal time for this work they determined to appoint seven men who did. Still, they delegated the selection of the men who knew far better the "personnel pool" from which they would be drawn. The wisdom of the Master's selection of the twelve was continually confirmed.

All seven men selected were, logically enough, Hellenistic Jews, for each possessed a Greek name such as Philip, Prochorus, Timon, Parmenas, Nicholas and Nicanor. They were the ones most familiar with the neglect (and it is described as neglect, not "alleged" neglect) of the Grecian widows. Further, their selection and its manner demonstrated the flexibility and fluidity of the early Church in organization matters. Only an uninformed observer would argue that the early Church and her leaders possessed a total carte blanche organizationally. Still, the apostles displayed a wisdom which should be a touchstone and bellwether for churches two thousand years hence. The primary goal was "getting the job done well," and they were not throttled by organization forms. How the Church has ever and continually falls short of this aspiration is left to the individual Christian's judgment.

The power displayed by the apostles in this early Church difficulty was an early confirmation of the character of the apostles and of the wisdom of Christ's choice. None were grasping for power, and actually each man seemed fully committed to displaying the power, not of their offices, but of Christ. Evidently, the matter of the dispute with the "daily ministrations" to the widow was ameliorated, for we hear no more of it. Yet, it was starkly illustrative of a danger that was overcoming the Jerusalem Church. It had grown too large. That observation alone provides a hothouse for growth of disputations. Especially in modern times, in the hyperactive media age, we have become accustomed to being taught that the motto for a church should be "the bigger, the better." In the last few years, a new term has crept its way into common usage, the "megachurch." The first church in Jerusalem was a megachurch, and it was growing to a point where the potential for good had intersected with the certainty of the bad.

The Jerusalem church was an ancient church, the very first church, and its burgeoning size along gave it means and resources to engage in many benevolent activities. The "daily ministrations" to the widows provides an elemental fact that they took the longstanding Biblical enjoinder to provide for the weak and the helpless seriously. Among thousands of Christians in one place the talent pool must have shown an incredible depth, and thereby much good could be accomplished. Further, the size of this new Church alone drew attention, an attention much more difficult for a small band of faithful to attract. Not a word of these observations is untrue for large churches in the twenty-first century, but neither are the following observations of disadvantage any less true.

No group, no matter how small or large, is immune to factionalism. Nations, political parties, business enterprises and perhaps especially even families can see any cohesion and unity ripped to shreds by its national disunifying characteristics. The Jerusalem Church was in the initial stages of disunion.

Ancient Jerusalem was basically square shaped, with each side of the square approximately two miles long. Into this tiny area and likely its outlying environs were now packed thousands of Christians, excited, for the most part infused with the highest aspirations but crowded together too closely. Christ breaks barriers, but He does not re-form men and women in many ways. Two basic groups, Hebrew and Hellenistic, were trying to adhere, and their numbers and dissimilarities were increasingly difficult to handle. It is simply a basic incontrovertible fact of the human experience that generally persons of the same backgrounds, beliefs, and other similarities work better together than do the dissimilar. This is far from an unbroken rule but as a general observation it stands.

Besides, and even more importantly, the Church was not meant by God to be a spiritual island limited by the geographic boundaries of Jerusalem. It was Christ's commission to the apostles to "...go into all the world." The time had arrived for many Christians to return to their original homes, but what would be the means and methods of their prompting?

Before the study commences with a more thorough reflection on the last question it must be admitted that earlier only six names were given when identifying the men in charge of tending to the widows. The seventh man was named Stephen.

CHAPTER FOUR

THE FACE OF AN ANGEL

The first Church in Jerusalem had grown with an amazing rapidity and was now so large that it had become impossible for the non-Christian section of Jerusalem and Judea not to notice and notice with a gimlet eye of apprehension, dread, contempt and perhaps more than a mere modicum of fear. To the mass of the non-believing Jews the Church's internal squabbles and difficulties meant little or nothing. The nexus of hostility was found where the Church's teachings met the world and the lives of the Jews. Although the terminology is commonly employed still today few persons, much less institutions, are "overnight sensations," yet the infant Church was precisely so described. Born in one day with an initial legion of three thousand through the evangelical efforts of the apostles additional thousands were being appended swiftly to the Church's rolls. The apostles with Peter and John in the vanguard, already in a short time had attracted the same heated opposition from the same coterie of establishment conspirators who had crucified Christ and who in their hearts wished to do the same to the apostles. Their hands were stayed, though, and as has been described the Church remained a viable burgeoning young institution. As noted, as great as were the apostles in the performance of their evangelistic roles they were not without assistance.

At the risk of being pummeled with accusations of severe pedantry the assertion, nay, the certainty that not all are possessed of equal abilities is made. For example, in the canon of Western civilization and thought, many greats have written masterworks of literature, yet few have attained the strata of such as Shakespeare, Dante or Dostoevsky. Our history and culture is blessed with an abundance of great and beautiful music, but the roster of names to be included with Mozart or Beethoven is short indeed. Many are the compositions and melodies which have flowed from the minds of giants, but few reach such a pinnacle. The arts community is daily, even hourly, engaged in creating and endowing the world with their versions of truth and beauty, but how historically rare is a Michelangelo or a Rembrandt? The questions and answers are rhetorical, but they are not limited to these fields of the fine arts. The Bible, both Testaments is, among its endless stories, a tale of a certain few men and women supremely endowed with ability and faith and most of them employed in Divine works.

A supremely (in the literal meaning of the word) gifted man was Stephen, who makes his debut as one of the seven Hellenistic Jews appointed to tend to the needs of neglected widows in the first Church. Even in his introduction, though, he is a singular presence as only Stephen is described as "... a man full of faith and the Holy Spirit." Of his life's history we have but a general outline. As a Hellenistic Jew he could have been from almost anywhere in the Mediterranean world, perhaps from Greece or even Alexandria in Egypt. His age and physical appearance are unknown, although historically he has invariably been portrayed as youthful. Speculation may be fascinating, but it is now of little real importance. As with all persons of every age and era it was the conduct and character of Stephen which mattered. With the obvious exception of Christ, the Church's Founder, no person has ever had such an immediate and far-reaching impact on Christ's Church as did this one amazing man.

> "The word of God increased and multiplied," and the apostles themselves publicly recognized the seven men, but only one was given this recognition: "And Stephen, full of faith and powers, did great wonders among the people."

Great ability, great deeds, and great power, though, all became a midwife to great opposition. Likely by now the Jewish religious hierarchy had become somewhat accustomed to the apostles, although we find little indicia of a softening of their opposition other than that "... a great company of the priests were obedient to the faith." Stephen, though, was something and somebody new, not a Galilean fisherman, but a Hellenistic Jew, from his oratory and eloquence, likely highly educated and well read. His lot was common with much of humanity in one particular fact, though, in that the most heated and hated opposition to him was centered in the synagogues of these Grecian Jews:

> "Then there arose certain of the synagogue, which is called the synagogue of the Libertines, and Cyrenians, and Alexandrians, and of Asia, disputing with Stephen."

Numerically the opposition to one lone evangelist was crushing, but the majority was getting crushed:

"And they were not able to resist the wisdom and
the spirit by which he spoke."

The hands of these opposing Jews remained firmly gripped
upon the levers of human power and force, and they were about
to employ them. Yet, Stephen possessed in his life's arsenal the
elements that compose real power, sincerity, honesty, good
will, the Holy Spirit, truth and above all, the eternal support
of God. For the moment, though, the enemies of Stephen and
the Church had temporal control of the situation, and with an
eeriness not of mere resemblance but of exact replication we
find that:

"Then they suborned men, which said We have
heard him speak blasphemous words against
Moses, and against God."

Now, all the props, all the scenery, all the cast was being prepared for the latest offering in a long running hit series, which
could have styled "The Persecution of Christ." It began with
the Savior's Passion, was extended by not one, but two separate persecutions of the apostles. The performance in the off-
ing now was the destruction of the early Church's greatest and
most formidable evangelist, Stephen.

Being the object of another person's hatred is a terrible and
frightful experience. Hatred is almost impossible to define in
the sense that a phrase of explanation or elucidation would
comfortably fit into a lexicon or dictionary. Neither is it truly defined by a simple "hatred is the opposite of love." True
love has a substance and quality which may attain elements
of Divinity, even for mortals, for which there exists no true
antonym. Hatred is more than a word, a concept, or a feeling,

though it is all these things. It is an elemental force which grips a person and demands abject subservience and blind obedience to its dictates, no matter how illogical, irrational, or unreasonable. "Blind faith" is often employed as a pejorative, but more often it is "blind hatred" that is truly unseeing, unknowing, and heedless of consequences. The highest court in Judea, the Sanhedrin, the Great Council itself, had now reconstituted itself into a tribunal of hatred, a form in which it was becoming quite accustomed and comfortable. Approximately seventy in number they were the crème de la crème of Judean intelligentsia and law, men respected and feared for their knowledge of the Law and their collective power to hear cases and issue and enforce civil and criminal judgments. Their power was impressive, substantive, and real, but its limitations were now being discerned and highlighted in ways not seen before. Yes, they had to reckon with the Galilean carpenter, but with Rome's help hopefully He had been dispatched. The motley collection of the leaders of this new Nazarene cult were presenting a problem, but they ultimately must have rested in secure comfort that they could be squelched.

But now here was Stephen, and for some reason or reasons he excited hatred at a level and intensity not seen since Jesus of Nazareth Himself, but why? To a certain degree we must recognize an element of speculation in our answers to the inquiry. For certain, Stephen was an electrifying speaker. The ancients, certainly inclusive of the Jews, prized eloquence in speaking ability and oratory, and Stephen, with the never-failing Spirit of God, was fully endowed with it. (We may merely surmise the opinions which ancient society would have held of our media driven, heavily handled and scripted, and teleprompter addicted politicians). Stephen seemed fearless, incapable of being intimidated and possessed a knowledge both encyclopedic and intimate of Jewish law and history, a knowledge he was now about to demonstrate.

Today, the Sanhedrin was an arena of hatred, dozens of the black eyes of jurists fixed with disapproval of just one man, a man who had no one to speak for him. Stephen was a lone defendant in a powerful tribunal of dozens of powerful men, most united in a fierce hatred and empathy for his destruction. The Council was pulsating with hatred and power, but one man seemed to be not only without rancor or hatred but instead was another type of exemplar:

> "And all that sat in the council, looking stead-
> fastly on Stephen, saw his face as it had the face
> of an angel."

The self-possession of soul, love, faith, devotion, and courage which were shining forth now as the very definition of Stephen's character retain a power to move and inspire believers yet today. Finally, the high priest granted him leave to speak in his own defense.

Excluding any words or sermons of Christ, Stephen's response is one of the three greatest sermons in the New Testament (the other two being Peter's on Pentecost and Paul's before Herod and Felix). Stephen began his discourse in a spirit of respect, even reverence, and camaraderie with his audience and began to demonstrate a powerful knowledge of Jewish and Biblical history. He commenced in a spirit of friendship and respect, addressing his listeners with words such as "brethren and fathers," and in a manner still worthy of emulation issued expressions upon which all could and did agree. He spoke of the ancient Divine call of Abram from Ur of the Chaldees and the immense blessings which God would bestow upon him and all his descendants who followed. In other terms he began with the common ancestor of all Jewish, all Hebrew people, a powerful common denominator. From there Stephen led his audience through as true and concise summary of Jewish history, which can be found anywhere, even today.

Stephen continued bringing his judge and jury down the long historical road of the patriarchs, Abraham, Isaac and Jacob, the four-hundred-year long sojourn in Egypt commencing with Joseph and ending with the leadership of Moses and exodus of the Israelites from slavery. In intimate detail Stephen related the Egyptian story and Moses's role as the deliverer of the people. Perhaps unthinkingly this audience of the judges of Israel was becoming enrapt by Stephen's history, and that is itself not surprising. It is our natural human inclination to enjoy agreement and function in this speech of Stephen's for the Jewish savants to swell with pride as the history of their special nation was well, even brilliantly, recited.

Eagerly did the Sanhedrin listen as Stephen related the birth of Israel and the Law of Moses, upon Mount Sinai. How especially must they have delighted in this unexpected recognition of the Mosaical Law, a codified legal system which meant almost everything to these men. Likely at this juncture many in the Sanhedrin may have been thinking that perhaps we have misjudged this man Stephen, and he was able to continue uninterrupted. The atmosphere now began to blacken, though, as Stephen introduced them to a reminder of much of the darkness of Israel's past. Even while on Sinai, Moses's brother Aaron and the Israelites began to turn from a God to whom they had no deep allegiance and construct and worship idols. Stephen remembered and related their ancestors's love affair with pagan idolatry, especially that of the Canaanites. From there he leaped forward and discussed King Solomon's construction of the Temple, which contained the Holy of Holies and the Mercy Seat and to many Jews, especially these priests and councilors was the very embodiment and the alpha and omega of their religion. To this Stephen:

> "Howbeit the most High dwelleth not in temples
> made with hands; as saith the prophets. Heaven
> is my throne, and the earth is my footstool: what
> house will ye build Me? Saith the Lord:

or what is the place of My rest?"

Two thousand years later we may also hear the shuffling of feet, see the looks of indignation, and hear the scornful statements in the ranks of the Sanhedrin. Now they knew why this Stephen was on trial, for his disrespect of Moses and likely even worse, the Temple. How familiar, how sadly, morosely, pathetically familiar this all was. Yes, now they saw that this previously unknown Stephen was a "worthy" successor to the Galilean upstart, who had stated that he would destroy the Temple but then raise it up again in three days. The intensity and fierceness of anger continued to rage and boil within the hearts of the Council members, yet even now with their opposition becoming apparent and tangible this Hellenistic intruder would not cease his prattling about the historic disobedience of their revered Jewish ancestors. Moreover, the tenor of his voice began to rise and now he linked the present Jewish leaders with all the past that not Stephen, but rather God, had upbraided and condemned:

> "Ye stiff necked and uncircumcised in heart and
> ears, ye do always resist the Holy Spirit: as your
> fathers did, so do ye."

With this excoriation Stephen was approaching the ultimate in insult to this assemblage of learned Jews, a clear statement that they were "uncircumcised in heart and ears." Physically and ethnically, yes, they were Jews, God's original Chosen, but in their hearts, they were ... Gentiles. Stephen said and revealed again that their holiness and spiritual leadership of the Jews was a tired, a very tired, masquerade which Christ, not Stephen, had revealed to the world. To be labeled effectively a Gentile, a 'hypocritical Jew" by this nobody who had come from nowhere was a body blow to the Sanhedrin's spiritual psyche, yet Stephen had even greater denunciation to deliver:

> "Which of the prophets have not your fathers persecuted? and they have slain them which showed before of the coming of the Just One; of whom ye have been now the betrayers and murderers. Who have received the law by the disposition of angels, and have not kept it."

How they must have been hating Stephen by this point in his speech, likely now being delivered amidst the tumult of catcalls and insults. In smoothly eloquent yet clear, sharp language the Jewish religious hierarchy was hearing words with the strong echoes of that Galilean carpenter's, "... scribes, Pharisees, hypocrites." They had preened and prided themselves on being the true keepers, interpreters, and guardians of the Law, yet here they are denounced as the Law's despoilers, traitors, murderers, and worst of all to the Semitic pride, "Gentiles." A man such as Stephen, with his talents, eloquence, knowledge, and penetrating insight was a man who was easy to hate. As they did with Jesus, and were haltingly attempting with the apostles, Stephen had to be destroyed. Again, their unconvincing logic, which was actually unrestrained emotion, led to their belief that the destruction and eradication of the messenger would mean the end of the message. These calm, cool, sober elders, and leaders of the people in actuality were propelled forward not by judicious and judicial reasoning but by the mentality of the mob, their own high ranking, highly prestigious lynch mob.

In the event the Great Sanhedrin was tired of listening to anything Stephen might utter. Whatever their religious and historical hypocrisies may have been, no hint of hypocrisy, falsehood or insincerity moved them now. So intense, so deeply internal, even visceral had their hatred for Stephen, his words and deeds become that:

> "When they heard these things, they were cut
> to the heart, and they gnashed on him with their
> teeth."

So deep, vile, and galling was their antipathy and hatred for him that these judicial masters of Judea gave life and reality to an old adage that someone was so angry that he was literally "... foaming at the mouth" as a rabid dog. Yet, even as the inevitable final few minutes of Stephen ebbed away his every word and thought glorified Christ:

> "But he, being full of the Holy Spirit, looked up
> stedfastly into heaven, and saw the glory of God,
> and Jesus standing on the right hand of God."

Stephen thus became the first of only three New Testament recordings of disciples who were allowed to look into Heaven. The eternal magnificence of what his eyes beheld needs no further explanation or interpretation. As the earthly environs and realms were enclosing and encasing Stephen with darkness the path ahead grew with an intense luminous brightness. In many respects, emotionally and spiritually Stephen had already passed into the next world. The waiting, baying mob who sought his blood had not, though, and were firmly bound to this terrestrial sphere:

> "Then they cried out with a loud voice, and stopped their ears, and ran upon him with one accord, And cast him out of the city and stoned him."

This time a well-armed and accoutered coterie of Roman soldiers was not to be seen, and the hill of Calvary was bereft of crosses. This death was to be a production wholly engineered and directed by the Jewish aristocracy and the Sanhedrin. It had not the thinnest veneer of legality other than its physical locale of the Sanhedrin. No judicial pronouncements, no questioning of witnesses (other than the suborned individuals who began the charade), nothing. It was mob action by a group that was esteemed as the foremost authorities of the Law of Moses. Hatred, though, cuts through so many barriers, and it was that envenomed emotion which led Stephen outside the Jerusalem city walls to meet his death by stoning. Again, the Jewish legal intelligentsia rigorously observed the letter of the law since an execution with Jerusalem's municipal limits would profane the holy city.

Stoning was among those methods employed by ancient cultures to deliver capital punishment, and still retains a legal presence in many Islamic countries. The criminal miscreant would be led before his executioners and pelted with stones until the accumulated trauma brought death. Some have estimated that

a stoning could require as long as thirty minutes, but that of
Stephen's was unlikely to have been that excruciatingly long.
He would have been surrounded by dozens of men who delivered death blows with hateful enthusiasm. To enhance their
strength, they removed their outer garments of clothing for
more freedom of action. The size, velocity, and rapidity with
which the stones struck Stephen is sickening to contemplate,
much less to have witnessed.

Stephen, though, Christianity's first martyr, was the man
who ended this scene of macabre and grotesque drama, but true
to his character and magnificence he uplifted and still infuses
the spirits of all Christians yet today:

> "Stephen, calling upon God, (said) Lord Jesus,
> receive my spirit. And he kneeled down, and
> cried with a loud voice, Lord, lay not this sin to
> their charge. And when he had said this, he fell
> asleep."

The similarity of Stephen's benedictory words and those
to whom they were directed is too obvious to require further
observation.

Stephen's fellow brothers in Christ tended to his remains,
buried his body and in Luke's haunting phrase "made great lamentation over him." Great as he was, though, as exemplary as
was his life, neither Stephen, the twelve apostles, any of the
disciples, or any being could have realized what we may confidently assess and assert today. A common phrase worn thin
and almost transparent by historical over-usage is that some
event or moment constitutes a "turning point" in history. This
is regrettable, for the persecution and martyrdom of Stephen
was a turning point of gargantuan effect and importance. Just

as this great man's death did not come without pain, sorrow and disappointment neither was the growth of the early Church unaccompanied by anguish. Who can reckon in numbers of the many new Christians in whose lives were now introduced wanderings from home, resettlement in other widely dispersed lands, heartbreak of absence and outright tangible persecution. None of it, though, was in vain and it all served a higher, the highest purpose:

> "Now they were scattered abroad upon the persecution that arose about Stephen traveled as far as Phenice, and Cyprus, and Antioch, preaching the word to none but the Jews only."

Only the uninformed, the deliberately blinkered (seemingly always the majority) could still view this as only another Jewish sect.

Stephen's death and heroic martyrdom was the bridge over which the Christian religion first crossed. From a growing but tightly packed community in Jerusalem and its environs Christians and the Truth to which they adhered began to spread, to be dispersed to Samaria, Galilee, even into Europe, to the high culture of Greece and to the dynamic power of the city on the Tiber, to Rome itself. Eventually into the north, west and east of Europe and fifteen hundred years later the cross was planted in the New World of North and South America. Into the lands, the mysterious miasmic Eastern realms of India, China and Japan the Spirit of Christ was taught. Islands, large and small, in the vast Pacific Ocean, became dotted with churches and the uplifting and saving message of Jesus Christ. It never stopped, has not stopped and never will it be halted.

His time upon the Biblical stage was truncated by the hatred of religious hierarchy of his fellow Jews, but the short, exemplary life of Stephen helps light the way. Stephen was a meteor that streaked across the sky and helped illuminate the brighter Light, the one true Light of Christ. When Stephen passed from this temporal life to that of eternity Satan must have shivered with the exhilaration of power the death of this man brought his efforts. In reality, though, how strange this was. The life and martyrdom of Stephen delivered a blow to Satan and his minions from which they have yet to recover.

CHAPTER FIVE

NEW REALMS: NEW CHRISTIANS

If any region was ready for the spread of the Truth, it was Samaria, a fact which had always shone brightly in the teachings of the Master. Samaria, a small region sandwiched between Galilee to the north and Judah to the south had long been a stepchild of the Jewish nation. It was a stepchild held in contempt, despised as racial mongrels, neither truly Jews nor Gentiles. The latter was certainly true for most Samaritans possessed a mixed ethnology, some Jewish with a likely predominance of Gentile blood. As with most racial divides and animosities, the opprobrium which Jews and Gentiles had for one another was neither baseless nor rootless. Besides the ethnic distinctions the Samaritans, still two hundred years after the event, received Jewish scorn for their ancestors not fighting in one of the proudest battles in Jewish history in the 160's B.C. the Maccabean War for survival against the tyrant Antiochus Epiphanes IV. And so it went, never relenting, always building in the vile richness of the venom of ethnic hatred until the time of the Advent, when most Jews equated Samaritans with street refuse, scavengers, and dogs.

One man, a Jew, did not share or endorse this bill of indictment against the Samaritans, and that naturally was the Master. Christ's teachings and references were strewn with the term "Samaritan," including giving us both a teaching and phrase still employed today, the Good Samaritan. It was to the oft-married woman at the well, a Samaritan, to whom Jesus first proclaimed His identity as the Savior. Among His final words to the apostles was to take the gospel to Samaria. Yet it was not an apostle, but rather a man with the apostolic name of Philip who first heeded Christ's charge. This was Philip the Evangelist, one of the seven men appointed to serve the church in Jerusalem, and thus a co-worker with the late Stephen. His success in Samaria was spectacular, for when Philip preached and taught many became Christians. As did Stephen he was Divinely gifted:

> "For unclean spirits, crying with loud voice, came
> out of many that were possessed with them: and
> many laden with palsies, and that were lame, and
> healed."

Philip's success in the city of Samaria was phenomenal, the disciples' number skyrocketed, and the notoriety of healings, signs and wonders spread as always. A stunning, perhaps more appropriately a man of startling traits, was in that first wave of disciples. This, in reality, though, was no ordinary man, for his fame, prestige and presumed special powers had burnished his image to a golden hue among the Samaritan people. Luke, with both his customary and terse manner, well describes him:

> "But there was a certain man called Simon, which
> before time in the same city used sorcery, and
> bewitched the people of Samaria, giving out that
> himself was some great one: To whom they all
> gave heed, from the least to the greatest, saying,
> This man is the great power of God."

Simon, whose character bears and suffers no aspersions upon his belief and obedience in Christ, yet his lifetime's pursuit of wealth, fame, and the esteem of the multitude. Simon, though, had risen to fame and acclaim through the pretext of being a "sorcerer." A magician, a dealer in witchcraft and the occult, all activities roundly and specifically condemned in the Old Law.

Philip's success in Samaria was so great that the apostles Peter and John journeyed there from Jerusalem, hoping to add to the victories being won by Philip. When they came, and as was their power entrusted to them by the Messian Himself, laid their hands on certain of the new disciples and imbued them with the plenary power of the Holy Spirit, endowing them with the miraculous ability to perform signs and wonders. Simon, a man whose stock in trade had long been awing the crowd by supposed miracles and Divine gifts, positively salivated with jealousy and desire when he saw this and confronted the apostles:

> "... (H)e offered them money. Saying, Give me
> also this power, that on whomsoever I lay hands,
> he may receive the Holy Spirit."

Aghast at such a brazen sacrilege Peter upbraided Simon with a scathing denunciation:

"Thy money perish with thee, because thou hast thought that the gift of God may be purchased with money."

From the olden days of Simon the Sorcerer to the present many scorners and skeptics in each generation anew believe in their own ingenuity and thoughtful inventiveness and that they can paralyze God and his supposed gullible followers with some variation of the observation that "Religion is a racket," and that people, scandalous scoundrels, are in it only for the money that may be theirs. We mortals, no matter how strong and sincere is our faith plausibly may be moved by such arguments that religion has become a racket and that all Christians and especially their leaders are irredeemably, although this itself is a dubious proposition. Maybe we can, though, but God cannot.

Twisted, distorted appeals to monetary gain and personal aggrandizement have been a part of religion from the beginning in the Garden of Eden, where Satan's temptation was that "... ye shall be as gods." Eight hundred pagan priests, reprobates to a man, "...ate at Jezebel's table." Even more to the point and relevant to the Christian age is the sad status of the Jewish religious establishment in the first century, the century of the New Testament, and the spread of the gospel. It was a period of the revelation of the hearts of many publicly pious men, who were shown to be careerists, prestige driven and addicted to the material rewards of religion. So, there is nothing new about Simon or his ideological, moral, and spiritual successors of the past two millennia.

Nonetheless, the rage of the apostle Peter was real, and he spoke with a scalding, scathing reality to Simon:

"Thou hast neither part nor lot in this matter; for they heart is not right in the sight of God. Repent ... for the thought of thine heart may be forgiven thee. For I perceive that thou art in the gall of bitterness, and in the bond of iniquity."

The observer's mind naturally makes a referential comparison to that moment not so long before where for the only recorded Biblical instance Christ flashed bolts of violence upon the money changers in the Temple, the men who were desecrating the worship of God by making a fast profit. His quickly constructed whip flailed the backs of the blasphemous money grabbers, but Peter referenced from such a demonstration with Simon. Instead, his upbraiding of the sorcerer seemed to accrue at least partial change:

"Then answered Simon, and said, Pray ye to the Lord for me, that none of these things which ye have spoken come upon me."

Christianity and the Bible teach realism about the human condition, but they also offer the blessings of an ultimately optimistic view of life. Simon "the sorcerer" has now disappeared from the Biblical chronicle, but yet our hopes are great that truly he repented of his vile attitude and grew in grace and favor. In any event thus did the Church in Samaria, as it became an early center of strength as the apostles fulfilled the Savior's Commission.

The Queen's Treasurer

The Jews were and so remain a remarkably talented and accomplished people. Because of centuries of national calamities and disasters they had dispersed (the "Diaspora") throughout the world, but generally acclimated themselves well into any surroundings, often obtaining positions of influence and authority. An apparent example was a man who is scripturally nameless but ever since his appearance has been given the nomenclature of the "Ethiopian eunuch" or the "Queen's treasurer." He was a man who lived in Ethiopia, (for a time, Abyssinia), and held that position under Candace, queen of Ethiopia. He is encountered on a road south of Jerusalem to Gaza, to the former place he had come to worship. Again, Philip, well named "the Evangelist" is key as an angel advises him to join the eunuch on his journey south. As the man, of obvious prestige and authority was riding in his chariot, Philip ran, hailed him, and offered to join him on his journey. Philip was welcomed into the chariot and noticed that the treasurer was reading from the Old Testament book of Isaiah. Philip, who had been guided by the Holy Spirit, made a serious inquiry:

"Understandest thou what thou readest?"

The man's short response is alone a sermon of souls and is a rebuke to the self-pride that all humans possess to some degree.

"How can, except some man should guide me?"

Such an attitude is a gold, maybe even a platinum, mine, to both student and teacher. It abrogated the pride that is a barrier to so much learning, it revealed a heart eager for knowledge and indirectly asked for the help of a more knowledgeable teacher. Such an attitude, yet two thousand years hence is the commencement point for great learning and potentially magnificent results. Intelligence, self-confidence, and self-assurance are certainly not incompatible with this quality. Cockiness, arrogance, and intellectual pride are, and they have stunted and even doomed the learning capacities and even the souls of multitudes for:

> "God resisteth the proud, and giveth grace to the humble."

If the treasurer had responded to Philip with the false pride that is present in some form and quantity in every person, with a dismissive "...of course, I understand it" likely his story, life and the trajectory of his spirit and soul would have gone forth as before, in uninterrupted ignorance of the scripture. Blessedly he asked a question of Philip, and it proved to be a question of remarkable presence:

> "I pray thee, of whom speaketh the prophet this?
> Of himself, or of some other man?"

Philip, the proverbial "right man in the right place at the right time" was well worthy and splendidly suited to the task of the moment:

> "Then Philip opened his mouth, and began at the same scripture, and preached unto him Jesus."

The key word, the term of treasure in Philip's response, was "Jesus." The knowledge of Philip's background is not available to us and whether he was a disciple who was personally acquainted with the Son of Man is not within our ken. He well understood, though, what has seemingly been so easy to slip from the emotional and mental grasp of the Church throughout the ages. The attraction of Christianity is the person and life of its Founder, Jesus Christ. Neither its history, its great men and women, the truth of its moral teachings nor its inherent beauty are the lures which God's fishers employ to catch men. It is the Savior Himself, and the beauty of His personality, character, life, and teachings. In Philip's instruction to the eunuch obviously was one of those teachings, for the eunuch's response was:

> "See, here is water; what doth hinder me to be baptized?'

The teaching, the response and the man's conversion to Christ Himself was incomplete without the fulfillment of the directive to be baptized, given by Christ, preached again by Peter on Pentecost and a specifically integral element of every Christian conversion story in the New Testament.

Philip's response was majestically worthy of the question for his eyes affixed upon the eunuch, and he spoke:

> "If thou believest with all thine heart, thou mayest."

The Ethiopian then confessed the foundation truth, the Rock, upon which Christianity is built that:

> "I believe that Jesus Christ is the Son of God."

Philip and the man went down into the water, where he was immersed and away went the Queen's treasurer, rejoicing, but never heard from again. Or is this so? In the 1500's and 1600's and beyond when European colonialists, businessmen, missionaries, and others began to plunge into the great expanses of sub-Saharan Africa naturally enough the continent was basically devoid of Christianity – save for one nation. A form of Christianity through the Coptic Church was practiced in the nation of Ethiopia. Perhaps the chariot on the road to Gaza that day contained not one, but two great evangelists.

Cornelius

He was the backbone of the magnificent and mighty Roman army, the real animate force that had given Rome much of the world, including the small eastern province of Judea. His title was centurion because he was originally the commanding officer of a "century," a unit of one hundred soldiers. Still today he is invariably defined in such terms, but the extensive army reforms of 107 B.C. engineered by Marius revamped the army's organizational structure, and though the centurion still commanded a century, now it was a unit of eighty men. A centurion was selected for many reasons, and his resume' was no flimsy padded piece of puff. He was to be physically in top condition, not just a leader but a proven soldier of ability with battle experience. His mental acumen was required to be high, and the successful centurion possessed certain indefinable qualities which mark every real leader. Such a man was stationed and lived in Caesarea, the major Judean seaport, and the administrative center for the Roman occupation of the land. Centurion Cornelius was in the "Italian band," a true Roman unit. He was Roman, Italian, and carried a Latin name, a true "Roman's Roman" dwelling in the world of the Jews.

Undoubtedly, he was a seasoned professional soldier of great experience and high ability, for like all nations Rome had its share of fools and buffoons in political leadership, it did not gladly suffer fools in such military leadership roles as centurion. The scriptures though, are otherwise silent on the military career of Cornelius, but he is introduced. From pagan Rome this Gentile agent in the conquest of the Jews was:

> "A devout man, and one that feared God with all
> his house, which gave much alms to the people,
> and prayed to God always."

One afternoon at about three o'clock, in a vision an angel appeared to Cornelius and told him that not only had God heard his prayers, but they were being answered in a manner and with a bounty greater than could be anticipated. Cornelius was directed to send men to Joppa and go to the house of Simon the tanner, where a man named Peter temporarily was lodging. Send for him, he was directed, and Peter will tell you what is to be done.

If Cornelius was a "Roman's Roman" then the apostle Peter was a "Jew's Jew." From a Galilean fishing village, a working man, he had been taught from infancy that Jews were different. Truly they were God's Chosen with a special and exclusive Law, the Mosaical Law, and moral standards far above those of the Gentiles, who were at best unclean and at worst, Satanic dogs. Peter was overjoyed to be a friend of Jesus of Nazareth and happily and well did he go forth as a prominent apostle in Christ's mission to redeem Israel and save all Jews.

Like Cornelius, a man with whom he was unacquainted Peter was a paragon of prayer. At Joppa, while praying at noon he was given a strange, even eerie vision of the skies opening and a great sheet descending to earth. Upon the sheet were all sorts of animals, and according to the strict Jewish dietary restrictions some were clean and some unclean. A heavenly voice directed the apostle to "kill and eat." Peter, true to the consistency of his personality and character fended off his instructions with his presumed self-knowledge of God's will superior to God Himself:

> "Not so Lord, for I have never eaten anything that is common or unclean."

The voice from Heaven reinstructed Peter with:

> "What God hath cleansed, that call not thou common."

Then, forever establishing that the Creator has both a sense of irony and a sense of humor Peter was told thus three separate times. The vision soon ended, and Peter was told by the Holy Spirit that downstairs three visitors from Caesarea were waiting to see him. With these three men, the messengers from Cornelius, Peter made the requested journey to the centurion's home in Caesarea.

In Caesarea Cornelius was awaiting Peter, but in the meantime, he had demonstrated the attention and thoroughness which a good Roman centurion would give to any task. Cornelius was ready, his home was ready, his family was ready, and he had also "... called together his kinsmen and near friends." Finally, Peter, a humble rustic Jewish fisherman arrived at the home of Cornelius, a Roman officer of great influence and authority and even as Peter was just entering the house:

> "Cornelius met him, and fell down at his feet,
> and worshipped him."

Peter, an apostle, had spent three intense years of his life with the only man who has walked this earth who is worthy of such worship and obeisance and immediately:

"Peter took him up, saying, Standup; I myself also am a man."

It is so elementally easy to find and comment upon the coalescence and combination of evil, but that of its opposite is but infrequently mentioned. A mental tableau of this scene should be etched in every psyche. It is a pictorial not just of goodness but rather of greatness. Cornelius, an important Roman possessed of commanding authority and power humbling himself before a ragged Jewish fisherman, who was totally bereft of such worldly power. Only the power, the real power of Jesus Christ could have brought these two men together.

Cornelius related to Peter his story of the Heavenly voice, the instructions to send messengers to Joppa and his promise of more to come. The apostle responded with a phrase which doubtless read, studied, quoted and in his own fashion believed the entirety of his life:

> "Of a truth I perceive that God is no respecter
> of persons: But in every nation he that feareth
> Him, and worketh righteousness is accepted
> with Him."

Simon Peter was a good man who became a great man, one of the most important and greatest men who ever lived. Like all men and women then and now, even those with good hearts turned towards God he had a blinkered understanding of certain matters. Jesus of Nazareth, who he passionately loved and followed had come to redeem Israel and save all Jews. Now, though, the heavens had literally opened to him and finally he understood the true message and meaning of Jesus Christ, that the Savior had come to save from sin the souls of all men and women, Jews and Gentiles. The majestic power of Christ still washed over Peter, and its blessings were now about to be received by, of all humanity, a Roman officer, his friends, and family. At Peter's command this party of believers was baptized, and thus became the first Gentile Christians and disciples of Christ. Through Peter, a seemingly odd choice, the truth was first preached to the Gentiles. In Cornelius, an even more noteworthy selection, the first Gentile Christian was found. Not a pious farmer, laborer, fisherman or carpenter but an army officer from far distant and hated Rome. Only God had the resolution and the power to bring these two men together in this story of salvation and inspiration (as an aside it is worth the observation that almost all references to the character of Roman centurions in the New Testament places them in a positive light. Even the officer in charge of the crucifixion with his admittance that Jesus was the Son of God thus glorified God).

What may rightfully be termed the Christian version of the Diaspora had begun, and the truth, Christianity and churches spread into new realms. Seemingly but not surprisingly great success had been found in a northward direction with the truth's penetration into Samaria. With Philip the Evangelist, another man of splendid talents but strangely often overlooked in Church history accounts, great success was reaped in Samaria. Hardly should this have been a surprise. The Master Himself had always gone out of His way, sometimes literally as with the woman at Jacob's well, to deliver truth to this nation and to positively reference them. Philip found a special eagerness among this mired breed, neither Jew nor Gentile, and so many seemed ecstatic to embrace Christ and His teachings. Even Simon the Sorcerer, a Samaritan burdened by a serious albeit quite common moral failing, avarice, is left with a penitent heart and our hope that he overcame the mercenary cancer of greed that plagued him.

With the queen's treasurer, the eunuch from Ethiopia the Church and the message of Christ traveled to a far distant land, Ethiopia, a nation yet extant today and populated by an entirely different race of people. With his joyful conversion the truth traveled far afield to an African nation south of the practically impassable Sahara Desert. Once again, the prime mover in the drama was Philip the Evangelist.

It is with the third of our three spotlighted converts, though, that Satan absorbed the greatest and most surprising blow. To see a Roman centurion, by profession a servant of the gods of war, and likely at sometime in his life a worshipper of Rome's bellicose pagan gods follow a Prince of Peace is a marvel. As we have seen no further mention is made of Cornelius, but likely his career took him to other postings in Rome's immense empire. The heart of Cornelius was Christ's port of entry into the Gentile world, a field which would be far more fertile for the spreading of Christianity's seed than that of Judaism, whose rejection if Christ is embittering to this day. Just as importantly and more specifically this was the genesis of Christianity's incursion into Europe and Western Civilization, where historically the faith has maintained its greatest growth and influence.

Not exclusively but more and more predominately the Truth of Christ would spread into Gentile realms and the remainder of the Bible would be a story of its growing pains, persecutions, and triumphs among the Gentiles. With the violent murder of Stephen Satan may have preened himself on his great victory in an early destruction of the great evangelist. Instead, it was an unmitigated disaster for the Prince of Darkness since Christ's teachings spread rapidly throughout the world. As an added blow the victim Stephen easily elided directly into Heaven and the Arms of His Redeemer.

God's thinking is not that of humanity. It would seem that the Stephen was the logical figure to bring light into the darkness of the Gentiles, or perhaps even Philip the Evangelist. The Almighty's choice for that role, though, would come as a staggering shock to friend and foe, as now to the centrality of events would come the greatest individual change of course in all history.

CHAPTER SIX

BORN OUT OF DUE SEASON

In the Roman world of the first century A.D. three cities stood above all others as centers of learning and education. Rome itself was many things, but it still lacked that patina of intellectual pride and glory which had seemingly enabled the cities of Alexandria, Athens, and Tarsus. Alexandria, on the northern coast of Egypt, was the most famous of the apparently limitless numbers of cities and places which had been named after Alexander the Great. In addition to the famed Lighthouse of Alexandria, one of the Seven Wonders of the World, it boasted a magnificent library which contained perhaps the world's largest collection of recorded knowledge.

Athens, Greece, is a name that even in the twenty-first century evokes images of splendid architecture, the philosophy of Socrates, Plato, and Aristotle, the first great dramatists, scientists, astronomers, mathematicians, and luminaries in all other types of learning and the arts. Its glory had faded a bit by the first century AD, but as long as Western Civilization is honored (a decreasing likelihood) so will be Athens.

Tarsus is a city in southwestern Asia Minor (modern Turkey), and in antiquity was located but twelve miles inland from the Mediterranean coast. It had become a cosmopolitan metropolis, an east-west gateway for the far-flung Roman colossus, and to some, especially outside of Rome the very crossroads of the Empire. Its past glittered with historical glamor, for it was through here Alexander and his Greco-Macedonian army marched on their way to conquer the Persians. Two of history's most noted star-crossed lovers, Mark Antony and Cleopatra here first met, two powerful souls who historically embody the fate of those who grasp for too much power. Academically and intellectually the shining jewel in its panoply of municipal glory was the University of Tarsus. The first century Greek historian Strabo opined that by his time Tarsus had surpassed Rome, Athens, and Alexandria as a center of learning. Its most famous citizen pithily described Tarsus as "no mean city," and further it was a Roman "free city," wherein all free adult males had been granted the valuable honor of Roman citizenship. Certainly, even laughably, it was no backwoods Galilean village such as Nazareth or Capernaum.

That person who today is still reckoned as the most famous of all the dwellers in Tarsus made his historical and Biblical debut at the murder of Stephen, when the murderers stoned him and:

> "... the witnesses laid down their clothes at a
> young man's feet, whose name was Saul."

Why Saul himself did not actually participate in the stoning of Stephen remains a matter of conjecture but his heart, spirit, and life itself utilized the death of Stephen as a springboard for the savagery the first Christians endured:

"As for Saul, he made havoc of the Church, entering into every house, and haling men and women
committed them to prison."

We have been privileged with no contemporary biography
of Saul other than the bulk of the New Testament, which is to
follow him, his companions, and travels relentlessly, but that is
for later. Who was this young man so eager to kill Stephen, and
to destroy the recently established Church?

Saul was an extremely talented and gifted young man. From
his own writings we may glean that he was raised in prosperous, perhaps even wealthy circumstances. He was not just intelligent, but instead brilliant, at a young age taught under the
tutelage of Gamaliel in Jerusalem. It was Gamaliel who was
the most revered of all authorities on Jewish Law. Saul, by his
own later self-description was a Jew's Jew, a 'Pharisee of the
Pharisees," the strictest of all Jewish sects. He was a "good"
youth, no hypocrite to be sure, for he kept the strictures of the
Mosaical Law from childhood.

Being raised in Tarsus gave Saul special intellectual and cultural advantages. Tarsus's being a center of Greco-Roman culture he spoke Greek, certainly spoke Hebrew, and almost certainly was fluent in Latin as well. He could converse smoothly
on Hellenistic art, prose, poetry, and philosophy, but his greatest love and devotion was to God and the canons of the Hebrew
law. These few comments are but a skim on the waves of the
many and varied talents of young Saul. So much had coalesced
into this one youthful person. Certainly, youth, with its unique
advantages, not just intelligence but brilliance (more likely
genius), education, prosperity, public acclaim, boundless energy, and explosive ambition, both spiritually and personally.
Moreover, perhaps most importantly of all, he was one hundred

percent certain of the truth, righteousness, and efficacy of his own beliefs. Young Saul was a dangerous man, of a type that is easy to hate. What was worse, though, he was about to become not just a dangerous young man, but a dangerous young man with power, real power which he had every intention of wielding with severity and without mercy.

In those days following the death of Stephen, Saul exuberantly coveted a place in the front rank of the persecution that the Jews were unleashing on the nascent Church, nowhere bettered described than by Luke:

> "And Saul, yet breathing out threatenings and slaughter against the disciples of the Lord, went unto the high priest, And desired of him letters to Damascus to the synagogues, that if he found any of this way, whether they were men or women, he might bring them bound unto Jerusalem."

Now this bright young man with boundless energy had in his hands' edicts, orders, warrants, writs or whatever the high priest could authorize, the authority of the Jewish religious establishment now placed in the control of its rising young star. The arrested were to be brutally taken from their homes and families, thrown into the fetid filth of an ancient prison to await who knows what fate. Their unpardonable crime had been to become disciples of the Prince of Peace. As Saul and his companions journeyed somewhere on the road from Jerusalem to Damascus, a distance of over two hundred miles, suddenly Saul fell to the ground as a bright light from Heaven glowed and a voice was heard by the terrified Saul:

> "Saul, Saul, why persecutes thou me?"

Saul, doubtless terrified, responded with an inquiry as to identity of the Heavenly speaker:

"I am Jesus, whom thou persecutes: it is hard for
thee to kick against the pricks."

To the modern ear the last phrase is strange until explanation is offered. Pricks were sharp instruments, darts of a sort, utilized by herdsmen to control and drive animals. Considering, though, that Saul was neither sheep nor cow nor any other creature perhaps the gist of Christ's meaning in light of the character of the hearer is more likely"

"What are you going to say and do now, smart guy?

For once you are not the one in control."

Saul, "trembling and astonished," asked for directions, whereupon Jesus instructed the sojourning Saul, now blinded by the light, to continue to Damascus where he would be given further instructions. As astonished as he was his fellow travelers were no less so, for none of them heard or saw anything. Nonetheless the formerly self-assured, swaggering Saul was taken by the hand and led into the city, where for three days he ate or drank nothing.

Rarely do young men, brilliant, ambitions, hubristic young men such as Saul grant themselves time for true self-analysis and contemplation. Like petulant and misbehaving children often they must be temporarily confined to keep their bodies, minds, and ambitions from overheating. So it was with Saul, who was now in a sort of solitary confinement mentally, emotionally, and spiritually harsher than any modern maximum-security prison. He was blind, his appetites recoiled at the ideas of food and water. Only prayer and self-contemplation remained, and any observations on their structure and substance are truly speculative. Of a certainty, though, a mind such as Saul's never halted and now, he likely explored depths and places in his psyche the existence of which he had been unaware. After three (a Biblical number if ever there is one) the clay was ready for the Master's touch.

God's employments of dramatic power is often paradoxical. His chosen vessels are almost always ordinary men and women, but perhaps better described by placing the modification "seemingly" to precede ordinary. A disciple in Damascus named Ananias was directed by God to go to the house of Judas on a street named Straight where Saul of Tarsus awaited him. This command was terror-inducing for any sentient Christian. Saul of Tarsus? The chief persecutor of the early Church and a man whose hands had dipped deeply into the blood of the martyrs? Ananias had no shyness in expressing his reservations, but the Lord assured his safety, and he became the first man to hear God's plans, which two thousand years later are still taught:

> "Go thy way; for he (Saul) is a chosen vessel unto Me, to bear My name before the Gentiles and kings, and the children of Israel. For I will show him how great things he must suffer for My name's sake."

We should always be discreet and judicious in our employment of superlatives; however, the text of these forthcoming events demands a suspension of that principle. In Ananias, of whom we otherwise know little, God had found a true disciple, a man on intelligence, caution, resolve, courage, and obedience, for despite his natural fears of meeting with a maniacal persecutor we next find him speaking plainly to Saul. Ananias went straight (yes, a pun) to the street on which Saul was to be found, went into him, likely carrying a rapidly beating heart, laid his hands upon Saul and:

> "Immediately there fell from his eyes as it had been scales: and he received sight forthwith, and arose, and was baptized."

The chief persecutor, the Jewish establishment's point a man for prison and death was to them now and forever would be, a turncoat, that most despicable of all persons, and a disciple to boot, of the hated Galilean rabbi.

As for Saul, as self-assured and self-possessed as any young man who ever lived, through the Damascus Road miracle, the teaching of Ananias and receiving sight again he became not Christ's chief persecutor, but a specifically appointed apostle to all, especially the Gentiles. No quicker or more startling and complete reversal of direction is to be found in all the long history of humanity.

The greatest adulatory paeans of praise, though, are reserved for the Deity. Who but God and Christ could or would have done this? Even in the midst of the thick forest of resentment, hatred, and overt persecution of God's own people, His children, He saw that the soul and true character of Saul was not to be discarded to oblivion but to be converted to discipleship and the lead role in the evangelism of the world. To the cynic and the scornful the words are trite, but to the believer they are truth. Only God Himself could be so forgiving, so patient and so full of foresight as to make straight a path for Saul. Christians take it as a foundation of faith that God is forgiving to a degree and an intensity which even the finest of His fallible disciples never attain. Yet Saul had been prominent in the murder of Stephen, was "breathing out threatenings and slaughter" and was on his way to add more names to the list and more luster to his own name as the rising, fair-haired star of Judaism. God, though, not only accepted Saul but He made him the chosen vessel to kings and to the Gentile world. Saul was not the "first" apostle (no such office existed) but with Peter became the most prominent apostle of the early church. Only God had the forgiveness, the patience, the knowledge, and the foresight to literally throw Saul to the ground on that long road to Damascus, to forgive him and to make him a prime mover in the success of the early Church.

The changes effected in a man such as Saul may only be attributed to the Divine Agency of God Himself. Our gaze and thoughts return to Christ's selection of the original twelve apostles, an event which preceded this selection by only a few years. Galileans to a man, the majority fishermen, the records reveal no opposition or antipathy to Jesus before their selection. Each had his own character and personality and frequently easily discernible faults and flaws. None offered resistance to the Savior, and for certain none were His persecutors. Saul, though, was different, different in many tangible and important ways. Whereas the originals were basically "small town" Jews from Galilean villages, humble, hard-working, intelligent, but no great formal education, Saul was a Hellenistic Jew, from the metropolis Tarsus, no "mean city" and a hub of learning and education. Saul was familiar with Gentile ways, customs, languages, religious, etc. perhaps to an extent the others had not attained. He was on speaking terms with the high priest, a prize pupil of Gamaliel and inured to walking among the self-regarding "very important people." Still, His selection gives us reason to pause for a brief summation of Christ's judgment of human character. No man or woman would have chosen the non-descript original dozen men as apostles, the very foundation of the eternal institution, the Church, which he was building. Neither would any but the Master have chosen the Church's worst enemy, Saul of Tarsus, as the apostle "born out of due season." The old scriptural admonition that God's ways are not our ways, and neither is His thinking ours was once again renewed.

Still, what was the reaction of the existing Christians, particularly and maybe especially the apostles, to having their previous worst and most identifiable enemy in their midst, as one of them? Unsurprisingly the Christians at Damascus reacted as all Christians in any age would react. They recoiled in bafflement and suspicion and inquired:

> "Is not this he that destroyed them which called
> on this name in Jerusalem, and came hither for
> that intent, that he might bring them bound unto
> the chief priest?"

To go to a service of the Church and notice among the congregants the man whose very name was electric with terror and fear must have been an emotional trauma for any Christian. "By their fruits ye shall know them" Christ had taught, and the fruit of Saul had always been imprisonment or death for any Christian. Likely, it is no farcical exaggeration that by this time with many Christians Saul's name had become synonymous with the Devil. Here he was, though, one bright Sunday, sitting serenely and placidly among them, their friends, neighbors, and families. It was too much, even among those in whom the Spirit of Christ dwelled, to demand or ever expect a sudden and joyous acceptance of Saul as a brother in the faith. As talented and persuasive as was Saul, on his own actions he could not find full acceptance. The new apostle, though, was not on his own, and this assertion is not intended to have a Divine exclusivity.

Certainly, God was with Saul, but so were many disciples, and in particular one man whose spiritual courage and heroism are oft overlooked. This was Barnabas, one of the great leaders of the early church, a wealthy man in the forefront of missionary efforts and a partner of Saul's in those early endeavors.

Saul had made a surreptitious nocturnal escape from Damascus (more of which later) he had made his way to Jerusalem, there to join what was still the core, the very centrality, of early Christianity. Now, in the locale where Truth's blood had run and would flow in veritable rivers, from the days of the prophets, through the Passion of Jesus Christ Himself and from Stephen, the first martyr, whose death was a culmination of a conspiracy of which Saul had been a key player. The Jewish Christians in Jerusalem were no more eager to welcome the new "convert" into the fold than were those at Damascus:

> "And when Saul was come to Jerusalem, he assayed to join himself to the disciples: but they were all afraid of him, and believed not that he was a disciple."

Afraid they had a right to be, and fear is not magically, easily, or quickly overcome, even by the assurance of another man or woman. To banish fear often requires time and not just a preponderance of evidence but that which is "beyond a reasonable doubt" to clear the fearful heart and mind of all trepidations. One man, Barnabas, stepped forward and began the comforting process:

> "Barnabas took him, and brought him to the apostles, and declared unto them how he had seen the Lord in the way, and that he had spoken to him,

and how he had preached boldly in Damascus in
the name of Jesus."

The waves of fear, which had been almost a tsunami began to
subside, and the apostles accepted their new fellow:

"And he was with them coming in and going out
at Jerusalem."

Saul, always a busy young man, perhaps best described in
the modern phrase as hyper-active, now a new creature and imbued with a mission and an energy charged by Christ, began
a life which withstands little comparison with any which was
ever lived. Yet, the price, which was paid, constantly, continually, and incessantly was so great that it will fulfill the Master's
promise that "... he must suffer great things for My name's sake."

Later in the scriptures Saul provides a detailed inventory
of the calamities and even catastrophes which befell him in a
lifetime of serving as Christ's apostle. Many, if most, of these
are transfixed by times, dates, people, and places, but two difficulties which Saul always battled were so insidious that they
become part of the very fabric of his existence. The first is
what he experienced upon first becoming a Christian, which
encompassed a reluctance or even a refusal to be trusted by
other Christians, a deeply rooted distrust of his motives and a
general sense of the recurring question of "What is this char-
latan Saul up to?" These resentments and hatreds never went
away, but they abated and in time Saul's full acceptance by most
Christians was his enjoyment.

The second of Saul's lifelong troubles was the one which
not only followed him to his grave but provided an enthusiastic
escort to the cemetery. Our text has noted that soon after his

conversion he left Damascus for Jerusalem. While Saul's original entrance into Damascus was burdened by his own fears, temporary blindness and being led by the hand as if he were a child, it was of minor difficulty in comparison with his exit:

> "The Jews took counsel to kill him, But their laying await was known of Saul. And they watched the Jews day and night to kill him. Then the disciples took him by night, and let him down by the wall in a basket."

To the early Christians the newly converted Saul was a curiosity and certainly a man whose acceptance of a new faith would raise eyebrows. Yet to the members of the Jewish religious establishment, of which Saul had been a proud and prominent member, and a rising star Saul had become a toxic piece of refuse, that worst of all characters, a heretic, a turncoat, and a traitor. From this time forward their desire was never to "trip him up," to harass him or to make life difficult, but rather their desire was to kill him. The desperate measures they would take and the emotions which Saul, their one-time hero, had engendered in them would force many to go to absurd, almost comical lengths, to destroy Saul. Their hatred of a former champion was a river of bitterness, which would eventually carry Saul to his earthly demise. Still, we are getting ahead of the narrative, for the questions is now, what did Saul really do in that first period after becoming a Christian and an apostle?

Saul of Tarsus was a man with few idle moments in his life. He was now a Christian and an apostle and he joined fully with the other apostles "... coming in and out of Jerusalem." As a true believing scion of the Jewish establishment Saul was no wallflower, never reticent and now, in turn:

"He spoke boldly in the name of the Lord Jesus, and disputed against the Grecians: but they went about to slay him."

No person's life, especially one such as Saul, can be summarized in one sentence, but the above is an accurate though compact rendition of the remainder of Saul's life on this earth.

As intelligent as he was, as courageous, bold, enterprising, oratorical ad infinitum each of the other twelve apostles possessed one thing which Saul lacked. They had spent three years with the Master, living with Him, laughing, and loving Him, had witnessed His signs and wonders, and had absorbed three golden years of His teaching. In many ways until his very end Saul was sensitive, notably conscious of the fact that he was the self-described "apostle born out of due season," different in so many ways from he other chosen. Later he exclaimed that he was "not one whit behind the chiefest apostles," likely not because of any egoism but to suppress accusations that his teachings somehow had less authority than these of the other apostles. Though Saul was the latecomer he revealed in his own later writings that like the other twelve he too had received his teachings and training directly by the revelation of Jesus Christ. Regardless, though, this was a reality that would accompany Saul the remainder of his earthly trek. To many, especially Christians with a Jewish heritage, he would always have a certain suspicious cloak about him. To them he was insincere at best and a complete, maybe malicious fraudster at worst. These accusations, which matched the tenure of his apostleship were annoying, and exasperating, yet it was not his fellow Christians, whatever their national and religious heritage, who actively worked to harm Saul. His great enemy remained his one-time cohorts, a group in which he had moved to the front rank, the unbelieving Jews. From the beginning of his Christian mission to the end of his life they were incessant and fanatical in their attempts to destroy Saul. Many were the schemes, the plots, the chicaneries employed to trap and crush this apostle to the Gentiles. On their own, though, the Jews failed to deliver the death blow, and for that they required the very center of the world, the power of powers, the centrality of force, Rome itself.

Still today power in any era cannot be discussed without a thorough recourse to the city, the society and the nation that remains synonymous with the word power itself, Rome. Our introductory chapter was a very brief summary of high politics in Rome in the century before Christ and throughout his brief life. It was an unending narrative of titanic clashes between well-known historical figures such as Marius, Sulla, Crassus and Pompey and men whose fame, achievements and the wielding of the state's sword and power have woven their names into the cultural fabric of Western civilization. Men of the renown of Julius Caesar, Mark Antony and Augustus Caesar had their days in the sun, and the stories of their power radiated to the present and likely for all history. Yet by the time Christ founded His Church these men were long gone, and others had arrived to replace them. They and their understanding of power and its implementation invite us to refocus our attention upon Rome, where events, but events made by men are leading Rome unknowingly, but inexorably to the first struggle and clash of power between the mighty Empire and the fledgling Church.

CHAPTER SEVEN

ROMAN ADVENTURE

I f all roads lead to Rome, then just as assuredly those same roads lead away from Rome. Certainly, this was true in the first century, as that city on Italy's Tiber River needs no additional acclamations as the epicenter of world political power. This work's initial chapter attempted a brief summary of the political history of the century before the birth of Christ and even a few years beyond to the death of Augustus Caesar in 14 AD. Our focus since has been upon the amazing, phenomenally powerful Church in Judea and then beyond. Still, though, whether it was the first century world of the West or the hyperactive twenty-first century world, for this period of time Rome and power were synonymous. No one thought of the tiny, conquered nation of Judea as a world power, and even less so was that consideration given to the tiny Church which had arisen from its soil. That would have been laughable.

What was not laughable was the empire and the emperor's power which Augustus Caesar bequeathed to his stepson, Tiberius Claudius Nero Caesar, when Augustus died in 14 A.D. at the then advanced age of seventy-seven. Before delving into the identity and nature of Augustus's successors it is appropriate to offer a brief word on the lengthy reign of Rome's first emperor (although he himself always eschewed this title). Augustus left a political, economic, military, and to some degree a cultural heritage which the ancient world had never seen, and arguably that it has yet to view today. All southern Europe from the Iberian Peninsula (modern Spain and Portugal), Gaul (modern France and Belgium), all Italy, of course, Greece, Macedonia, the Balkans, much of what we today term the Middle East, all of Africa north of the Sahara from Egypt in the east to Morocco in the west bore the Roman suzerainty. A road system, marvelous and practical engineering works which benefited the population, growing and prosperous economies and a stable legal structure were the glory of Rome and redounded to the benefit of millions of otherwise disconnected people. For certain it had been built by military conquest, and Augustus, while still call Octavian Caesar, had risen to the pinnacle of power after one of the most violent and bloodiest centuries in history. So successful was Augustus's reign that it began a two-century period known as the Pax Romana (the "Roman Peace") which lived for some two centuries. Rome was in its prime of fame and power and even after the demise of Augustus would so remain for generations. Augustus Caesar was the most successful ruler in antiquity, and it is not preposterous to assert of all history. The great, powerful emperor, was dead now, and who or what would succeed him?

The answer to the question is the "Julio-Claudian" line of emperors, although even with that answer a technical inaccuracy appears. This was the blending of two ancient Roman aristocratic, or "patrician" families, whose lineage is interesting but not here relevant. Actually, the first of the line was Augustus himself, succeeded as noted, by Tiberius, and then (employing the names by which popular history recognizes them), Caligula, Claudius, and Nero. This succession of rulers has been (and continues without abatement) to be the subject of torrents of literature, biographies, analysis, motion pictures, television shows and documentaries. They are endlessly fascinating, decadent, salacious and perverse in their personal proclivities and appetites, and on and on ad nauseum. More to our interest, though, they were evil and any one emperor in his day was the most powerful man in the world. On one level, it is fortunate that they lived when they did, for Rome had ceased being an expansive power and was essentially content with its imperial boundaries and map. Although the span of the Julio-Claudian line is of considerable duration, excluding Augustus, 37 to 68 AD it was peaceful and prosperous. It had always been most interesting to us for two basic reasons: (1) the bizarre and often atrocious personal lives of its principals and their usage of power; and (2) its effect upon the Church, for remarkably the length of the dynasty closely coincides with the history of the early Church, found in the Book of Acts.

Although the personal lives of the high and mighty may excite our attention it should never be forgotten that these were the most powerful figures on earth, and even their personal lives could have great bearing on all people, events, and institutions, including the fledgling Church in far-away Judea.

Fortunately for Rome and especially for the individuals involved the transition from Augustus to Tiberius was relatively smooth and entirely non-violent. The latter fact alone places this transfer of office in a position of singularity in the Julio-Claudian line, for all other transfers of power had to some degree a measure of violence. So now Tiberius became the first "official" emperor of Rome, and his personality and character demand at least a modicum of attention. He was a soldier by profession, a Roman general of considerable success and in that sphere was a great asset to the imperial power. He inherited all the power and authority of his stepfather Augustus but coming with that bequest was little or nothing of the great reputation which Augustus had attained.

The Pax Romana continued to flourish under the new emperor, although there remained flashpoints of violence and insipient and aborted rebellions in obscure places such as Judea. At that eastern extremity of Empire occurred the Passion, the suffering and death of the unusual religious figure, Jesus of Nazareth. Historically, it seemed to be only a momentary flashpoint, and it is most likely that the emperor Tiberius lived and died with no knowledge of its existence.

The reign of Tiberius, again especially in its early phases, was generally a time of peace and prosperity. The powers of the state, fully and absolutely in the hands of Tiberius, were rarely employed in personal persecutions of the emperor's enemies, real and imagined, and the person and power of Emperor Tiberius was really a non-factor in the lives of the mass of Rome's citizens and subjects. Age was beginning to overtake the emperor, and probably for an admixture of reasons he moved to the Isle of Capri, a resort in the Mediterranean Sea off the western coast of Italy in 26 AD. He was certainly growing tired of the affairs of state, and he had found a man in whom he could place absolute trust as a form of prime minister. His name was Lucius Aelius Sejanus (20 B.C. – AD 31), who had become Prefect of the Praetorian Guard; the emperor's private army, in AD 14. By the time Tiberius left for the comforts and pleasures of Capri, so trusted had Sejanus become that he was effectively the in-absentia emperor. Tiberius, though aging, indulged his proclivities for sexual perversions, deviancies, and pedophilia, while on Capri. Sejanus, in his absence, for a time, was a de facto emperor as much as any man who ever ruled Rome.

Sejanus consolidated his personal power and that of the Praetorian Guard, which became a type of ancient Nazi SS with power independent from the regular army. With the power which had fallen into his increasingly grasping hands he kept apace by an increasing number of accusations, indictments, and treason trials against prominent men, including high ranking senators. All this resulted in increasing executions of the victims, and the power, the real power of the might of Rome had seemingly fallen into the hands of this soldier. Effectively, the de facto emperor of Rome was Sejanus. Yet "de facto" is still not complete, for the "de jure," or legal power, remained with Tiberius, who continued to luxuriate on Capri. News of all this traveled from Rome to Capri, wherein the Roman world was to discover that Tiberius had not yet reached the final stages of senility. Sejanus had reached the pinnacle of power, and the ancient historian Cassius Dio so observed:

> "Sejanus was so great a person by reason of his excessive haughtiness and of his vast power, that to put it briefly, he himself seemed to be the emperor and Tiberius a kind of island potentate, inasmuch as the latter spent his time on the island of Capri."

Sometimes, though maybe not as often as we hope, history, drama (or melodrama) and truth coalesce in one storied historical moment, and one of those moments belongs to the faded glory and memory of Sejanus. Just at the heighth of what he hoped was to be the attainment of absolute power Tiberius, through a cache of still loyal followers, accused Sejanus of treason before the Senate. He was summarily arrested, imprisoned, strangled to death and his body dragged down the Gemonian stairs, where the ever fickle and violent mob tore it to pieces. It is highly unlikely that the once powerful Sejanus had ever heard the words, but the man most associated with peace provided an epitaph most fitting for the would-be usurper of the throne:

"For all that take the sword shall perish with the sword."

As for Tiberius, a man who lived for some seventy-eight years, he remains a bland figure historically, and certainly he was not one of history's, or even Rome's prime historical figures. If remembered at all he is an answer to a sort of religious "trivia" question of "... Who was the emperor when Christ was crucified." Yet, Tiberius was no persecutor of the early Church, especially since he was probably unaware of its existence. What men and women do, especially kings and emperors, has a lasting, even an eternal importance, well beyond their lives. Tiberius was father to a man named Drusus, who became like him a Roman general of rising fame. The relationship between father and son was close, and also Tiberius had become a father figure to a young man from the east who had been sent to Rome. He was a friend of Drusus and some others in the royal lineage, and his name was Marcus Julius Agrippa, as Roman a name as can be conjured. As a youth and into early adulthood he must have had a certain magnetism, for he never lacked friends and admirers. He is known to all by the name Herod Agrippa, and he was the grandson of the notorious Herod the Great, the Jewish-Edomite king who had alternatively been an ally of Mark Antony and then Octavian and the later king of Judea, among other lands, and the would-be murderer of the baby of a Nazarene couple named Mary and Joseph. He lacked no friends in Rome, although he maintained a network of connections in Judea. In Rome he became friends with Caligula, the grandnephew of Tiberius and Claudius, the son of Drusus, and nephew of Tiberius, each of whom in succession would become emperors. Herod Agrippa's life in Rome was really the performance of a caricature, for he was known for his good-natured bonhomie, a certain Falstaffian gusto for life and huge gambling debts, for which he lacked the means to pay. His rank and position were no absolute shield, though, and he was imprisoned for debt. Discretion and modesty were never among his strengths, and one day he was heard wishing for the death of Tiberius and the elevation of Caligula. Overheard by the wrong persons again he was cast into prison. This is our introduction to Herod Agrippa, a man lacking in power but bloated with ambition. The remedying of his void of power will be a subject deferred to the next chapter.

As for Caligula (12 AD – 41 AD), whose full name was the properly Latin Gaius Caesar Augustus Germanicus, he was the son of Germanicus, the most glamorous Roman general since Julius Caesar, the conqueror of many German tribes, but a victim of an early death. Caligula, while still a relative youth had ingratiated himself with Tiberius and apparently leveraged a shared perverse immorality into a friendship with the old man, which had delivered. For the final six years of Tiberius's life Caligula lived with him on Capri, and by the machinations and consummate acting ability of the younger man the two became fast friends. A contemporary said of Caligula:

> "Never was there a better servant or a worse master."

In other terser terms, Caligula was a toady to Tiberius, yet it worked inasmuch as Caligula was designated his successor. At last, in 37 AD the old man succumbed either to natural causes, or perhaps to his being suffocated at the direction of Caligula. In any event the old man, not history's greatest villain, but for certain a dweller in the darker regions of human existence had expired, as did his grip on power.

So now, by hook or crook the young (25) man known as Caligula had come to supreme power. The name "Caligula" itself was a moniker given him while a little boy playing soldier in the army camps of his father, the great and esteemed Germanicus. It meant "little boot" and as the few years of Caligula's life rolled by it seemed to have a certain superficial accuracy, for everything about him seemed small. The descriptions of him delineate a young man of slight, thin stature with thinning hair and no special strength in any of his facial features. The physical man seemed to be the perfect embodiment of a tiny, but ferocious, soul. All about Caligula was not only petty but luminesced with a glow of macabre weirdness that his character has retained well into the twenty-first century. The one outstanding aspect of his character that was not inmature was the absolute power he wielded for four years as Emperor of Rome. Into the hands and the perverse mind of this deranged deviant had been placed a vastness of power greater than that possessed by any other man or woman. At his direction, the world's greatest army would march, huge sums of money would be expended, and heads would and did roll (literally).

Surprisingly, though, Caligula's early days as emperor were somewhat aglow with the promise of brighter days to come. The upstart tyrant Sejanus was gone, and the old wizened "good-for-nothing anymore" Tiberius was in his grave, though likely at the hand of Caligula. The new young emperor certainly had friends, supporters and well wishers, among whom was Herod Agrippa, more mature now and ready for great responsibility.

As for Caligula's debut he was hailed by many Romans as "our baby" and "our boy." Although his initial actions as emperor were certainly politically motivated, they seemed to reflect not harshness, but a generosity of spirit. Bonuses were granted to all soldiers, especially members of the vital Praetorian Guard, treason charges instigated by Tiberius against many Romans were dismissed, and he sponsored many public spectacles, including gladiatorial games, always a key element in maintaining the support of the Roman public. Further, he had the aura of being the son of the famed Germanicus, the youthful godlike figure fallen in his prime without the expected fulfillment of his imperial destiny.

Still, Caligula is remembered little at all for any of this, but rather for his increasingly maniacal and sadistic exercise of power, of which he never had enough. Caligula's exercise of power seemed to flow in two separate channels, but each supporting the other one was the bizarre and whimsical, an attributable which has been dramatized (perhaps excessively) in modern entertainment. For example, he appointed to consul, the state's highest office, his own horse, although in this gesture it is easy to read contempt for the pretensions of high-ranking Roman politicians. Often, in the imperial palace he would assign to the Praetorian soldiers the daily and nightly passwords, and he displayed an adolescent's delight in giving them sexual crudisms and vulgarities, especially of a homoerotic nature, which they were humiliatingly compelled to repeat.

The other stream of his power had little or nothing of the whimsical to it. Shortly after becoming emperor, he had his own cousin and adopted son, a boy named Tiberius Gemellus executed for no reason other than his being a potential threat to Caligula's throne. Most importantly Caligula alienated the Roman Senate, an aristocratic, proud, and egocentric body of men who publicly, at least, portrayed a zeal for their own power. The young emperor increasingly sought to constrain the remaining power of the Senate, much of which they had already delegated to previous emperors.

Finally, it was all too much, especially for officers of Caligula's own Praetorian Guard. The emperor continually mocked them with sexual innuendo, and one man in particular, Cassius Chaerea, possessed of a high-pitched voice was savagely mocked by Caligula for seeming to be effeminate. One day a carefully planned action was undertaken, and Rome's young emperor received the knife wielded by Chaerea and many other wounds from his fellow soldiers and ingloriously expired. As Caligula's blood drained from his unimpressive body so to, did all his power.

Chaos ran unchecked in the imperial palace. Caligula's close personal guard, all Germanic soldiers, went on a rampage of revenge killing the guilty and innocent alike. This day truly was a day for soldiers, but those of the Praetorian Guard were worried. Should republican sentiment, which was raging, prevail, the imperial dynasty would cease with no further need for the specialized Praetorian Guard. When chaos is rampant so is fear, and members of the imperial family had reason to fear. Cassius Chaerea, leader of the assassination conspiracy went above and beyond the conspiracy's pre-set boundaries and had both Caligula's wife and baby murdered. None of the Julio-Claudian Line was safe, especially one as close to the emperor as his uncle, Tiberius Claudius Augustus Germanicus ("Claudius" to history), who was found by a soldier named Gratus as he was cowering behind drapes. According to the ancient historian Tacitus, Gratus and many of the elite Praetorian soldiering quickly settled upon the thought of Claudius as the new emperor. With a large cohort of highly trained and experienced soldiers standing at his back Claudius seemed a strong choice. Without those men of arms, though, it appeared to be a ridiculous idea to all. Claudius was half-deaf, spoke with a stutter and walked with a limp. To modern audiences he was immortalized in the BBC's 1976 production of I, Claudius, where all these handicaps are acknowledged, compounded by a perceived mental deficiency (which effectively did not exist). A harmless crippled man of dull wits? Yes. An emperor? No. Effectively, the Senate wished no new emperor but, in some manner, would have to accede to such. Claudius had little, or no, support except for the soldiers at his back, and an old friend who by now had been highly trained in the affairs of state at the highest levels. This was Claudius's longtime comrade, Herod Agrippa. For a non-Roman, or actually for any individual, Herod had demonstrated a lifelong affinity, even a genius for making friends in the highest of places. Claudius, no fool, was reluctant to accept the power of the throne, but Herod encouraged him otherwise. With the sage advice of his old friend, the prestige and power of the Praetorian Guard, and a Senate which was increasingly emasculated, Claudius consented to the grasp of power, and Rome now had its third emperor.

Although Claudius Caesar historically has borne a certain patina of dullness, perhaps attributable to his physical maladies, the period of his reign (AD 41-54) is of monumental importance to the rise of Christianity. Neither Biblically nor historically is there found any juncture of Claudius and this new religion, but both spiritual and peculiar sources record the emperor's expulsion of Jews from the city of Rome. Historically the records reflect that this was at least the third time that this eastern sect had been banished from the imperial city. This time, though, it was likely different. Many historians, even those with no particular bent towards Christianity, assert that the banishment was really directed at the Jewish Christians, who at this time were still deemed by the Romans as no more than a particularly noisy, obstreperous Jewish sect.

Like so many kings, rulers and officials of all types, Claudius, without the emperor's office, would have been a total non-entity, known today by only a few of the most detailed and diligent scholars of ancient history. Under his reign his good friend and confidante, Herod Agrippa, would see his power expanded from the post of Tetrarch of Galilee and Perea to also be made King of Palestine, including Judea, Galilee, Perea and Balanaea eastward to Trachonis. His authority and power was great, as widespread as his grandfather of infamy, Herod the Great, and effectively even greater.

Herod Agrippa's sojourn in Rome, his masterful synthesis of two distinctly different cultures, Rome and Judea, was reaping huge dividends. His own talents, which were considerable and the immense power and energy, both sycophantic and synergistic, created by his comradeship with two emperors, Caligula and Claudius, was harvesting huge and bounteous advantage to King Agrippa I. It also proved the perfect backdrop for the clash of three great powers, pagan Rome, the entrenched Jewish establishment, and Christianity. It is the manner and outcome of this clash which remains of consummate interest.

CHAPTER EIGHT

HEROD AGRIPPA BECOMES A GOD

I t has been remarked that all political careers end in defeat. While we leave the exactitude of that remark for another day's discussion the generality of its truth may be recognized. The historical titans (of power and fame) so remind us. Julius Caesar died in a bloody heap, the victim of twenty-three knife thrusts from presumed friends and colleagues, Alexander the Great expired far from his Macedonian home, ill in bed at the ridiculously young age of thirty-two and Napoleon Bonaparte gasped his last breath in exile on a barren rock of an island in the South Atlantic. Although his historical stature is not close to the level of such figures as these, King Herod Agrippa's life, especially in its latter stages, is a fascinating object lesson of both what was and what might have been.

In this story of the history of the early Church, to this point Herod Agrippa has played no part, and even in our brief scan of the Roman's history he has been but a minor figure. Now, though, for a brief moment Herod assumes a major role in the history of both institutions, Rome and the Church, for to date

113

Herod is that most envied of all persons, a "winner." He had spent many prime years of his life in the Eternal City and its environs and knew Rome, its culture, its manners, and its idiosyncrasies well. Herod had become fast friends with two successive emperors, Caligula, now dead, and Claudius, fully ensconced in his emperor's might. From these friendships he had parlayed and finagled royal appointments to the very zenith of the power possessed by his illustrious grandfather, Herod the Great. In modern parlance he was superb at networking, and readily employed what many of the strata of his class would have deemed a charming personality. In short, in his lengthy sojourn Herod Agrippa had acquitted himself exceptionally well, and not many persons, Roman or Jewish, could boast of having the emperor himself as a close personal friend. He had become a familiar figure in the corridors of Roman power, and except for Tiberius, now long in his grave, he seems to have had no real enemies. The powerful winds of Rome were at his back. They would be needed.

By AD 41 Herod Agrippa was king over a political realm the equal or perhaps the superior to that of Herod the Great, but he was relatively new to the role. Most of the subjects over whom he ruled as a sort of Roman viceroy, were Jews, whose enmity for Rome had never diminished. Herod, ethnically to be certain was part Jewish, but even more salient and more to the relevant point he was Jewish by religion. Actually, his life had demonstrated a certain sincerity (at least of a partial nature) for Judaism, for Herod Agrippa had an abiding interest in Jewish customs and religious practices. In a pure political sense Herod needed to demonstrate this interest, inasmuch as the Herods and the Jews they ruled had always maintained a prickly relationship. If Herod Agrippa was to win the favor of the Jewish people and increase his power, overt action was requisite.

For many millennia politicians have asked the question "How do I make myself more popular, more loved?," and one of the undying answers to this inquiry is to find a person, an idea, in effect a scapegoat that can be excoriated as an emblem of vitriol and hatred alike by the ruler and the ruled, and so Herod found one. It is now the early AD 40's, and the Church founded by Christ is beyond its infancy but continuing with the metaphor it is still in its toddler years. At first an exclusively Jewish institution, with the apostle Peter's taking the truth to the Roman Cornelius, the Gentile world had been breached. Increasingly the Church was assuming a Gentile complexion, its early momentum in the Jewish community had begun to lag. It is not unfair or prejudicial to observe the simple reality that a high percentage of the Jews hated the Church. Wise, crafty Herod had found common cause with his subjects, and he tossed the apostle James into prison. This was the James of Jesus's inner circle, which included Peter and John, the same James who was present with the Master in Gethsemane where his agony wrought drops of blood from the Savior's brow. He was a prominent apostle, a prominent leader, and a prime Herodian target:

> "Herod the king stretched forth His hands to vex certain of the Church. And he killed James the brother of John with the sword."

As coldly clinical a case study in the unfettered employment of raw power as these words provide, they are emotionally exceeded by the next sentence:

> "And because he saw it pleased the Jews, he proceeded further to take Peter also."

If one cold-blooded murder of an apostle is good, two is even better (and more beneficial to my image and popularity) thought Herod. So, Peter, to date the most prominent of Christ's chosen twelve, was confined, undoubtedly with a diabolical severity, to await the next blow of the executioner's sword.

Within that foreboding world of brute force in which so many power seekers reside, whether by desire or reality, Herod Agrippa was now operating from its highest altitudes. His word alone, as the king, could sever the head from any body which was subject to his word. Whether they realized it or not (and most likely did not) all in his kingdom were living only by the whimsical employment of the king's powers. Herod's power as king was as real as power comes, although he was already far down a path that destroys power seekers. He was working and acting on the assumption that his power was inviolable, that it was endless and would yet grow stronger. The king of Judea failed to account for the entrance onto the stage of another power. Herod's power had not diminished, but he was about to be shown its limitations.

His prize prisoner, Peter, an apostle yet still a lowly working-class fisherman, had assigned to his person sixteen soldiers to keep close guard upon him. Even more directly he was chained to two soldiers and slept between them at night, any night of which he was likely expecting to be his last. One of those night's Herod finally sent for Peter, but so had God:

> "And behold an angel of the Lord came upon him, and a light shined in the prison; and he smote Peter of the side, and raised him up saying, Arise up quickly, And his chains fell off from his hands."

Quickly, the angel prodded Peter, and as he put on his garment and shoes, they exited the prison:

> "And he went out, and followed him; and knew
> not that it was true which was done by the angel;
> but thought he saw a vision."

With the angel's departures, though, Peter regained his equilibrium and "... knew that the Lord hat sent His angel, and hath delivered me out of the hand of Herod." God's power, real power, had bested Herod Agrippa, and it had been exercised quietly under the night's mantle of darkness.

Affairs, though, were not as quiet back at the prison for in the morning:

> "...(T)here was no small stir among the soldiers,
> what was become of Peter."

With their wonderment these men of arms had added a fear, a stark terror, of what Herod would do because of the sudden absence of his prized prisoner. Peter had made his way down to the house of the mother of John Mark, a disciple and author of increasing importance, and his appearance startled, even terrified, all the disciples who had gathered together in a prayer for the release of their most prominent brother and for their own safety from the terrors of Herod, whose thirst for blood had yet to be slaked. When Herod found that his prize prisoner had vanished the king personally examined the keepers at the prison. When they, probably trembling in terror at what was soon to be visited upon them, could give no explanation satisfactory explanation to Herod he had them "... put to death," i.e. murdered. As life still daily demonstrates it is not wise or advisable to ever be caught in the angry, crosshairs of the high and mighty.

For the moment, though, King Herod Agrippa had his fill of scruffy, bedraggled fishermen and their nonsensical, blasphemous religion. He had greater, more important, more spectacular matters on his agenda, namely his own self-glorification and apotheosis.

A fuller, more complete understanding of King Herod Agrippa and of his activities, requires an assiduous undertaking of the complicated background of the man. In current twenty-first century terminology Herod Agrippa could have passed the "diversity" tests and hurdles of all but the most exacting and prudish of diversity monitors. We have identified him as the grandson of King Herod the Great, husband of many wives and father to many children, most of whom he murdered for various reasons. Herod the Great, historically the "first" Herod, was neither Jew nor Gentile. Herod the Great, born in 72 B.C. was partially Arabian and partially Edomite, a people who traced their origin to the famed Esau of the Old Testament. This Herod, though, was raised as a Jew, and for his purposes had the good fortune of being raised and maturing during some of the most dynamic years of ancient history. At various times he become friends and allies or conversely antagonists and enemies with historical figures of the highest rank, that is Octavian, later the Emperor Augustus, Mark Antony, and Cleopatra. His life is the subject of plentiful biographies, and its details are not fully relevant to our present interests. Nonetheless, he was an adroit politician and was masterful at staying on the good side of the Romans. Most specifically, he ingratiated himself with Octavian, and when that rising star became sole ruler of Rome in 31 B.C., he quickly named Herod the Great the King of the Jews, a position which he held until his demise in 4 B.C. By no means universally popular most of his subjects respected his political and administrative skills, and in some ways, they benefited from the massive construction projects which were a hallmark of his reign. To many traditional, devout Jews, he remained a figure of hatred. The Pharisees particularly had an easy enmity for Herod. He was only half-Jewish (and that Edomite), and he became increasingly enamored with introducing Roman and Greek cultures into the Jewish way of life.

Whatever one's opinion of King Herod the Great, though, all Jews were united by a common emotion, the fear of him and his power. It would be tedious and essentially needless to attempt a catalogue of his tyranny, so let us be reminded that the one action for which Herod the Great is most remembered through the centuries is the infamous Slaughter of the Innocents, the hell-borne but failed plot to kill the infant Christ.

The Herod ancestral tree to the death of Herod the Great is complicated, but thereafter it assumes an intricacy and a bizarre quality that makes Herodian lineage almost impossible to decipher. Herod the Great's offspring included Herod Antipas, the most noteworthy and infamous of his children. He was married to Herodias (as if the Herods had not already created sufficient confusion). It was Antipas, at the trickery and instigation of Herodias who himself was one of the "sinful men" to whom Christ Himself was delivered before his crucifixion.

Herein our principal actor Herod Agrippa I, was the grandson of Herod the Great and the son of Aristobulus and Berenice, which also made him the brother to Herodias. Hopefully, with brevity we have introduced the lineage and background of Herod Agrippa I with the abbreviated mentions of his more famous relations. Herod Agrippa was well trained by family history and his own observations while growing up upon the value and the premium which all his kin placed upon the attainment and exercise of political power. To this date, though, almost all the Herodian power had been exercised over the Jews, and rulers and ruled had become somewhat accustomed one to another. It was Herod Agrippa, well-schooled and perhaps even genetically programmed to exercise power over the Jews, who had been given the advantageous award of many his younger years being spent in Rome, and in a Roman world where he seemed to move essentially as an equal with emperors and future emperors such as Augustus, Caligula, and Claudius. The diversity of his knowledge, comfort in two distinct cultural worlds and his own, still unfulfilled ambitions fashioned him as a man to be watched.

It was now the moment for this highly self-regarded man, Herod Agrippa, to return to the city of Caesarea, the administrative center of his kingdom. This was a city built by Herod the Great on a beautiful plain which lay on the Mediterranean coast of Judea. It was the home of three noted Roman governors who lived there during crucial Biblical moments, Pontius Pilate, Festus, and Felix, and it had also been the home of the Roman centurion, Cornelius, the first Gentile Christian. It was the site of a large 30,000 seat hippodrome (the fictional locale of the famed chariot race in Ben Hur), and a large amphitheater for public gatherings. Judea could be a hard and harsh land, but nothing of this sort characterized Caesarea.

Tyre and Sidon are famous Biblical cities, so noted by Christ Himself. They were Canaanite (more properly Phoenician to the Romans) and lay just north of Galilee, adjacent to Herod's kingdom. For whatever reason Herod had become highly displeased with these cities, certainly two locales which could not withstand the might and power of either Herod or Rome. The Phoenicians, though desired peace, and through an intermediary named Blastus, they had apparently calmed the waters between themselves and the great king. A wise Roman official, whatever his title, was expected to maintain peace, and it was a celebratory moment when this was achieved under the auspices. Great moments where kings have done great things require great crowds of people where the king's greatness may be made resplendent and shown to his subjects.

Power, especially political and religious power, is a peacock which loves to preen and display its presumed singularity of dazzling beauty to all its subjects and to those lesser mortals which compose most of the world's teeming population. The Romans, of whom Herod Agrippa was the present monarchial agent, were masters at this particular skill. The triumph given to a conquering Roman general was an ornate and majestic parade honoring one man through the lengthy streets of Rome. It could last days and was often a prelude to the hero's elevation to greater glory and in some instances even deification. Disdainfully people of the West have often ridiculed the ornate, glittering self-adulation and worshipful aspects of Eastern potentates, but history records that we have kept pace. The medieval monarchs increasingly were characterized by the finery of their clothing and jewelry, but outpacing them were glitterati of the medieval church, with its popes, cardinals, bishops, and lesser acolytes being costumed in finery the value of which likely surpassed the life's earnings of the average working man.

We modern men and women, buoyed by tacit societal agreement that with our pseudo-democratic mores and manners still replicate the pomp and circumstance of earlier supposedly benighted ages. The high fashion industry and culture shows no signs of abatement, and for certain neither does the endless array of an increasing variety of celebrity awards shows which provide a perfect opportunity for the display of peacock finery. In the plainest terms it all screams and bellows "Look at me!"

for the bearer of power, of celebrity and of fashion and fame is by his or her declaration severed rungs above the common people on any societal ladder. Any account of this human phenomenon and failing would be remiss if it failed to note only a single Biblical reference to the clothing of either Christ or His apostles. As He was dying on the cross the Roman soldiers gambled for title to the few garments the dying Savior possessed.

Herod Agrippa, in the fullest of his power and glory was set to carry his spectacular aura of splendor to stratospheric heights few before or since have attempted to scale. His audience was to be his fellow Roman officials, their Jewish counterparts, the many and varied sycophants which parasitically draw succor from the high and mighty and quite apparently a large audience of Jews over when he ruled and had yet won over to his side. They awaited with needles of excitement and anticipation. In his account the physician and historian Luke is typically both terse and informative:

> "And upon a set day Herod, arrived in royal apparel, sat upon his throne, and made an oration unto them."

The simple statement is direct, vigorous, and well explanatory, but for an even greater vision of Herod's performance we must consult another famous ancient historian, Flavius Josephine. Herod Agrippa and Josephus lives had only a slight overlap in years, and they are not really contemporaries. The two bear an eerie similarity to each other, though. Herod was half-Jewish but had been reared in the Jewish tradition and the Mosaical religion, while Josephus was entirely Jewish. Herod bestrode both the Gentile and Jewish worlds and ruled his own people as an agent of the Romans. Josephus had been a military commander of high rank among the Jews, but later switched to the Roman side. All the sophistry of historical analyses and neat arguments cannot alter the reality that both men were traitors to their own people. Nonetheless, Josephus became the greatest of ancient Jewish historians and thus records the appearance of King Herod Agrippa:

> "On the second day of the spectacles (in honor of Caesar) Herod put on a garment wholly made of silver, of a truly wonderful texture, and came into the theater early in the morning. There the silver of the garment being illuminated by the fresh reflection of the sun's rays, shone out in a wonderful manner, and was so resplendent as to spread awe over those that looked intently upon him. Presently his flatterers cried out, one from one place, and another from another, (though not his own god) that he was a god; and they added, "Be thou merciful to us, for although we have hitherto reverenced thee only as a man, yet shall we henceforth own thee as superior to mortal nature."

The silly, sycophantic mob had in this moment transformed Herod from a man to a god, but to this, Josephus records "...the king neither rebuked them nor rejected their impious flattery." The echoes of long ago in the Garden must have enticingly massaged the ears of Herod:

> "For ye shall be as gods."

Herod's power hunger, his brilliant display over a lifetime of befriending and flattering the right people at the right time, his masterful ability to win power and acclaim from the Romans in the west and the Jews in the east had allowed him to scale the greatest heights of power, to where he was but a trifle from its pinnacle, perhaps rule in Rome itself. He had become a god.

No king, emperor, or ruler of any ilk for one moment had received greater accolades and adulation than did Herod Agrippa, King of all Judea. None ever had a greater, more precipitous fall in a scintilla of time than did Herod Agrippa. He went from the acclaim of the multitude and the self-assumption of the divine to, in Luke's account:

> "Immediately the angel of the Lord smote him because he gave not God the glory; and he was eaten of worms, and gave up the ghost."

Josephus, as was his custom provided a more graphic illustration of the life and power which had begun to drain from the royal body of Herod Agrippa:

> "A severe pain arose in his belly, striking with a most violent intensity. (H)is pain became violent. Accordingly he was carried into the palace, and the rumor went abroad everywhere that he would certainly die soon. And he had been quite worn out by the pain in his belly for five days, he departed this life, being in the fifty-fourth year of his age."

Thus did the rising meteoric star of the entire Roman political world reach the apogee of his acclaim only to quickly plummet to earth into a putrid, stinking, fetid heap of rotting flesh beset by crawling, wriggling worms, maggots, and God knows what else (in the literal meaning of this expression). It had taken this Herod, marvelously well placed and gifted (or cursed) with enormous political gifts to attain a realm as great as his storied grandfather Herod the Great only fifty-four years to achieve power and acclaim wherein he was virtually knocking on the door of Rome itself.

We beg the reader's indulgence as now we offer a time worn cliché, i.e., that the life of Jerod Agrippa had its ups and downs and peaks and valleys. So do all lives. Herod, though, captures both a religious and a historical interest because, while not historically unique, he was able not only to stride confidently in two worlds, the Roman and the Jewish, but to be dazzlingly successful in each. Only half-Jewish, and not at all Roman, he built a power base in Rome by apparent ease of movement and force of personality to where he became close friends and confidantes with two successive emperors, Caligula and Claudius. This was the heart and soul of his Roman political power, and it as well as his name prompted to the title of King, wherein his power likely exceeded that wielded by his grandfather. Herod Agrippa's Roman flank was secure, while simultaneously he built increasing power and favor among his supposed "countrymen," the Jews. Any popularity the Herodian dynasty had with the Jewish populace was always tenuous at best, yet Herod Agrippa seemed to find the pathway into the hearts of the Jewish leadership and establishment through the persecution of the Christians, commencing with the apostle James' murder, that of Peter, who escaped only through God's miraculous grace and who knows what to follow, likely a general persecution of the new church. It was not to be, though.

On that day in Caesarea almost two thousand years ago four powers were present on the stage of the great amphitheater when Herod Agrippa was proclaimed a god. Of course, the Romans, the reigning military and political power, dominated all. Ultimately, Herod Agrippa I answered to Rome, and he was its agent. Likely, though, his demise, while shocking, caused little stir or consternation among the Roman powers. Quickly, Herod's son, Herod Agrippa II succeeded him, but only in part, for he was denied Judea and was limited in scope.

It was Judea after all where this strange event transpired, and the Jews had given a great impetus to Herod's powerful forward momentum. Although beholden to the Romans the Jews maintained enormous religious influence. Herod Agrippa I had become their man, and he was to be both a spear point and a powerful battering ram in their ongoing persecution of the Christians. Again, such was not to be.

In his brief tour de' force upon the ancient stage King Herod Agrippa I was becoming not a shining star, not a superstar, but a supernova, a star which burns brightly but briefly and then dies. Whatever light emanated from Herod it quickly dissipated as his grotesquely diseased entrails were dissolved by the slithering and ravenous maggots and worms.

The fourth power of the drama seemed somewhat inconspicuous and reticent. Yet this power, the real power, is omnipresent and briefly mentioned by the historian Luke as he closed his chapter on this strange story:

"But the word of God grew and multiplied."

Power, real power.

CHAPTER NINE

THE JOURNEY BEGINS

The growth and multiplication of churches and Christians did not occur of itself, for now the Church, in spite of opposition and outright persecution, had begun a period of growth and expansion that in two thousand years hence has never seen an equivalent. Now its growth was shared by two cultures always believed and taught in traditional Jewish history to be anathema one to another. The Gentiles (all the world but the Jews) culturally had always been kept at arm's length by serious, observant Jews. Religiously, though, they were pariahs, but as the earlier chapters have disclosed this was beginning to change. Peter had brought the Truth to the Roman soldier Cornelius, and the Jew of all Jews, Saul of Tarsus, had himself become not only a Christian but an apostle. Thoroughly committed to Christ, brilliant in mind, indefatigable in labors and of an almost fanatical singularity of devotion he is known today, as he was in the New Testament, as the apostle to the Gentiles. All true but two modifications are required. Not to the Gentiles only but also to the Jews did this astonishing man minister. Further, the very Jewish name of Saul was dropped, and henceforth and ever after he has become known as the apostle Paul, a more Gentile sounding appellation.

Commencing with the death of Herod Agrippa, as related in the previous chapter, the second half of Luke's great history of the early Church is the story of the dissemination of the good news of Jesus Christ told primarily by using the life of Paul and several of his companions as the protagonist evangelists who spread that word. Briefly Paul and several others were congregated at the city of Antioch of Pisidia in Asia Minor, a site forever immortalized as the place where the disciples were first called Christians. Here the Church experienced a spectacular burst of growth, and here it had an abundance of teachers of high ability, most notably Paul and Barnabas. The latter has already appeared in our narrative, and he is certainly a man of great spiritual stature and depth. In these days and for some time following he was closely associated with Paul and appeared to have garnered the same amount of fame and praise, though, not of ridicule and hatred. He was a Hellenistic Jew from the island of Cyprus, a man of some wealth and a talented public speaker.

Barnabas's home of Cyprus was soon visited by him and his companion Paul when they came to Salamis and there established a pattern which was oft repeated. It was a template for behavior and a script for conduct that maintained a large, ever changing yet remaining static cast of characters. That pattern was repeated at Antioch, and it is here that Paul and Barnabas began to achieve an early special notoriety, and for our immediate interest it is in this famous city where we have an extensive record of speech from Paul, the man to the present day stands as Christianity's most famous and to man, its greatest evangelist.

As Jesus Himself said it was first to the Jews that the gospel would be taught, and Paul, the greatest Apostle to the Gentiles was not excepted from this ordination. The custom of Paul and Barnabas was to first go to the Jewish synagogue for Sabbath, i.e. Saturday, worship. In Antioch they did so, and as was their manner arrived, were seated and were as quiet and inconspicuous as possible. The Sabbath service progressed as usual and at its conclusion the rulers of the synagogue asked these visitors if they had anything to say. Paul, physically an unprepossessing and inconspicuous figure, arose, beckoned the Jewish audience of another great orator only a few years previous. It was essentially the same sermon offered by Stephen to the Jewish Sanhedrin, a sermon most certainly heard by Paul while he was still the zealous Saul of Tarsus. It is a sermon made for a Jewish audience and these two sermons by Stephen and Paul engraved a template that was continually used for teaching the Jews.

The sermon was tailor-made for a knowledgeable Jewish audience. Little direct teaching on morals was included, for the assumption (correctly) was made that an informed Jewish audience was already well-versed on the moral principles of the Mosaical Law, little changed by Christ. The Jews were and are a people of exceptional mental ability and acuity, very learned, extremely thorough, and quite rigorous intellectually. So, Paul began with Moses and the Exodus and continued down the centuries long path through the Law, the establishment of the nation of Israel, the era of the Judges, the Kings, the Prophets and even beyond what Stephen delivered, for it was there that Stephen had so antagonized his fellow Jews that they stoned him. Paul, though, was granted leave to continue and he was able to introduce the birth of the Savior, John the Baptist, the Passion of Christ and culmination in the resurrection and the gift of forgiveness for sins. To a non-Jew, or to any person of indifference it would have been of little interest, boring and perhaps more than a bit pedantic. The interest and observant

Jews, though, being a people of intellectual rigor, which often encroaches into the realm of pure legalism, listened.

The sermon and teachings of Paul and Barnabas had a noticeable effect upon the Jews:

> "And when the congregation was broken up many of the Jews and religious proselytes followed Paul and Barnabas: who, speaking to them, persuaded them to continue in the grace of God."

The reactions of a multitude of Jews, as it had been since Pentecost, was positive, and such was the true for the Gentiles as well:

> "And when the Jews were gone out of the synagogue, the Gentiles besought that these words might be preached to them the next sabbath."

Paul was achieving splendid success in his labor as apostle to both the Gentiles and the Jews, but there remained a growing fly in the ointment that became an integral, yet unwanted, element in the remainder of Paul's life. As yet, however, the joy and success of the Christians was unmarred and still growing for on:

> "... the next Sabbath day came almost the whole city together to hear the word of God."

Such an outpouring of interest and support in a major city such as Antioch certainly did not go unnoticed:

> "But when the Jews saw the multitudes, they were filled with envy, and spoke against those

things which were spoke by Paul, contradicting
and blaspheming."

The timeless consistency of the established order of the
Jewish political and religious hierarchy was astonishing. The
reactions, the emotions, the hatred and the criminality began
with their opposition to Christ Himself, then the early confrontation with Peter and John, the martyrdom of Stephen and their
fanatical hatred of Paul.

Lest the world ever forget, though, at the Last Supper it was
the Savior who told the original apostles that:

"If the world hate you, you know that it hated Me
before it hated you."

This hatred was now not only inclusive of Paul, but as time
progressed it became an emotion of white-hot intensity with
so many, especially the self-denominated "righteous" and
"religious" Jews. Yes, Paul engendered hatred among certain
Gentiles, but to the mass of the unbelievers he and his fellow
apostles seemed to remain more an object of curiosity than
an article to hate. Certainly, at first many of the Jews became
Christians, but apparently but a few of the ruling hierarchy,
the scribes, the Pharisees, the high priests, and such retained
only hatred, certainly for Christ but also for Paul. To them this
one-time star of Judaism has become a detested renegade and
turncoat. He was to be especially feared, an intellectual force
in whom they once had great pride, a zealot for the Law and
traditional Judaism, a dynamic speaker and tireless worker.
Now, all these qualities in which they had taken such pride had
been turned against them as he became a servant and an apostle, the most prominent at that, of the despised carpenter from

Nazareth, a man whose death had proven even more problematic to them than His life.

The primary theme of the New Testament is the saving power of Jesus Christ, yet in this most densely textured and informative book room is found for many subordinate themes. Not the least of these is the antipathy which the Jewish religions establishment felt and displayed towards Paul. The apostle born out of due season did not display hatred in return, but he became increasingly filled with shock, disgust and likely a little sadness at his fellow Jews.

The Jews were a people of great intellect, but the opposition to Christianity, which gradually became to have a duality of focus on the religion itself as well as the person of the apostle Paul, was not a mere mental dissent. As will be seen increasingly it came with the violence of persecution, which no doubt was nourished by, to them, the brazen conduct of Paul and Barnabas, for:

> "... (they) waxed bold, and said, it was necessary that the word of God should first have been spoken to you: but seeing ye put it from you, and judge yourselves unworthy of everlasting life, lo, we turn to the Gentiles."

Antioch, its suburbs, and environs was proving to be fertile ground for the truth, so much so that as the first century progressed the center of gravity for the Church gradually slid northward from Jerusalem to Antioch. Yet, the days of Paul and Barnabas in this region gradually dwindled to zero as:

> "... the Jews stirred up the devout and honorable women, and the chief men of the city, and raised

persecution against Paul and Barnabas, and ex-
pelled them from their coasts."

The welcome mat of Antioch unceremoniously had been
jerked from beneath the feet of Paul and Barnabas, but men
such as these rarely spent much time in a despondent malaise
of reflection, but instead:

"(T)hey shook off the dust of their feet against
them, and continued unto Iconium."

Before leaving Antioch for the journey to Iconium it is imperative that Paul's remark of turning away from the Jews to the
Gentiles be given a brief examination. Did he actually do this?
The answer is a simple but resounding "No." Even great men
and spiritual giants such as Paul and Barnabas are subject to
the many faceted failures of human emotions. Paul was caught
in a whirlpool of emotions, disgust and shame for his fellow
Jews, anger at their intransigence, unfair, vile, and threatening
behavior, and simple hurt for being in this manner by his fellow Jews and onetime compatriots. The remainder of the New
Testament furnishes a plentitude of evidence that Paul never
abandoned preaching and teaching the Jews.

For the moment, the apostolic mission to Antioch was over,
and Paul and Barnabas were blessed to have absconded with
their lives. The "ending" of an episode, though, is often only a
brief terminus, a line of demarcation, for the Church continued
to grow and greatly prosper in Antioch. The two great evangelists, their companions, and associates, had become victims of
a skillfully wielded power play by the influential and self-im-
portant Jews of Antioch, and how they must have beamed and
gloated at their public success. Power is often a proud peacock

of an emotion, often preening itself publicly for all to see. Sometimes, though, power, the real power, is a quietly growing and strengthening force, as it was at Antioch. The only lasting power of any man or woman can claim is growth in Christ, and Luke records:

> "And the disciples were filled with joy, and the Holy Spirit."

Meanwhile, the evangelists departed Antioch, and awaiting them in Lystra was a dramatic reception.

Iconium, Derbe and Lystra

As the dust which Paul and Barnabas shook from their feet was settling into the ground once again, they continued their great missionary journey in a generally southeasterly direction in Asia Minor, making their way into the cities of Iconium, Derbe and Lystra.

Their first stop, Iconium, may serve almost as a prototype of the typical reception they received. Their efforts, which again were centered in the local Jewish synagogue, were graced with a marvelous success as "... a great multitude both of the Jews and the Greeks believed." This was a duplicate page from the story book of Antioch, but so was the following:

> "But the unbelieving Jews stirred up the Gentiles, and made their minds evil affected against the brethren."

An ever-repetitive consistency is here to be observed. It was never enough for a multitude of the Jews who rejected Christ to simply not believe and then go about their lives. Their disbelief, their spiritual hearts and their animosity demanded an active, even a criminal opposition if necessary. So, it began with the criminal conspiracy against Jesus, and as He foretold to the apostles the time would arrive when they would kill you and believe they were serving God. That time had begun to arrive. Here in Iconium the opposition to Paul was as great as at Antioch and perhaps even more widespread and better organized:

> "There was an assault made both of the Gentiles,
> and also of the Jews with their rulers, to use them
> despitefully and to stone them."

Not wishing to perish needlessly, an apostolic and indeed a Christian virtue, Paul and the others, upon becoming alerted, fled to the Lyaconian cities of Lystra and Derbe, where welcomes, both familiar and strange, awaited.

To a disciple of Christ, a moment of healing an infirm person, while ever startling and magnificent, was not unique. The apostles had been granted authority and power by Christ Himself, yet they were not profligate in its employment. To the uninitiated and especially in a predominantly Gentile city such as Lystra its occurrence was of stunning and revelatory importance. A piteously handicapped man, "...a cripple from his mother's womb" heard Paul speak. The apostle, perceiving the man's faith made him whole and the man "... leaped and walked." To this marvel the reaction of the multitude of people was nothing short of both rhapsodic and blasphemous:

> "And when the people saw what Paul had done,
> they lifted up their voices, saying in the speech
> of Lycaonia, The gods are come down to us in the
> likeness of men."

Barnabas was named Jupiter, and Paul, the chief speaker of the two, was given the appellation of Mercurius, both gods in the pantheon of Roman mythology. The priest of Jupiter, the chief god of the Romans, came and draped garlands of flowers at the city gates and made a religious sacrifice of animals. The emotions of the evangelists kept pace with those of the multitude, yet in the entirely opposite direction. They rent their clothes and spoke to the teeming multitude of celebrants:

> "We are men of like passions with you, and preach unto you that ye should turn from these vanities unto the living God, which made heaven, and earth, and the sea, and all things that are therein."

So ardent was the people's enthusiasm for their newly minted heroes it was with difficulty that Paul and Barnabas restrained the mob from offering sacrifices to them.

Of this day in Lystra long ago much can be said, but in the interests of succinctness two points are to be noted. The first is the wisdom displayed by the Savior in His selection of the apostles and the other teachers of repute in the early church. How tempting it must have been for these men to bask in praise and glory and feel empowered by the crowd's adulation. The Bible records not a single instance where any did, and in fact, they were remarkably quick and agile in deflecting all credit and glory to Christ. Repeatedly and with an unanimity no matter what signs and wonders they performed or how much reverence was offered them, they would quickly assure all that they were just men. The contrast between the real article, the apostles, and many religious leaders in the Bible and throughout history is starkly revealing.

The backdrop for the second lesson in this narrative has yet to unfold, but it is coming. Paul and Barnabas were literally chased out of both Antioch and Iconium by recalcitrant Jews, a people if for nothing else must be grudgingly admired for the terrible tenacity of purpose. After a journey of over one hundred miles, they arrived in Lystra and began to rail against the evil doctrines of Paul.

A second great lesson from Lystra must be described as more than just a lesson, but rather an entire curriculum. For the sake of brevity herein we describe as the fickleness of the mob, from first century Lystra to twenty-first century America and all points between. As Luke's narrative progressed the reader becomes swept away by the esteem and wonder in which the crowd at Lystra holds Paul and Barnabas. It is an adoration that literally had reached a destination of apotheosis where these mortal men are to receive sacrifices and be recognized as gods, rather than men. Literally, the next verse shows the change of course:

> "And there came thither certain Jews from Antioch and Iconium, who persuaded the people, and, having stoned Paul, drew him out of the city, supposing he had been dead."

The multitude of Lystra, the deifiers of Paul and Barnabas, upon hearing the excoriating venom of the Jewish enemies of Christ, who in their own manner were doubtless eloquent, turned 180° and become the would-be executioners of Paul, who had just escaped their enfolding "love" as a would-be God. Now, they pummeled him with stones of death.

How frequently has such a scene been staged since the very onset of time. Those familiar with Shakespeare's famous play

"Julius Caesar," once a foundational stone in the Western canon of literature (before the advent of woke progressivism) are versed in the instructive sequence where after the assassination of Caesar, the play's protagonist and the leader of the conspiracy, Brutus, addresses a street crowd in Rome. Brutus, a man of no small substance and oratorical talent, succeeds in persuading the crowd of the justness of their cause, wherein he leaves the public podium with the deafening cheers of the crowd. As he exits, Caesar's right-hand man, Mark Antony, makes a superb dramatic entrance carrying the body of the freshly murdered Caesar. Antony gently lays the body of Caesar in front of the mob and begins one of the most famous of all speeches "Friends, Romans, countrymen..." His (actually Shakespeare's) oration begins with a mock humility, but then the river of words flows into a bitter satire and mockery of Brutus and his associates and climaxes with the effective deification of Julius Caesar and the mob's baying for the blood of the assassins, the same "assassins" who but moments before were to the mob the saviors of the republic.

Since our subject is power it must be recognized hat the multitude, the mob, the horde, etc. can be a great power, but its greatness of power is fickle and ephemeral. No one understood this more than Jesus Himself, who was besieged by multitudes of people, especially in the early days of His ministry. Yet He knew why most of them were there and that their "power" was as vanishing as a vapor. One of Christ's most famous miracles, the feeding of the five thousand, merits consideration. One of the lasting and still modern images of Christ is that of a man trailed and surrounded literally by thousands upon thousands. This is apparently true, but only to a point. Jesus with His apostles had spent a day teaching this multitude who were now hungry. With a mere five barley loaves and two fishes He fed the multitude miraculously, but still they followed Him. Christ knew, though, why most followed, and later when they approached Him, He remarked to them:

> "I say unto you, ye seek me not because ye saw
> the miracles, but because ye did eat of the loaves
> and were filled."

From this statement He developed a lengthy message, a trumpet of joy, grace and all such things but also of personal sacrifice which Christ required. At that, the crowd ceased to be a crowd and:

> "From that time many of His disciples went back,
> and walked no more with Him."

The Master knew the multitude could be uplifting, exciting and inspirational, but He knew as well it was both a transitory and essentially an illusory power, here today, gone later today. Neither were the apostles, including Paul, non-apprehensive of the essentiality of the truth, for Paul suffered his apparent demise from the mob's stoning of him at Lystra.

But really, was Paul another shooting star as was Stephen, fated for only a briefly bright and brilliant streak across the heavens before departing the transience and temporality of the present world? Stephen, the apostle James, and countless others had been martyred already, but God had additional labors for Paul, as Luke recorded:

> "Howbeit, as the disciples stood around about
> (Paul), he rose up and came into the city: and the
> next day he departed with Barnabas to Derbe."

Through the lives of Paul, Barnabas, Peter and so many other magnificent men and women Satan's world would yet have to contend with the truth of the resurrected Christ.

Leaving Derbe, Paul and Barnabas returned to Antioch (itself an act of unparalleled faith and courage) and gave a report to the Christians of Antioch, a report so beautifully summarized by one phrase of Paul's when he spoke that "...God had opened the door of faith unto the Gentiles."

Jews, Gentiles, Creeks, Samaritans, Roman and on we go with names, and it naturally can become confusing to us. Little should we be embarrassed, though, because this conglomeration and admixture of people, many of whom had been anathema, to one another, would now provide the first "doctrinal" crisis of the early Church.

CHAPTER TEN

THE FIRST CHURCH TROUBLES

All human organizations of whatever size and purpose have problems, and it is a commentary on the strength of any organization of the manner in which it deals with these problems. Not only religious skeptics but also many Christians have felt the Church founded by Jesus Christ Himself should be exempt from such human frailness. The skeptic maintains that problems and even disagreements invalidate the Church's claim to be a Divinely ordained institution, while sometimes Christians feel as if the entire holy structure is collapsing if differing views and methods clash. Both groups, however, are wrong, for problems even to the point of schism are a partially defining trait of any institution. Problems and difficulties, though, do not necessarily equate to disintegration.

The first human organization and the one remaining most prevalent is the family. Quickly we admit the reality that masses of families do collapse, and their members spun off in all directions, but it is the surviving family unit that here demands our review. As time worn as is the cliché, nonetheless it is true that all families, all marriages, all parent-child, and all sibling relationships, even the best, deal with difficulty. The best survive, grow closer and prosper. Nations, be they empires, monarchies or republics seem to be fueled by problems, ever present disagreements, and ferocious fighting between contending factions. If done peacefully and with even a modicum of decorum it is what we call the political process. If this collapses the resort most often is civil war, and even the most rudimentary compendium of the world's civil wars requires a full volume. Even the United States suffered through one of the worst civil wars in history before a reconciliation that produced a nation of great strength and stability, the latter presently being challenged and threatened by the childish nomenclature of "red" and "blue" states. On we may go, but our purposes are repetitive after the principle is established, which is that all organizations are prone to conflict. So, is the Church exempt from problems? Of course not, it never has and in the earthly span of time never will it be.

The first half of the New Testament history of the Church establishes with incredible precision and specificity that the Church for many years ethnically, culturally and in spiritual training and tradition, exclusively Jewish. With the conversion of the Roman centurion, Cornelius, the Light of Christ had found its access of entrance into the Gentile world, and now with the leadership of Paul and Barnabas the early Church began to grow, and Gentile Christians could not help but be objects of notice and perhaps a bit of fear to the Jewish Christians. All the obedient were one in Christ, but they remained Jews and Gentiles. That is an easy and effectively unchallengeable assertion, but really what does it mean? Even with the purest of intentions from our perspective of two thousand years hence likely it is close to impossible to decipher let alone describe and define the tremendous chasm that lay between Jew and Gentile.

The distinction was not merely race, and probably race itself was not as determinative as the modern race-addled world would wish to think. Due to geographical proximity many of the Gentiles with whom the Jews dealt and sometimes mixed were like the Jews, Semitic peoples whose physical appearance would have been close to that of the Jews. It was in the realm of culture and the spiritual, frequently overlapping realms, where the distinctions were greatest. The clash and attempted merging of these two distinct civilizations, the strict and tightly bound Jewish community with the free-wheeling Greco-Roman world may have hid more distinctions than were actually revealed openly. Still, the chasm between Jew and Gentile was great, the extent and depth of which is beyond this work, but here in the Church's early days it approached a flashpoint.

The believing Jews (and lest we forget our present discussion is of Christ's followers only) stubbornly began to accept the Gentile men and women who were flocking to Christ but yet they issued one major proviso. Simply, but effectively, it was that before a Gentile could be accepted as a Christian brother, he must first become a Jew. As taught by the "believing Pharisees" before a male Gentile could be accepted as a Christian brother he had to submit to the rite of circumcision, as had been ordained by the Law of Moses for over one thousand years. Anyone with but a cursory familiarity with the New Testament knows that this became a divisive issue of more than transient controversy, as it was beginning to divide Churches. Modern humanity, with its almost reflexive resort to ironical humor in the face of any serious issue, will tend to dismiss this as a type of "tempest in a teapot," a silly, even ridiculous dispute over what is now regarded as a medical issue. Most decidedly, it was not funny, not ironical but rather of such concern that Paul and Barnabas "... had no small dissension and disputation with them." So great did this issue become that it was determined that the two great evangelists should go to the earthly hub of the Church in Jerusalem and there meet with the apostles and elders to determine the question. Nothing less than the health and vitality of mission efforts to the Gentiles and the harmony between Gentile and Jewish Christians was in the balance.

Thus, Paul and Barnabas journeyed to Jerusalem for what was effectively the first great Church council. They passed through Phoenicia and Samaria and found a great historical city the tensions of irresolution of divisive issues was as great as it had been in Antioch. To this day the attendance at councils, conferences, symposia, and conventions will give any observer and/or participant a clear view on how people who come together to find agreement often unearth the opposite. All the apostles and elders come together, their number a conspicuous omission in the text, and not unsurprisingly no more agreement is found among these men than Paul and Barnabas had known in Antioch. The scene was of "much disputing," a nice Biblical term for argument, when a man who was well versed in Jewish-Gentile matters spoke up. The apostle Peter, as Jewish and as committed to the Old Law as any man who ever lived, spoke of his honor at being given the responsibility of first offering the Truth to the Gentiles. The roughhewn Galilean spoke:

> "And God which knoweth the hearts, bare them witness, giving them the Holy Spirit, even as He did unto us; And put no difference between us and them, purifying their hearts by faith."

Among other things this statement is a remarkable tribute to the changed heart and attitude of Peter, who not long before had considered the Gentile world as anathema. Still, to be added, though, was a statement about the Law which so many Jews could or would not recognize:

> "Now, therefore why tempt ye God, to put a yoke
> upon the neck of the disciples, which neither we
> nor our fathers were able to bear?"

This pierced the heart of the Jewish-Gentile dichotomy, a division which many Jews still today will not accept. To Christ there is no distinction between a Jew and a Gentile. Ethnicity, race, and culture are not the lines of spiritual demarcation. The line now, is no more or less, Jesus Christ Himself alone, who said "there is neither Jew nor Greek." The Old Law, a necessary, but heavy burdensome yoke had been removed, and no need or commandment regarding circumcision was extant for either Jew or Gentile. As a pirouette to his address Peter added the central reason for everything, then or now:

> "But we believe that through the grace of the
> Lord Jesus Christ we shall be saved, even as they."

Such was either the personal authority of Peter or his message, likely a combination of both, that the assembly fell silent, and then listened to Paul and Barnabas recount their efforts. Finally, a man who had emerged as the most influential figure of the Jerusalem Church, James, rose to speak. This was the same James who was a younger brother of Jesus of Nazareth, and a man who in the early stages of Jesus's mission was not an adherent. From Nazareth, raised in the same home and by the same Mary and Joseph, the parents of Jesus, James was but a man. Still, he was a man of growing stature and influence, later to be the author of the Book of James, that he obviously imbibed freely from the teachings and character of his older brother, Jesus. He was in no sense the sole ruler of the Church in Jerusalem and was not the final arbiter in this Church council; still, however, he was a man whose opinions and judgments weighed heavily with Barnabas, Paul, and the other apostles. When he rose to speak James offered nothing less than the purest wisdom, which would soon be distilled into four directives to the many newly forming Gentile churches: (1) that the Jewish law and the ritual circumcision of the Jews was not binding upon the Gentiles; (2) that they abstain from eating food sacrificed to pagan idols; (3) that they adhere to the longstanding prohibition of the gross practice, long common among the Gentiles, of drinking blood; and (4) that they abjure the practice of "fornication," i.e. sexual immorality.

An observer's initial inclination is to assert that by these four instructions James had followed two principles in teaching the new Gentile Christians. The first was that the Law of God, now found fully in the person of His Son Jesus be fully followed and secondly, that the burdens of the new Christians not be increased. Actually, the two principles were conjoined by James more succinctly into only one, and that being that the Will of God is that the burdens of his children be eased. This is the same God whose only Son declared of His Messiahship:

> "Take My yoke upon you, and learn of me; for
> I am meek and lowly in heart: and ye shall find
> rest unto your souls. For my yoke is easy, and my
> burden is light."

The thoughts and recommendations of James seem to have been born from this statement of Jesus, and further the entire Council found an accord in this, for it "...pleased the apostles and elders, with the whole church, to send chosen men of their own company to Antioch with Paul and Barnabas; namely, Judas summoned Barnabas, and Silas, chief men among the brethrens." They were to take letters to the churches in Antioch, Syria, and Cilicia, announcing the desires of the council. Before our narrative thus presses forward it will be advantageous that a further thought or two be expressed about the four points of decision. Of circumcision and its nonessentiality we have spoken. "Pollutions" to idols were nothing more than the remains of animals which had been sacrificed to pagan idols and then offered for sale in a marketplace known as "the shambles." Nothing innately sinful was connected with the eating of this meat, but such practice seemed to be an adherent to the old ways of heathenism.

Eating "things strangled" was a grotesquerie of Gentile culture and resulted in the consumer's not only eating the flesh of an animal but in drinking its blood. It was common in the Gentile world, still prevalent today and always abhorrent to God. The practice remains prohibited under Jewish dietary law, was codified in the Law of Moses, but further was forbidden from the outset of the world, long before Moses. It was wrong and remains anathema to God.

The final instruction is the easiest to understand, but even today remains the most difficult to practice, the abstinence from sexual immorality. The ancient Gentile world, even, maybe even especially that of the historically ennobled Greeks and Romans was a macabre theater of sexual perversions, the most extreme of which perhaps would jolt even the libertine modern sector of society. Further, it was a realm of moral practice where the teachings of the Gentiles and that of serious Judaism were as diametrically opposed as could be imagined. The later letters of the New Testament reflect that it long remined a problem in the early church. James and the others effectively signed off on the insistence that with this issue no compromise could be affected between Christ and Gentile pagan practices. All in all, though, the intention of James, the apostles, the elders, and the council was well summarized by James in this observation:

"For it seemed good to the Holy Spirit, and to us, to lay upon you no greater burdens than these necessary things."

Would that those who followed in their paths and offices since had understood the same appreciation of God's desires. These early leaders had the Spirit of Christ, teaching morality but as much as possible expounding freedom in Christ, which was inclusive of a life not beset by extraordinary burdens. At times, the two-thousand-year history of Christendom has closely paralleled the errors of the Jewish establishment at the time of Christ, in which they "lay burdens, grievous to be born" upon the backs of the disciples. These things were roundly condemned by Christ, and His Spirit moved with this desire upon His true followers. People have always turned from what they perceive to be Christ and His Church for many reasons. Christians and Christian leaders should give them no more than those which they possess. The Christianity as propagated by the apostles required no liturgy, eschewed formalism, the" teach not, touch not, handle not" thinking of which Paul later spoke, but rather grants true moral freedom to serve Christ.

God had men well placed for handling the first great Church controversy, but too frequently wisdom is not given a warm reception by those who hear it. Happily, though, this was not the fate of the council's messengers. Initially, the evangelists, Paul, Barnabas, Silas, and likely others returned to Antioch, which had rapidly become one of the twin hubs of the early church (Jerusalem being the other), where their deliverance of the message was met:

> "Which when they had read, they rejoiced for the consolation."

Although the initial direction of doctrinal issues with the Gentile Christians was well accepted, unfortunately the New Testament record is a chronicle of ever continuing difficulties caused by the merging Gentile disciples with the original Jewish base of the Church. For the moment, though, a deeper insight into these matters will be deferred.

The Church grew, and that is the essential reality of its early days. Regardless of tyrannical rulers, internal strife, and doctrinal disputes the Body of Christ was triumphant overall, especially Satan. Still, the Church had other problems because it is composed of humans, who are fraught with woes and difficulties. At Antioch evangelistic plans were developed, the most known and studied of which is known as the Second Missionary Journey of Paul. Its planning and its beginnings, though, were not without their own struggles, and as we will observe even the best of Christians can be the receptors of sparks which fly between them.

Schism Between Paul and Barnabas

Jerusalem needed no more religious teachers. Even today, well into the twenty-first century the name Jerusalem connotes so many matters, but none more than religion. It is easy to over-look that for all its well-deserved historical fame and notoriety, geographically was a relatively small area, perhaps a two mile by two-mile square. Into this crowded space were most of the apostles, many church elders, an untold but like a rather large number of Christians, including a sizable troop of converted Jewish priests. The city, as do all, needed more Christians, but not more teachers. The remainder of the world, the Gentile world, was dying of thirst for the truth, and it was to this end that Paul and others, especially Barnabas, were selected by God. With enthusiasm this marvelous pair of supremely talented men left Jerusalem for Antioch, from which point they would embark on a great missionary journey. So, they did, but facts, personalities and perhaps God intervened to alter and even enhance these efforts.

The similarity of background, ability, and perhaps even personality between the two men, Paul and Barnabas, who had quickly emerged as the leading actor in taking the truth to the Gentiles was remarkable. Both were Hellenistic Jews, Paul from Tarsus and Barnabas from the island of Cyprus. Paul, as is known, was marvelously well educated and likely Barnabas was as well, and each, especially Paul, for whom we have a more extensive record, seemed almost preternaturally intelligent. Scriptural evidence establishes that they each were of some material means, maybe even wealthy. The two were superlative speakers, fully dedicated to Christ and possessed of unquestioned courage. Their ages are omitted, but likely they were in the prime of life and physical vigor. On the First Missionary Journey overall they were enormously diligent and worked together hand and glove. The clock, though, had begun to tick, and its chimes would soon mark the end of their personal working relationship.

The organization for the second missionary trip had commenced and as Paul said to Barnabas:

> "Let us go again and visit our brethren in every
> city where we have preached the word of the
> Lord, and see how they do."

They apparently did not intend to go by themselves, and here the seed of contention to where it grew into a chasm and eventually a personal schism Barnabas wished their party to include his cousin, a young man named John Mark, but Paul bristled at the very idea:

> "But Paul thought not good to take him with
> them John Mark, who departed from them from
> Pamphylia, and went not with them to the work."

In the plainest of speech Paul saw John Mark as a "quitter," and a man so dedicated and driven (and yes, obsessed) as Paul, has extreme difficulty in abiding such a man. Barnabas, too, was a man of great substance and as are most successful men, quite confident in his own beliefs, opinions, and preferences. Our observer, Luke, seemingly one of the most astute and levelheaded men who ever wrote:

> "And the contention was so sharp between, that
> they departed asunder one from the other: and
> so, Barnabas took Mark, and sailed unto Cyprus;
> And Paul chose Silas, and departed, being recommended by the brethren unto the grace of God."

So, who was right and who was wrong? From the perspective of two thousand years, we are not called upon to judge. At the conclusion of this rift Paul and Barnabas likely were of the same character and personality as before. Both were strong men, not just pillars in the early Church but part of its very foundation yet today. Each was a man of enormous integrity and commitment to God, and it is doubtful that few intelligent persons, friend or foe, ever doubted this. Plainly we are not supplied a sufficiency of narrative to really make accurate judgments, but that is no prohibition to speculation, perhaps to the ends that we may learn when Christians suffer similar disputes today.

John Mark was a young man, and we are provided no other facts of his departure from Paul and Barnabas other than that "...he returned to Jerusalem." Likely, for whatever reason he left home sickness provided a strong element to the mixture. It is the rare young man or woman who has not experienced the haunting hurt of homesickness, for the inclusion of "sick" in the word structure is well made. Especially for the happy and contented, even those with ambition and desire, it is difficult to make the break. For whatever reason he left, good or bad, John Mark returned to the work, and was no inconsequential figure in the early Church. Only a few men were entrusted with the writing of the New Testament, and he was among the few. The Gospel of Mark literally will live forever, and its writer, John Mark likewise.

A final word on the participants in this early Church rift, Paul and Barnabas, each on his own a towering figure of strength and lasting influence in the early Church. The prior sentence itself may contain both the genesis and the heart of their problem over John Mark. The stars of Paul and Barnabas, now two thousand years hence, have never seen their brightness dimmed. The Christian remains inspired and motivated by the steadfastness and strength of men such as these two beacons. All this, though, does not signify that their working in tandem indefinitely was going to be profitable to either themselves or to God. They were masters of their occupation, i.e. the evangelization of the Gentile world, and in the loose context of the word it would not be amiss to ascribe to them "genius." Such men and women are needed but are not best suited to being yoked with another of like character and ability. They demand so much of themselves and often demand too much of others. Perhaps this was at the heart of Paul's rejections of John Mark as a working companion. Perhaps not.

Paul and Barnabas separated but each remained true to their commissions and faithful to God. As for the latter, His Hand in some manner obvious or not, was moving in the entire episode. Originally the journey was a single effort planned for one group of evangelists. It became a dual mission, manned by those well competent to work in smaller groups. Paul and Barnabas never again worked together, but ultimately the Church did not suffer. Mozart and Beethoven never worked side by side to compose a symphony, Michelangelo along directed the painting of the Sistine chapel, and Shakespeare authored his masterworks as their sole creator.

Neither Paul nor Barnabas sought power. No one had to bow to either, no soldier killed or himself perished, and no lands, cities and villages were overrun. Each went on his way, serving the same God, and it was His power they preached not their own. Ahead for the apostle Paul lay much grueling work, rewards, and afflictions, but in the immediate future he would lead the way to the establishment of a new culture so influential that it would itself be labeled a "civilization."

CHAPTER ELEVEN

THE INVASION OF EUROPE

As continents go Europe is not particularly imposing stretching from the British Isles in the west to the steppes of Russia in the east and from the snow-covered tundra of the Arctic in Scandinavia to the sunny Mediterranean lands of Italy, Greece, and Spain in the south. It is crowded. Crowded not just with population but with diversity of cultures, nationalities, ethnicities, tribes and once upon a time, with religions. Withal, it has always been a place of productive timberlands, endless coastlines, some of the most pleasant and temperate climates in the world, rich agricultural lands, mineral wealth and for the most part productive and diligent populations.

In Biblical (and later for that matter) no threat of invasion from the north or west existed. Invasion from the south was possible and did occur, but only to those with seafaring skills. It was from the east, that its paucity of natural topographical barriers made for the potential invaders the opportunities for conquest and even colonization. That realm where Europe blends into Asia is mostly flat with few, if any, intimidating major river barriers. The geography itself has historically seemed to beckon the bold and the daring to come try their hands at conquest and rule.

First came the Persians. Not only were they the first foreign power to seriously threaten the new European civilization that was still in its infancy, but they remain the instigators of what to this day remains the most "glamorous" of would-be conquests. Centered in present day Iran the Persian Empire at the beginning of 500 B.C. was the mightiest and most far flung on earth. Comprised of some 128 provinces in 490 B.C. its emperor Darius the Great sent forth a mighty imperial army to crush an incipient rebellion on its western fringe in some small Greek colonies. Little and ever divided but under the leadership of the city of Athens the Greeks repelled the Persians on the plains of Marathon, and there the European dreams of Darius died. Still, but fifteen years later his son Xerxes, whose appetite for conquest was voracious, organized an army of several hundred thousand soldiers with the intent of marching on all Greece and smashing its strange nascent civilization. At hitherto unknown and obscure sites the dreadfully outnumbered Greeks, first under the inspiration of Sparta and then the leadership of Athens met and ultimately repelled the Persian horde at Thermopylae, Salamis, and Plataea. Greece would remain Greek, and its culture flourish.

Almost another three centuries elapsed, as a political and military power, the strength of the states of Greece were in irreversible decline, and the center of power had begun to shift to the central Italian city of Rome. On the south shore of the Mediterranean was the city of Carthage, a Phoenician (Canaanite in the Bible) colony possessed and an ancient navy second to none. The city challenged Rome for Mediterranean dominance, and in 218 B.C. under a young general named

Hannibal Barca invaded Europe through Spain, he and his army crossing the Alps north of Rome and emerging in the Italian peninsula to threaten Rome itself. In a series of military campaigns which defined military genius Hannibal destroyed one Roman army after another. Still, Rome did not break, and Hannibal was chased back to north Africa where he was defeated, and Carthage eliminated as a military power. Rome's strength grew to massive proportions, and invasion now came from, not to, Europe.

All earthly powers, though, have a temporal lifespan, and by the late 300's AD Rome was obviously weakening, with invading nations gnawing at the fringe of its borders, with none achieving more lasting fame than the Huns. A character who is part historical and part mythological, Attila the Hun, led a multi-tribal group into northern Italy in AD 452. Attila, though failed in his conquest of Rome, died the following year, and the Huns became assimilated into European culture.

Beginning in the eighth century the Moors came from northwest Africa, spanned the Straits of Gibraltar, and made their way into Spain, where they remained until the historically fateful year of 1492, and then were driven from Spain by the reigning monarchy and Roman Catholic Church. Their effect upon Spanish culture is well beyond the scope of this work but suffice it to observe that the Moors made a lasting impact on the Iberian Peninsula. Their attempts to drive further into Europe were little rewarded with success.

From the other side of Europe in the 1220's came the Mongol hordes from deep in Asia, notorious for cruelty which was synonymous with sadism. They, under Genghis Kahn, had begun to carve for themselves in central and east Asia the largest land empire in history. Relatively a small population, though, they were thwarted in their drive to penetrate deep into Europe, and withdrew in the 1240's. Perhaps they left some lasting footprints in Russia, where their presence was greatest, but the Mongol invasion's lasting alterations of European culture was minimal to non-existent.

From the southeast came the extended Ottoman invasions, their onset being in the 1300's B.C. and continuing into the seventeenth century. Generations of unrest followed the Turk's attempts at the imposition of a strange Islamic culture. Their cultural colonialism was met with lasting success in portions of the Balkans but never penetrated central, western, or northern Europe. The Turks were dealt a staggering blow at the naval battle of Lepanto in 1571, and gradually the Ottoman tide began to recede back into Asia. Our summary could continue almost indefinitely to the present and notation must be made of the great twentieth century conflagrations which began in Europe and spread to the world as World Wars I and II. Yet even they ceased, and seemingly even their influence may be waning. Still, one other European invasion and its influence must be confronted, and with it we return to the first century.

On an otherwise innocuous day circa 50 AD a small wooden boat (then there were no other kind) made landfall in the Macedonian city of Neapolis. The craft bore at least four passengers, Paul, the leader of the group, Silas, a proven man of great ability, Timotheus (hereafter "Timothy"), a young man half-Jewish, half Greek and the protégé of Paul and Luke, a physician, highly esteemed, the chronicler of these events and perhaps the greatest and most exacting of ancient historians. They had been busily occupied in mission efforts in Asia Minor when a vision appeared to Paul, beseeching him to come to Macedonia and teach the gospel. This famous "Macedonian Call" resulted in the introduction of Jesus Christ to the great continent of Europe. As has been demonstrated Europe's was a history of invasions, but this arrival of four unarmed, non-descript men in a small port city was the one whose effects would shake not the continent of Europe alone, but eventually the still unknown world of the west, North and South America, the lands of the unseen South Pacific and the heretofore impenetrable barriers of the dark continent of Africa. From this time, often slowly, sometimes swiftly, often gloriously, too often with gross impurity and even hypocrisy the teaching of the Savior would spread inexorably. Western Civilization was a structure for which the Greeks had laid the foundation of intellectual attainment, freedom of thought and great artistry and upon which the Romans were still building with magnificent political, engineering, and organizational talents. Yet it was these four men who carried the banner of freedom, liberty of the mind, spirit and ultimately the soul, a liberty that in its finer parts would glorify and exalt any land or people it touched. It all began in this tiny seaport town in Macedonia, the birthplace of Alexander the Great.

The greatest of events, even of epochs, may begin in the most mundane fashion. Paul and the others had moved inland to Philippi, a Roman colonial city and the capital of Macedonia. On a Saturday they went to a local riverbank where certain women often convened for prayer and religious services. Among them was Lydia, a seller of purple (a substance used for the dyeing of expensive clothing) who with her entire household believed and were baptized, becoming the first resident European converts to Christ (and the answer for two millennia to a popular Bible school question).

Religion and money is a marriage made in hell, and the Bible itself is not shy about the nuptial announcements, which never cease. In Philippi was a young woman "with a spirit of divination," which "brought her masters much gain by soothsaying." She continually hailed Paul and Silas about the city, "praising" them until their nerves were collapsing. Finally, through God's power the girl was restored to her normal mental health, a natural cause of rejoicing to all but "... her masters (who) saw that the hope of their gains was gone." The religious charlatans brought them to the city's magistrates and accused them of being Jews (how ironic for Paul) who "...do exceedingly trouble the city." A truly ridiculous tumult ensued in the city, and the Roman magistrates, without an iota of concern and respect for any law or justice ordered Paul and Silas flogged mercilessly and thrown into prison.

The Romans, for all their advances and their civilized veneer, knew how to punish those who offended them. A Roman whipping undeniably was a ghastly experience, and then upon its completion to be denied any medical care is almost Satanic. Yet, the two prisoners, were to by punished further, for they were:

> "...thrust into the inner prison and made their
> feet fast in the stocks."

All of this, the injustice and illegitimacy of the savage beating, its humiliating degradation and then being shoved into the midnight blackness of a hellish ancient prison likely would break most ordinary men. But, oh, what a mistake their tormentors had made, for Paul and Silas were no ordinary men:

> "And at midnight Paul and Silas prayed, and sang
> praises unto God; and the prisoners heard them."

The young Saul of Tarsus was overcome with hatred for every vestige of Christianity, a fanatically supercharged executioner of Christians. Now, as the apostle he, in tandem with his marvelous associate Silas, could not be halted from praising God and Christ. The other prisoners, the soldiers and the jailers had never seen such a demonstration of pure human resolution and power, but another sort of power was ready for its violent appearance.

Philippi, in the eastern Mediterranean, was and remains in one of the world's prime earthquake belts:

> "And suddenly there was a great earthquake, so
> that the foundations of the prison were shaken;
> and immediately all the doors were opened, and
> every one's bonds were unloosed."

In accord with the harshness of even Roman law, the ancient tradition likely would have demanded the death(s) of the keeper(s) of the prison for the escape of any prisoners. The jailer of the prisoners well knew the fate which awaited him, guilty or not of any malfeasance:

> "And the keeper of the prison awaking out of his
> sleep, and seeing the prison doors open, he drew
> out is sword, and would have killed himself, sup-
> posing that the prisoners had been fled."

Guilty or not, Roman law was stern and unbending and demanded retribution. Paul and Silas were not ordinary men and were certainly not of the ilk that likely resided in this and most prisons. Quickly, Paul saw the jailer's sword poised and its wielder's death a moment away when he shouted "...Do thyself no harm: for we are all here." For the moment, this catastrophic moment of destruction, the mighty power of Rome lay in the dusty debris of the Philippian earthquake. The terrors which the officers, keepers and guards of the prison could visit upon its wretched inmates, and their swords now turning on themselves. Temporarily the power rested with the prisoners, as easily they could stride forth from the prism. Likely, many did just that. This option remained for Paul and Silas, but these were extraordinarily powerful men, fully committed to God and intrinsically aware of Christ's great Beatitude of "Blessed are the meek," for meekness is a controlled power. The two evangelists were given power to escape the Philippian dungeon, but they were aware of the greater power, need and opportunity the jailer's fears presented. Into the blackness of the inner dungeon came the jailer and fell down before Paul and Silas. As he brought forth his prisoners, still in terror he articulated the question which should reside in the heart of every human soul:

"Sirs, what must I do to be saved?"

Whether the jailer was proffering his inquiry in the spiritual or the worldly sense is surely open to differing reasonable interpretations. Likely, though, his immediate concern was not the salvation of his soul but rather a path of extrication from the dilemma of his own condemnation as a failed jailer. In the Spirit of Christ and the other apostles who had gone before him, Paul provided more than words, and more than the Philippians had ever dreamt, as Paul answered:

"Believe on the Lord Jesus Christ, and thou shalt be saved, and thine house."

First things first, and contrary to the reputed wisdom of the world the spiritual is always preeminent. Did not Christ in perhaps the key statement of His Sermon on the Mount declare:

"Seek ye first the Kingdom of God, and His righ-
teousness; and all these things shall be added
unto you."

The jailer's response was in all ways splendid. He (and in
this he is forever nameless) now tended to his penal charges as
would a nurse, cleansing their wounds and caring for them and:

"... was baptized, he and all his straightway. And
when he had brought them into his house, he sat
neat before them, and rejoiced, believing in God
with all his house."

When he had awakened that morning the Philippian jailer
was just another cog in the powerful Roman Empire whose rule
engulfed much of the world. Of a Gentile background, whether
Roman, Greek, or other, his hopes and expectations from life
were strictly limited. He had a responsible position with a living
wage, and he enjoyed the comforts of a family. Really, though,
what else could life offer him? His master and employer Rome,
the greatest power on earth, demanded labor from him in return for sustenance. Likely his prospects for advancement were
limited or nil, and the imperial favors would be bestowed on
other than lowly prison keepers. Instead, whenever he finally
retired for the night (perhaps another day or two) like those
healed by Christ, the lepers, the crippled, the blind, the plague
ridden, the despondent, even the adulterers, the change in him
and his family was sudden and lasting. Now, life had true value,
meaning and purpose, and just as the physically ill and enfee-
bled were healed and cured fully so were the jailed sins washed
away by the unconquerable blood of Christ.

In this drama, though, the mighty power of Rome was still a force which could not be ignored. Paul and Silas remained prisoners, but the city magistrates, shaken literally, emotionally, and perhaps in other ways, were ready to stamp "closed" on the file of their dealings with the strange Christian heralds. Early the next morning the sergeants of the guard were dispatched with the magistrate's word to "Let those men go." But what if the prisoners were not ready to go just yet, or suppose they had their own ideas about their manner of release? For we are reminded that Paul and Silas were no ordinary prisoners, but this assertion is not limited to their character or spirituality. It also extended to the realm of legality, and Paul was about to play a trump card which would rock the judicial establishment.

Unknown to the Philippian authorities not only was it a moral scandal to flog innocent men such as Paul and Silas, but also, they had committed a crime under Roman law. Such lack of knowledge did not extend to Paul and Silas, however, who refused to leave the prison quietly in the manner of whipped animals:

> "But Paul said unto them, They have beaten us openly uncondemned, being Romans, one have cast us into prison; and now do they thrust us out privily? nay verily; but let them come themselves and fetch us out."

The Roman antecedents of Silas are unknown to us. Paul, though, was a native of Tarsus, a Roman "free city," wherein Roman citizenship was granted to all free males. Indeed, it had its benefits, and to the point a Roman could not be treated in such an extra-judicial manner and could not be flogged. We may allow the spiritual lessons of this story to recede into the background for a moment and note the amazingly rapid reversal of the power structure. Paul and Silas, a few hours before were no-account prisoners and tossed away like garbage, possibly for quick dispatch by execution. Now, the single fact of Roman citizenship prompted different action:

> "(W)hen they heard they were Romans... they came and besought them out, and desired them to depart out of the city."

Power, like fame, is a fleeting thing.

They left, but before their exit from Philippi they stopped by Lydia's house, and here these freshly beaten victims of injustice "comforted" their fellow Christians. At two very important cities, Thessalonica and Athens, great events beckoned.

CHAPTER TWELVE

A TALE OF THREE CITIES

Being enshrouded and attacked by a mob of angry fanatics, beaten, and flogged within hailing distance of their deaths and cast into the Stygian blackness of an ancient prison, even these events in the aggregate, were not sufficient to deter men of the caliber of Paul and Silas. While they suffered and bled and had the fears, dreads, and anxieties of all mortals they were still on the mission of the Macedonian Call. Into Macedonia they continued, through the cities of Amphipolis and Apollonia, finally arriving in Thessalonica, the chief city of northern Macedonia, quite populous and the center of Roman administration for a wide area. A major metropolitan area into the twenty-first century (now known more commonly as Salonica or Thessaloniki) its name and story began in the sojourn of Paul and Silas and in a very obsequious manner. As he customarily did Paul began his teaching by attending Jewish synagogue services for three consecutive Saturdays. (So much for his prior diatribe that he was through with the Jews). He began with that message which two thousand years have neither dimmed nor reduced its centrality and essentiality:

> "Opening and alleging, that Christ must needs
> have suffered, and risen again from the dead;
> and that this Jesus, whom I preach unto you, is
> Christ."

In simple terms he expounded the death, burial, and resurrection of Jesus Christ. Always this was the message of Paul and Silas, Barnabas, the other apostles and all the early teachers. Even today it is not the best Christian message, but rather it is the Christian message. Many teachings remained on issues of conduct, worship, organization but all stand secondarily in the shadows of the Great Message, that Christ died for us and redeemed us so that the path to eternity was open. These apostles and their associates, those great men, never forgot this.

The message of Paul and Silas was well received:

> "And some of them believed, and consorted with
> Paul and Silas, and of the devout Greeks a great
> multitude, and of the chief women not a few."

Women and men, Gentile and Jew, were becoming disciples, and further a foundation for one of the first century's great churches was being laid in Thessalonica, a church to which Paul would later devote two New Testament books. Dissension, opposition and outright and open hostility, though, now visited the scene, and they were more than a shadow or a specter.

The introduction of this opposition is worthy of having its first line from the great chronicler of events, Luke, quoted: "And the Jews which believed not, moved with envy, took unto them lewd fellows of the baser sort, and gathered a company, and set all the city on an uproar, and assaulted the house of Jason, and sought to bring them out to the people."

This same story, ever cacophonous in noise, was beginning to play in dull repetition wherever Paul went. He and Silas would have great success with both Jew and Gentile, but the disbelieving Jews, often the priesthood and the other leaders, would attack Paul with an ever-increasing aggression. Here, their opposition encompassed those who would "harbor" a heretic such as Paul, and such was their power that they were to drag Jason, a Gentile convert, before the city's Roman magistrates. Their charge against Paul resounded with the terrifying echoes of the night of Christ's Passion:

"(Paul and Silas), whom Jason hath received: these all do contrary to the decrees of Caesar, saying that there is another king, one Jesus."

Search the New Testament with a microscope, and no reference will be found where either Christ, Paul, Peter, or any early Christian teacher ever made a single political reference, other than a general admonition for Christians to obey laws. Yet once again an almost cultic type connection between the radical Jewish haters of Christ and the ultimate civil authority, Rome, resulted in a confluence of power that ejected the evangelists from Thessalonica. To their dismay, though, the Church in Thessalonica grew to be one of the strongest of the first century world and given a modicum of time it can be surmised that God ultimately won this power struggle.

Finally, though, again under cover of darkness before Thessalonica became the scene of martyrdom the Christians sent Paul and Silas to a city approximately thirty miles southwest of Thessalonica. Still in Macedonia, its name was Berea, and historically it is the recipient of a superlative introduction.

BEREA

The pattern continued apace, whereupon their arrival in Berea Paul and Silas immediately went to the Jewish synagogue. There they and the Christian message received a splendid response:

> "These were more noble than those in Thessalonica, in that they received the word with all readiness of mind, and searched the scriptures daily, whether those things were so."

In English "noble" is truly an apt term, for knowledge, combined with a desire to acquire more and view it all with a spirit of inquiry and a discerning mind. This is true receptiveness in large and deep quantities, and it well illustrates a principle on which the world often makes false accusations of Christians. Sadly, such persons and attitudes are too often a minority, even in the Church, but at Berea they were a substantial force. Christianity pleads for self-examination just as its founder, Jesus Christ, asks every man and woman to examine his own heart. No body of leadership, no formal priesthood, no College of Cardinals, no Christian school, no minister, and no teacher is to make the determination of the direction of a person's life and beliefs. A man or woman who thinks and studies for themselves, as did the Bereans, has unearthed real power. No good teacher desires a student body of the ignorant but rather the delights of the well-read, the well versed and the well-spoken. This leads to even greater rewards, as Paul and Silas experienced in their short time in Berea. Men and women, of both high and low social rank, both Greek and Jew, learned and unlearned became Christians and the church at Berea a shining star in the Christian firmament. In this world rarely is any experience an unmixed blessing, though. While the native opposition to Paul in Berea may have been minimal to non-existent to the establishment Jews Paul remained a thorn in their flesh. These enemies of Paul and of Christ recognized no niceties such as jurisdiction or municipal boundaries and continued to hound Paul like a pack of savage jackals:

> "But when the Jews of Thessalonica had knowledge that the word of God was preached of Paul at Berea, they came thither also, and stirred up the people."

The observer may stand aside in a type of repugnant awe and amazement of the opposing activist Jews. The typical man or woman in any time or place gives no thought to some haunting specter that a group of people, bent on his harm and destruction, is going to drop everything in their daily lives and follow him on a journey from place to place to destroy him. Paul's enemies, though, were in no sense of the term ordinary. Likely, many were at one time his co-workers, co-believers in Judaism and co-haters of the new Christian religion. They hated the religion, they hated its Founder, Jesus Christ, and with a rabid intensity hated Paul, not only its foremost proponent but to them a man who had morphed into the very definition of a heretic and a traitor. To the very moment of Paul's eternal transformation, he would be plagued mercilessly by his one-time cohorts.

The Berean Christians, not only mature in faith but with a well-developed sense of reality and impending danger knew the fate which awaited Paul by a continued stay in their city. Macedonia had been a success with strong congregations of Christians established in Thessalonica, Berea, and other places, but for the sake of his survival Paul was conducted away from Berea. Silas and Timothy remained there, but Paul's Berean companions led him away from Macedonia and southward into the Greek heartland of Attica. In its capital city Paul would await the expected later arrival of Silas and Timothy. That city where he would reside for a bit was named Athens.

ATHENS

Athens was (and is) the largest city in Greece, located east of the Isthmus of Corinth, that elongated neck of land which separates Attica from southern Greece, a basically square shaped block of land called the Peloponnese. The ancient land of Greece contained such fabled realms as Sparta, Thebes and Corinth, but there was only one Athens. Three cities of antiquity retain to the present a special cachet, Jerusalem, Rome, and Athens. Such a bold assertion requires a brief explanation, simplistic as brevity is so often. Jerusalem, the Holy City, the City of David, and the City of Christ's Passion retains a religious preeminence. All roads led to Rome, and historically many still do, for it was the center of the largest and most extensive empire the world had seen. It was Athens, though, synonymous in the minds of men and in history texts for over two thousand years that was the "Birthplace of Western Civilization." For so small an area with a limited populace its cultural and scientific achievements remain unmatched. Rising from the mists of a pre-literate time, even in the storied history of Greece, Athens several centuries before Christ, developed a roster of fame, talent and accomplishment that is staggering.

Especially in the sixth, fifth and fourth centuries before Christ were the feats and legacies of this one city on the rocky plains of Greece so prodigious. Its political leadership included men such as Themistocles, Pericles, and Demosthenes, not always paragons of morality to be sure, but great orators and the focus of many policies and events. Athens began to unleash ideas and ideals of governance, still honored today, perhaps more in the breach than in fact, such as representative government, democracy, freedom of speech and equality of rights.

The Athenians were respectful of their past and their ancestry, and from its populace emerged the first two great European historians, Herodotus and Thucydides. Athen's population was quite human, and its citizenry of all classes hungered for entertainment. How fortunate they were, for from their ranks arose many writers and dramatists, the three most celebrated being the trio of Sophocles, Euripides, and Aeschylus. Their plays, the great tragedies, are intensively studied and performed even today. No names are more historically and culturally linked to Athens than the great philosopher threesome of Socrates, Plato, and Aristotle. It was a city productive of great art and sculpture and architecture, some of which still stand in this third millennium hence.

Such a concentration of cultural and historical creation in one city, over a relatively short period of time and across so many disciplines has yet to be duplicated. It was here that Paul, a one-man compendium of accomplishment himself awaited the arrival of his companions Silas and Timothy. As was his already time-honored custom he began his stay by going to the local synagogue and "disputing" with the Jews and daily with "devout," or religious persons in the marketplace. From our discussion, though, we will bypass for once the Jews and direct the focus upon the Athenian Greeks in this most Gentile of all cities. Paul, a man of eloquence and high intellectual attainment found himself for the first time in this self-proclaimed and self-absorbed intellectual capital of the world, and he was disturbed by what he saw:

> "And while he waited for (Silas and Timothy) at Athens, his spirit was stirred in him, when he saw the city wholly given to idolatry."

The ancient Athenian Greeks in the mass may have been the most creative people this world has yet to see, and hopefully these few words have added to the tributes that they have received ad infinitum. Our record, though, speaks both accurately and eloquently of another creative jewel in the city's crown. It was their ability to create deities, hundreds upon hundreds of gods and goddesses to receive the plaudits, monies, and obeisance of the people. In this respect their behavior approximated the traditional Old Testament foe of the Jews, the Canaanites, whose prowess in the creation and worship of idols remains legendary.

The Athenian Greeks, of course, were Gentiles and Paul was Christ's chosen apostle to the Gentiles. The two were fated, or rather ordained, to meet. Paul, to them a wandering Jew, and as a Jew unsurprisingly religious debated religion "in the market daily." Here, though, was no rough-hewn fisherman speaking in the coarse accent of Galilee, but rather an obviously educated man of breadth, learning and high intelligence. He prattled on about just one God, whereas the Athenians, creative geniuses as they were, worshipped an endless array of far away deities. At this point in the middle of the first century AD the "religions" and philosophies of Athens seemingly revolved around two poles, somewhat opposite, with their adherence to being known by two names that have entered and remain in the English language, the Epicureans, and the Stoics. Who were they and what was the impelling reason for their prominence and their confrontation with Paul?

Like all philosophies and religions subject to analysis by an outsider, the beliefs of the Epicureans and Stoics are easily subject to distortion. Nonetheless, they should be addressed. The followers of Epicurus, a one-time Athenian pedant believed that the earth itself, all its life forms, properties and characteristics are the result of accidental happenstance in the universe, maybe crudely expressed as an early manifestation of the "Big Bang Theory." The highest and most sensible goal in any human's life was the pursuit of pleasure, for life and existence is destined to end as suddenly as it began. It would be too trite to describe Stoicism as the opposite of Epicureanism; however, the stark contrast of the philosophies of the two groups should be noted. The Stoics taught the calm acceptance of the reality of the world, its questions, conundrums, problems, pains, and difficulties. All, the entire universe, our world, was controlled by the dictates of "reason," and the wise man or woman bore whatever came, or in modern English confronted any and all situations with "stoicism." In whatever guise, whatever drew and whatever accoutrements these two philosophies had current reign in the great Athens. Paul, though, excited both their curiosity and their contempt:

> "And some said, What will this babbler say?
> Other some, He seemeth to be a setter forth of
> strange gods: because he preached unto them
> Jesus, and the resurrection."

Babbler? A man as educated (and he would soon offer proof) as any of them, was a "babbler" because he taught something new. The pseudo and self-congratulatory contempt of the intellectually smug oozes down the flanks of the word "babbler." It is the same contempt found in the self-appointed and overly self-regarding academia and media of modern civilization. Certainly, it was no newly discovered emotion to Paul because he himself was not that long removed from the insularity of the Pharisees and the high Jewish religious establishment. Any criticism of the Athenian philosophers, though, should be tempered by an acknowledgment that they accorded this strange philosopher, Paul, an audience, and a stage. From the remove of twenty-first century America may we not ponder the question of how many major universities today would even allow a man such as Paul on their premises.

The stage for Paul's address to the philosophers was no other than the Areopagus, the great Athenian meeting place for its council and other historic assemblies. Paul's audience is worthy of one final description, again given us by Luke and two thousand years hence unsurpassed as a definition of intellectual dilettantism:

> "For all the Athenians and strangers which were
> there spent their time in nothing else, but either
> to tell, or to hear some new thing."

Here on Mars Hill, named for the Greek god of was stood Paul, superb ambassador for the Prince of Peace.

No man, whether poet, priest, politician, or preacher could speak with the directness of Paul. His Athenian observations, the apostle related, showed that they were so awash in religion and its deities. So, drowning in the effluvious of paganism as they were Paul remarked that in his travels through the streets, he found an altar with the inscription:

TO THE UNKNOWN GOD."

Then, these men of intellectual pride, the plaudits of themselves and the multitude, heard an allegation that rarely, if ever, burned their ears:

"(T)herefore ye ignorantly worship."

Ignorant? They were the crème de la crème, of the intelligentsia and this strange Jewish vagabond was declaring them ignorant? Although it is a worthwhile subject for a lengthy dissertation, it is to be observed that the Athens of the mid-first century was living on faded glory. The "glory that was Greece" was centuries before, its great personages dead and gone. It was totally shorn of political power, now no more than a province of mighty Rome to the west and its great creative intellectual spark(s) barely flickering or perhaps even extinguished. It still had its pride, that intellectual pride of which Christ proclaimed that God is resistant.

Paul did attempt to impress this gathering of highly intelligent men, but not with his personal intellect, of which he possessed copious quantities. He offered the only message he and the other apostles ever offered, for as he once said so well "We

preach Christ and Christ crucified." Paul, to bolster his standing with his audience but more to find common ground in belief referenced native Greek poets who taught that all humanity
was kin. He built on this theme, referencing the Creation, the
falsity of idols and affirmed that the days of God's "winking"
at the ignorance of the Gentile world were over. Ignorance,
though, was a quality these savant Greeks could never associate
with themselves, for while their land had been stripped of political power by the all-conquering Romans, they retained the
intellectual preeminence which awed the world. Not so, said
Paul, for without a real knowledge of God and Christ any man
or woman if fully bereft of real knowledge. No more to God
is there the dichotomy between Jew and Greek, and in a moving passage which both proclaims this truth and pays tribute to
Greek accomplishment:

> "For in Him we live, and move, and have our be-
> ing; as certain of your own poets have said, For
> we are His offspring."

Idols, golden images, elaborate, even eloquent mythologies
of gods and goddesses never served the interest of any people,
but now they had been irretrievably and irrevocably shown to
be junk, elaborate cultural bric-a-brac, because the true nature
of God had been demonstrated in the living, breathing life of
his own Son. Equality, equity, or its many and varied forms is
easy to say, and modern political systems have almost defied
the terminology. In reality, though, it remains difficult to accept, especially for any society's intelligentsia, which usually
views itself as a special breed apart from and above the herd.

Nonetheless, though, the Greeks did not seem to be enraptured by Paul's teachings apparently, they still accorded him

an audience, listening in deferential self-respect. To many, though, this strange, though obviously brilliant, Jew, an apostle (whatever that meant to them) finally strode too far with this statement:

> "He hath appointed a day, in which He will judge the world in righteousness by that man whom He hath ordained, whereof He hath given assurance unto all men, in that He hath raised Him from the dead."

Raised from the dead? Really? To so many, Paul was, for all his learning and eloquence, really just a "babbler." The taunting and mockery came swiftly:

> "And when they had heard of the resurrection of the dead, some mocked, and others said, We will hear again of this matter."

Mockery remains the common currency of opposition to detested ideas, for ridicule and taunting seeks no response or rejoinder, but rather is a missile aimed to inflict harm. It was not Paul who had bested this self-styled elite of scholars. Although this apostle was not a man lacking in intellectual and oratorical skills, he knew his sword was not that, but rather the truth. His own life, there on Mars Hill, and now, two thousand years later, is powerful evidence of the resurrection of Christ. A young man, Saul, was within sight of the pinnacles of prowess and power among his own people, the Jews, he in a flash abandoned it all for a life of servitude and suffering. Little did these hearers of Paul's message consider that the intervening fact in the radical change in Paul's life was his personal witness of the Resurrected Christ.

From the historical and scriptural silence, it seems that Athens was not an especially fertile ground on which the Church was to flourish. Paul's brief stay in Athens, though, was in no sense a failure. It concludes with a statement that certain men and women believed and became Christians, two in particular, Dionysius and Diana.

It was here on Mars Hill that a historic clash of powers unfolded. Not in the traditional sense of armies arrayed in battle or individuals engaged in combat. Numerically, the odds were overwhelmingly enormous. The proud but pagan Greeks with all their intellectual flummery walked away as proud as ever, and doubtless continued to make jokes about this crank, this "babbler," they had just heard. For all their intellectual firepower their only rejoinder to Paul was a taunting mockery. When he left, they went on to the next "new thing." In an intellectual dual between Christ and pagan thinking, the latter came to the battlefield weaponless. Paul, though, was undeterred and followed his brief Athenian stay with trips to Corinth and Ephesus, where the power of Truth would be fully displayed.

CHAPTER THIRTEEN

ETHEREAL AND VANISHING POWERS

The ancient city of Corinth lay just to the west of the narrow isthmus that bears its name, a narrow neck of land which connects Achaia, the province of Athens, to the Peloponnese, that block shaped body of land on which the storied city of Sparta found its niche. Corinth, an ancient city dating to the 700's BC was in the third and fourth centuries the major city in all Greece, the glory of Athens and the power of Sparta, in full fledged retreat. In 146 BC, though, Corinth, a victim of Rome's inexorable march of conquest lay in ruins, dormant for a century until Julius Caesar recolonized the city with a mixed group of Italians and Greeks. By the time of Christ, Corinth had regained its glory, perhaps even brighter than before, as it had become a major metropolis and a vital port city connecting the Roman West with Greece and the eastern Empire. As port and coastal cities are wont to do, from the ancient to the modern eras, it attracted an endless stream of seafarers, tradesmen, adventurers, and other wanderers with doubtful strains of morality.

Paul apparently did not tarry long in Athens, which had not given much promise of spiritual fertility and naturally the size, fame and proximity of Corinth drew him there. He met a married couple in Corinth, Aquila, and Priscilla, latterly from Rome from whence they had been banished by the emperor Claudius for being Jews. Paul fit gloriously well with this couple, they all being Jews and all both accepting Christ and testifying of Him. Further, they were tentmakers, the same occupation followed by Paul. (As an aside it is worthy to remark that even Jewish scholars and the intellectual upper crust were expected to learn a trade to support themselves. As an added boast to Paul's Corinthian efforts Corinth was the home of a large population of Jews, his fellow countrymen with whom he always began his teaching. Not only did Paul have a large city with which to work, new, committed companions in Aquila and Priscilla, but also Silas, Timothy and Luke had rejoined them from Macedonia. Doubtless with Paul and such a group the excitement of anticipated success was palpable, and never did a situation seem more appropriate for the earlier words of Christ Himself who spoke:

> "I say unto you, Lift up your eyes, and look on
> the fields; for they are white already to harvest."

Paul, a mature man, but for the Master he served a man of extraordinary passion "...was pressed in the spirit, and testified to the Jews that Jesus was Christ." Surely, this was the time and place for the gospel of Christ to forge a great breakthrough with the Jewish people. Then – all the promise and hopes collapsed.

The Jews, whose numbers are never mentioned, rejected Paul, and rejected Christ and rejected it all with a poisonous "blasphemy." Once again Paul's reaction to rejection was repetitive of past encounters:

> "He shook his raiment, and said unto them, Your blood be upon your own heads; I am clean: from henceforth I will go into the Gentiles."

How often he had spoken almost the same words, which had burst from the apostle in the twin emotional torrents of anger and hurt. This time, though, it seemed to be different, and from henceforth the Gentiles received the substantial portion (though not exclusively) of his evangelical efforts. Yet among the Corinthian Jews success could be found, for a man named Crispus, the chief ruler of that synagogue, became a Christian. For now, though, Paul had no scruples about enlisting the Gentile Romans in their efforts to destroy Paul (again, echoes of Christ's Passion).

The apostle and his companions continued working in Corinth for a year and a half until the Jews organized themselves into an "insurrection" and brought Paul before a judicial tribunal, the judgment seat of the real earthly power, Rome itself. Not for the last time did the rebelling Jews bring Paul before the Romans, but this time they placed themselves in an almost untenable position before the Roman magistrate, as they indicted Paul as:

> "This fellow persuadeth men to worship God contrary to the law."

The man before whom this was all occurring was no bureaucratic non-entity. He was Gallio, a brother to Seneca, who along with Burrus, were the chief advisors to the neophyte emperor

Nero and for several years the effective rulers of Rome. When hearing this charge from the Jews, of whom he had the likely ruling Roman attitude that they were all crazed religious fanatics, Gallio with perfect precision expressed the extant Roman attitude:

> "Gallio said unto the Jews, If it were a matter of wrong or wicked lewdness, O ye Jews, reason would that I should bear with you.But if it be a question of words and names, and of your law, look ye to it, for I will judge no such matters. And he drove them from his judgment seat."

The all-powerful Romans expected two signs of obeisance from the conquered subjects. The first was peace and order and equally important a steady flow of tax revenue. At least for now they had no official interest in internal Jewish religious quarrels. Power is real, and the Romans possessed the only real political power. Gallio's decision of Roman non-intervention was not only wise, but it confirmed Rome's mastery of the Jews and presumably any situation which would arise. As for Paul he stayed in Corinth for a bit, but with his entourage, now including Aquila and Priscille, traveled through Cenchrea, Syria and eventually to Ephesus.

The footsteps of Paul may never again have been heard in Corinth, nor his presence seen, and voice heard. The Corinthian church, though, was a success, primarily a large group of Gentiles that had been saved from heathenism by the teachings of Paul and his companions. His association with them was dear and he penned two lengthy epistles to the Corinthian Christians. It became a church beset with enormous problems, but one which retained the love of God, and the solicitous affections of

Paul. For now, though, Paul had other vistas in view and other congregations to found or to buttress, all along the way to his intended, and perilous, destination of Jerusalem. Much still lay ahead for this chosen apostle to the Gentiles.

EPHESUS

Ephesus was one of the splendors of the ancient Gentile world. It was a large metropolis located on the western coast of Asia Minor (Turkey) and the largest city in the area. Approximately one thousand years earlier it had been founded by the Greeks and through the centuries grew into a very impressive and quite wealthy urban center. As a strategically located coastal city its wealth grew through the centuries. Its population was quite industrious, and even in these ancient days they had developed many amenities which modern populations, especially Americans, find de riguer. Generally, a wealthy city its upper and upper middle classes lived in comfortable multi-storied homes, some of which had tile floors, marble walls and perhaps most importantly running water. Archaeological evidence of heated bathrooms, a twenty-first century necessity has been found.

Ephesus boasted many beautiful public buildings, and although its size and scope did not rival Rome and Athens its splendor and sparkle did. The architectural jewelry of Ephesus took second place to no one, and its most famous was a religious temple. Almost as old as the city itself was the Temple of Artemis, the largest structure in the Hellenistic world. It was constructed solely of marble, yet even this edifice's Greek name was secondary to its Roman nomenclature of the Temple of Diana, one of the Seven Wonders of the Ancient World. Diana, the "mother of the gods" was a special deity in Ephesus, not just for religious but for other reasons which will become apparent. All in all, Ephesus was a Gentile city, a hub of Greek culture and religion and with a self-regarding pride which probably rivaled that of Athens. So here came the oft beaten and bedraggled apostle Paul.

In Ephesus Paul found a man and his work, already under way, and we speculate perhaps the most important minister of the first century Church of whom so little is known. Apollos was a Jew from the great Egyptian cultural center of Alexandria. He was known for his eloquence, his remarkable teaching ability and perhaps most importantly his humility plentifully demonstrated in his dealings with Aquila and Priscilla. Apollos was evidently a major figure around whom so many Christians clustered. Apollos was among a dozen disciples, all of whom appear to be basically self-taught, who Paul encountered when he arrived in Ephesus. Their basic knowledge of Christian doctrine was somewhat checkered, but their intentions and spirits were strong. Paul embraced them as fellow Christians after they were baptized.

Paul, Apollos, and the other disciples, though, even in Ephesus, a pearl of paganism, did not begin with the Gentiles but rather with the Jews. Yes, again. For three months Paul taught and "disputed" with his fellow Jews in the synagogue, but at Ephesus he seemed to make little progress among his countrymen:

> "But when divers were hardened, and believed not, but spoke evil of that way before the multitude, he departed from them, and separated the disciples, disputing daily in the school of one Tyrannus."

The ministry especially to the Gentiles was a marked success, and both Jew and Gentile all over Asia (the province, not the continent, of which Ephesus was capital) heard the word and became Christian.

As an apostle Paul was endowed by God to perform certain miracles, and the power was amply used in Ephesus as many were healed of diseases and the "evil spirits went out of them." As Christ's own ministry superlatively demonstrated such conduct is not confined to a corner and may bring opposition, even of violence. Yet, God, through Paul, prevailed:

> "...and fear fell upon them all, and the name of
> the Lord Jesus was magnified."

So obvious were the miracles of God that the temporal force of a power that greatly plagued the ancient world and abides yet with the modern, began to crack:

> "Many of them also which used curious arts
> brought their books together, and burned them
> before all men, and they counted the price of
> them, and found it fifty thousand pieces of
> silver."

By whatever name it carries, be it the noted "curious arts," black magic, witchcraft, necromancy, or the occult, its progenitor, Satan, had suffered a real blow to his power in Ephesus. So great was the wound that Luke proclaimed:

> "Mightily grew the word of God and prevailed."

The powers of the Prince of Darkness, though subordinate to those of the Prince of Peace, are still mighty and they are resilient. Now Paul and companions, were to directly confront one of the greatest powers on earth. Not directly a political or military power or really even a religious power. This was power, real power, which grip on humanity remains as tight in the twenty-first century as it did in the 50's A.D. That power is the power of material wealth, or more tersely, money.

The study of religion is often the study of money. This averment of historical and commercial reality is not intended solely as a libel of all forms of idolatry and paganism. Even the most sincere and committed disciple of Christ should unhesitatingly concede that the worship of the one true God has been too often stained with the blasphemy of merchandising. The religious skeptic, the anti-Christian so often will with ill hidden smugness issue a blanket condemnation of Christianity as a "racket" and its adherents either hypocrites or manipulated fools. Whether these accusers are so aware many, if not most, Christians are willing to concede that too often the Truth of Christ has been tarnished with the stench of mercantile gain. The Bible from beginning to end makes no effort to conceal the horrors and outrage of many persons in utilizing religion for gain. A truncated list would include the eight hundred priests and prophets of Baal who "ate at Jezebel's table," the corrupt ancient priests of the Mosaical Age and into the Christian Age, the immovable Jewish religious establishment, Simon the Sorcerer, and countless examples from Christ's own parables. The falsity of professed but fraudulent worshippers who seek not spiritual and moral good but rather monetary gain in no way diminishes the truth of Christ and that taught by His apostles. For it was one of the apostles, Paul himself, speaking for God who proclaimed:

"For the love of money is the root of all (kinds of) evil."

Never is to be found a superior illustration of this than at Ephesus where the message of Christ was embattled with man's love of money.

Christianity has never been a religion of ethereal aestheticism. Its adherents and especially its leaders in its beginnings were active, productive working men and women, all of whom were material contributors to the extant commonwealth. Money is never condemned, but in that astonishingly apt phrase from the New Testament "filthy lucre" is abhorrent. Ephesus was a metropolis where filthy lucre itself had become a god, or more appropriately since this was the home of Diana, a goddess.

To this point in our narrative the pursuit of power has been an essentially narrowing lens to the great prize of political power, still sought and so it will ever be by many, but few ever really attain it. Money, though, in whatever form a particular society defines it, is a sine qua non for living. The power of money, essentially itself an amoral neutrality, is a power that to some degree all must possess. And so it was in the Ephesus of the first century.

The cult of Diana was more than a religion in Ephesus, for it was a way of life to many, and from the temple of Diana so many drew not spiritual sustenance alone but also their means for living. The Temple of Diana was literally the centerpiece of both the city of Ephesus and Ephesian society. This magnificent edifice was situated on a hill and the structure boasted one hundred marble columns which radiated brilliance in the sunlight. Inwardly, it contained the image of Diana so worshipped by the Ephesians and countless visitors to the city. Although a modern term it is not too far a stretch to aver that the great city of Ephesus was a "tourist trap." A modern traveler to historical sites and cities easily recognizes that in the midst of the undoubted historical and cultural value of so many places lies the demon of blatant commercialism, bric-a-brac and just plain junk. Ephesus lays claim, even now, to being in the front rank of such cities and places. The winds of idolatry and commercial greed were combining and would blow with a powerful hurricane force upon Paul and Company.

In two simple sentences Luke paints his picture:

> "And the same time there was no small stir about that way (i.e. Christianity). For a certain man named Demetrius, a silversmith, which made silver shrines for Diana brought no small gain unto the craftsmen."

Obviously, no intrinsic sin attaches to precious metals and neither does it adhere to statuary. The more successful Paul's message of Christ, though, the less in demand would be pagan silver statuary, the classic "graven image" always condemned by God. More Christ, fewer pagan images, fewer profits, and more silversmiths seeking new employment. Demetrius was a silversmith and a natural leader, organizing the silversmiths in an early form of a guild or union. To his fellow craftsmen he directed their attention to the obvious, that the message which Paul was teaching was spreading to the provincial trade and marketing area with potentially dire results to all of them. As with all antagonism and rabble rousing against God false slanders soon arrive:

> "...this Paul hath persuaded and turned away much people, saying that they be no gods, which are made with hands."

Paul's message was always Christ, and the exclusivity of Christ, not Paul, which condemned the other gods. Idols naturally fell in the wake of the truth. It is a natural human trait, though, that when one's means of making a living, the mechanism by which money is obtained is threatened a man or woman may react with unreasonableness and even violence. So, it was with the Ephesian silversmiths. So agitated did they become that they transformed themselves into a mob that they raised a chant:

> "And when they heard these sayings, they were
> full of wrath, and cried out, saying, Great is
> Diana of the Ephesians."

This is eerily reminiscent of the affair on Mount Carmel some nine centuries earlier the prophets of Jezebel chanted and implored for action from the god Baal. Now, at Ephesus this tumult and mindless chanting, so common to pagan religions, continued for over two hours.

Into the temple the Ephesian mob had coerced and dragged Gaius, Aristarchus, Paul's Macedonian companions and then Alexander, a Jew, who attempted to reason with them. No more is known of Alexander, a man who bore a very common name, but it is not an implausibility that as a Jew, likewise of a religion which condemned heathen idolatry, he wished to assure the Ephesian mob that the Jews had nothing to do with these economy wrecking Christians.

Paul made no personal appearance before the assembled mob, although his inclination was otherwise. When he had seen the mob, he was determined to venture into the situation, but the other disciples stopped him. A mob listens to no individual, yet it will likely heed the threat of either explicit or implicit power and force. That man appeared in the person of the town clerk; a man who will forever remain anonymous. But the "town clerk," really? He is so described but by virtue of the narrative's tone and description of his speech it must have been more than a clerical office, for he spoke as an official having executive and/or judicial authority. The man spoke with power and wisdom, a rare combination in any man or woman, much less a public official. Everyone everywhere knows the reputation of Ephesus as the center of worship of the goddess Diana and "...of her image which fell down from (the god) Jupiter." He instructed the mob to behave with reason and rationality towards the Christians:

> "...which are neither robbers or churches, nor yet blasphemers of your goddess."

If Demetrius and his followers had a complaint against Paul and his associates the courts were open to their petitions. With a parting statement that embodied both instruction and the hint of Roman force he said:

> "But if you enquire anything concerning other matters, it shall be determined in a lawful assembly. For we are in danger to be called in question for this day's uproar, there being no cause whereby we may give an account of this concourse."

Whatever this man's religious proclivities, which were certainly not Christian, he was fair-minded and faithful to his office. The sins of the Roman Empire were as scarlet, but its civilizing and legitimate virtues of legality and order must not be underestimated.

Neither secular nor sacred record speaks further of this event, and our logical assumption is that no civil action was ever pursued against Paul, his companions, the Church or, for that matter, anyone else. Certainly, the entirety of the population of Ephesus was not converted and consecrated to Christ, and doubtless Demetrius and his fellow craftsmen continued to ply their trade. The Ephesian silversmiths, though, deserve just a bit more notice. Mob action in any time, place or setting is deplorable, and its participants place themselves practically on the level of many of nature's beasts, which are subject to the herd instinct. The skilled craftsmen descended to the level of raucous, jeering chimpanzees. Likely, among any fair-minded observer there remains at least a modicum of sympathy for their plight. All humanity is burdened with the onerous tasks of making a living, of providing sustenance for our families and for ourselves, and we naturally should have a sympathy for our fellows whose livelihoods are imperiled. These artisans, though, were never attacked by Paul and the other Christian heralds, who were far more committed to proclaiming Christ. Any loss of income that they have suffered was within the purview of their powers to halt. Surely items other than pagan images could be fashioned by their skillful hands. The statuary of Diana was not only idolatrous but even in our modern times of greatly loosened standards most would view the images as pornographic.

Ephesus, this great commercial city of prosperity, art and religion had over three years been the scene of the confluence of four powers. The fanatics of the Jewish religious hierarchy, who sought nothing less than Paul's death, adhered to his ministry like barnacles on a ship. They would continue, but for now Ephesus was one more failure. The ruling Roman Empire actually demonstrated some wisdom and nobility, as it utilized its power properly as a means of keeping order and fair legal and judicial process. The third power was simply the love of money, a power which often distorts and configures itself in many shapes, and in this instance the shape of a mob. Legitimate authority prevailed, as God was not yet ready to lose so many to the mercenary howls of the mob. The fourth power was, as always, the quiet and peaceful power of the Spirit of Christ, found in the character and teachings of His apostles.

Ephesus itself would continue to flourish, but its path had been altered. Today, if considered at all this great city is inevitably coupled with Paul's epistle to the Ephesians, one of the primary Christian doctrinal texts in the New Testament. The city itself was eventually overcome by the increasing frequent wave of barbarian invasions from the north that began to plague Rome. In 252 A.D. Ephesus, with its marble edifice to Diana, was razed to the ground by Goths, Germanic warriors who were thorough in their destruction. Photographs of the hill on which the Temple stood in its magnificence gleaming in the sun, show a grass covered landscape with a few trees and scattered rocks and remnants.

As for Paul he continued undeterred on a very busy road. Yet on the horizon began to appear grayish clouds which would eventually blacken the sky.

CHAPTER FOURTEEN

I MUST GO TO
JERUSALEM

Modern travel is exhausting and even dehumanizing. Many modes of transportation are available, but by far for distance traveling airline flight remains the preferred method. It begins with booking or reserving the right flight on the right day at the right time and arriving at the airport at a safe time before the aircraft's departure. The process begins to intensify as soon as the traveler sets foot upon airport property. Especially in a large airport finding the correct booking counter is often a challenge and checking luggage and carry-on objects is often a flashpoint where the traveler incurs his first violation of some hitherto unknown airport rule. Following this the would-be trip taker is confronted with the dread of the "security check" where for a hoped for merciful short period he/she is subjected to the rudeness and questioning of overly officious federal factotums. Finally, after being released from this ordeal the traveler makes way to his/her assigned seat, and unless he/she is of the upper strata of the traveling classes, descends the weary body into an astonishingly narrow and cramped seat for several hours of uncomfortable travel. The arrival and exiting of the airplane and the airport are not exactly a mirror image of the departure, but they too, are quite taxing. Few persons enjoy travel today, but its serious benefits are not to be denied. Above those, two immediately come to the fore. First, modern travel is generally safe to an astonishingly high degree. Second, modernity has given the traveler the benefit of speed. Modern flight plans between any two points on the globe rarely extend beyond twenty-four hours, so the ordeal is over quickly.

The first century traveler dealt with all the detriments of modern travel (albeit in ancient form), and his presumption of safety was as great as that of the modern sojourner. Unless he was royalty or quite wealthy almost all travel was by walking on land or, if on water, small rickety wooden craft, which were not for the faint of heart. All the early Christian evangelists were traveling men, but perhaps none equaled Paul for sheer mobility, area places visited, and churches established. Following the famous events at Ephesus Paul and his companions departed in their wearying continuance of what has historically been styled his Third Missionary Journey. It began with a northward trip by land, sea, and land to Macedonia, where much success had met their original efforts. At varying points and for segments of his journey Paul's companions included Sopater, Aristarchus, Secundus, Gains, Timothy Tychicus, and of course, the great physician-historian Luke (who never once mentions his own name). This one instance, and one only, the itinerary for this journey we list to include Philippi, Assos, Mytilene, Chios, Samos, Tropylium, Miletus, Cores, Rhodes, Patra, Cyprus, Ptolemais, Caesarea, Tyre and finally Jerusalem. It was Paul who admitted that he had "no permanent dwelling place," and hos wearying must the hard travels have been for a man, who while not elderly, was certainly a considerable distance from his youth. But he prevailed, persevered and even triumphed, and physical complaints were not a part of the character of this amazing, yet strange man, the apostle to the Gentiles, Paul.

So, just what was the character of Paul? Not his curriculum vitae, for that can be summarized briskly and tersely while revealing little of his real character. Biographies of Paul have been written, and this work seeks not to add to the list, but a few salient traits of the famous apostle's life need to be noted and, in most events, even celebrated. One, perhaps somewhat downplayed, is the spirit of self-sacrifice. Certainly, all students and interested observers are aware of the thunderclap of change on the Road to Damascus which marked the beginning of the point of demarcation between Saul of Tarsus and Christ's apostle. The life he walked away from merits a brief examination. He was in his still youthful prime, brilliantly educated with an amazing mind and reckoned among the rising young stars of Judaism. He enjoyed the favor and confidence of the ruling priesthood, an insider and an executioner of major decisions, an honest ally, a fearful enemy and a "darling" upon whom all blessings seemed to fall. Later, it was Paul himself who hesitatingly gave a brief autobiographical sketch of his young life:

> "Circumcised of the eighth day, of the stock of Israel, of the tribe of Benjamin, a Hebrew of the Hebrews; as touching the law, a Pharisee; Concerning zeal, persecuting the church; touching the righteousness which is the law, blameless."

He was also well-born, perhaps even wealthy, loaded with prestige and youthful accomplishment, but now:

> "(W)hat things were gain to me, those I counted
> loss for Christ."

His language and feeling became more intense and earthy as he described it all, when contrasted to Christ, as "dung."

No one at any time or place in this world "has it all," but as a younger man Paul acknowledges that he possessed most of what he coveted, fame, prestige, the favor of the well placed, a fine education and obvious upward mobility. Was it courage or was it foolishness that caused him to sacrifice it all, and for what he received in return for his sacrifice we defer to the words of Jesus Himself, who directed Ananias to instruct the temporarily blinded Saul of Tarsus:

> "I will show him how great things he must suffer
> for my sake."

The young Saul willingly sacrificed so much, but scarcely a hint of a self-realization of suffering exists in his extensive writings. Instead as an old man, with death rapidly approaching he thus expressed:

> "To live is Christ, to die is gain."

Several times it has been remarked throughout this narrative that the singularity of Paul was amazing. Perhaps it was that trait, subordinated to the Spirit of Christ, that propelled him forward, through thick and thin and to be abased or abound. We need no intimate research or the gauziness of academic verbiage to define the nature of that "singularity." It is one word herein capable of being adequately defined by another word. His singularity was "Christ," no more, no less and no other. It was not fealty to some as yet inchoate religious doctrine that propelled, he and his great friend Silas to withstand the savagery of a Roman flogging before being unceremoniously dumped and shackled in the abyss of an ancient prison. The pedigree of his Hebrew ancestry, both temporal and spiritual, did not soften the brutality or smooth the edges of the stones that were pelted upon him at Derbe and allow him to recover from the diabolic hatred of his Jewish "brothers." His extensive and in-depth knowledge of his own religion and culture as well as that of the more celebrated Greeks, magnificent and useful as these traits were, did not give him the courage and energy force to stand alone and with singleness of purpose and person teach and debate the Athenian intelligentsia on Mars Hill. Beat him, kick him, stone him, chain him, no matter what fiendish action was so taken against him Paul would not be suppressed, and he would always bounce back. Many are the adventures and challenges which still lay ahead for this almost preternaturally committed and courageous man, and he would meet them all. Paul's mind was of a depth and complexity that foreclosed his thinking in sayings, creeds, or mottos. Still, the apostle himself succinctly summarized his methods and goals when writing to the church at Corinth:

"For we preach Christ crucified."

The message never altered, and this man, the author of fully one-half the New Testament from the beginning of his mission to the end of his days ever deviated an iota from this proclamation. He was a man of stamina, courage, single-mindedness which often morphed into obstinance and maybe self-will, honesty, and an eternal message. This was all good, and especially for the present. He would need all of this, for the foes he faced were relentless, personal and by their own reckoning would stop at nothing to destroy Paul. These were the recalcitrant and unrepentant men and leaders of the Jewish religious establishment.

This chapter began with a reference to travel and ultimately Paul's travels on this his popularly titled Third Missionary Journey. As Luke in Acts consistently relates, it was Paul's goal to go to the center of Judaism itself, the City of David, Jerusalem. This apostolic desire, and one may fairly call it an obsession, provides the structural trellis for all Paul's travels and activities. He was repeatedly warned by companions, fellow evangelists and Christians, the type men who themselves were courageous and certainly not naturally alarmists. Opposition, imprisonment, and death awaited this apostle to the Gentiles in the capital, national and cultural center of the Jews. The reader is entitled to voice and voice emphatically, "Why?"

To the Jews, Paul stated, Christ was a "stumbling block," an obstacle in their path. Was Christianity itself, and Paul personally, anti-Jewish or in the modern parlance, "anti-Semitic." Anti-Semitism is real, was real, has always been real, and will always be real, but is Christianity, the message of Jesus, itself the fullest expression of anti-Semitism? Even its accusation, whether or not true, is a powerful weapon, and can immediately put a person on the moral and cultural defensive. Christ Himself, on this earth a Jewish man, was accused of wanting to pervert and destroy Moses and the prophets, but as He painstakingly taught, He was not the destroyer of the Law, but its fulfillment. From Genesis through Malachi the message was explicit, implicit, implied, metaphorical, and proffered in any form that the Mosaical system was temporary, that the distinctions between Jew and Greek would vanish by the cleansing blood of Christ and that all were one in God's sight. This fundamental truth of Christianity, the Jews, en masse, did not then nor do they now acknowledge. Certainly, the exceptions are many and glaring, and after Jesus include all the apostles, the parents of Jesus, most of the great New Testament evangelists such as Stephen, Barnabas and Apollos, and the early Church itself. Gradually, though, and certainly after apostolic days the Jewish element in the Church began to fade, and within a shockingly few years the Church became and in the twenty-first century remains overwhelmingly Gentile. But does theology alone explain the almost eerily constant and steadfast Jewish opposition to Paul? This was an enmity so deep that once a group of Jews swore an oath that they would not eat until they had killed Paul.

The Jewish opposition was everywhere throughout the lands of the Diaspora, but it remained most concentrated and virulent in Jerusalem itself. Here was the Temple, the Great Council of the Sanhedrin, the cores of the scribes, Pharisees and Sadducees and the high priesthood. Familiarity should grasp the observer because this was essentially the same conspiracy which had crucified Christ. Paul would have been the first to declare that he was in no way as important as Christ, but it is no error to over that the Jewish hatred of the apostle equaled that of its bitterness towards the Messiah. At this time in the 50's A.D. Jerusalem itself was the home of the first Church and though numbers are not precisely calculable it is likely that Jerusalem's population included a substantial number of Christians. Generally speaking these Christians at this time were not in danger of physical persecution from the Jews, yet Paul's cold, dead body was a prized dream of theirs. Certainly, the Jewish hierarchy had little regard for these Jewish Christians, but so long as their numbers were of manageable proportions, they would grudgingly abide them. Further and perhaps most importantly an outright Jewish persecution of Christians would have been violent and disorderly, anathema to the Romans who retained a death grip on the city. Moreover, even the other apostles and James, the brother of Jesus, and a leader in the Jerusalem Church continued their activities unharmed.

Paul, though, was different and always was he different. The characters of the other apostles were the equal of Paul's, but their talents, great as they were, remained subordinate. Paul was effective, noticeably effective in his role as apostle to the Gentiles and also to their fellow Jews. This scholar from Tarsus certainly was intensely hated by the empowered Jews, the hierarchy, the establishment or by whatever name one prefers. Even on this point it must be recognized that their hatred for Paul did not grow from some seed in the other apostles to whom Jesus explained on that dark night of His Passion that the world hates you, but only because it first hated Him. This "apostle born out of due season" was every bit an apostle, but he was different, as his one-time colleagues well knew. It is likely not sufficient to say that they hated him because he had been "one of them." It was more. This constantly driven dynamo of a man had not been just "one of them," but rather he had been the most prominent of the rising stars in the traditional Jewish firmament. Paul had been the fair-haired boy of the entrenched Jewish ruling class, the recognizably brilliant protégé of none other than the great Gamaliel. He had served in a key role, the exact parameters of which are unknown, in the early martyrdom and murder of Stephen. So much a part of the inner circle was he that the high priesthood itself had given him charge of the Christian persecution north of Jerusalem all the way to Damascus, Syria.

As in a highly competitive school, a dynamic growing corporation with many ruthlessly aspiring young men or a military unit with young officers clamoring for promotion and rank so was Paul in the Jewish power structure. But he was more, not

Just one of many or one of a few, but he was the one. He was the young man, now mature, to be emulated, and by no meaning to trivialize the matter Paul was the class president, the sports hero, the top student of the class, ad infinitum. Then, one day, in Damascus he became not only one of them "in the way," a Christian, but quickly the most prominent of their number. As Judas Iscariot became for all time with Christians synonymous with betrayal, so did Saul of Tarsus earn this opprobrium from the Judaic establishment. Saul of Tarsus, though, betrayed no one or nothing except his own worldly ambitions, whereas Judas sold his soul for thirty pieces of silver.

The horde of persecutors which trailed Paul also hated him for his astonishing effectiveness. To high or low, rich or poor, male or female, Jew or Gentile, could Paul deliver Christ and with an amazing efficacy. The early Church in the Gentile world was a product of the indefatigable efforts of Paul and men of his caliber such as Apollos, Silas, Luke, and Barnabas. If a Jew loathed and rejected the truth of Jesus of Nazareth's being the Christ his detestation certainly would encompass his most successful teachers, of whom Paul was the most prominent.

Just about one generation had elapsed since Jesus had trod Judea as both the Son of God and the Son of Man. Always much changes in a quarter century, but the niche which the Jewish hierarchy held in the Judean and Roman world remained remarkably unchanged. The priesthood, the leaders of the sects, most prominently the Pharisees and Sadducees, and the scribes, self-anointed guardians of the truth, retained a quite comfortable and even powerful station in society, albeit their power was mortgaged to the far greater power of the Goliath in the west, Rome. Woe to anyone who threatened it, as was their perception of the message which Paul preached.

All the superlatives lavished upon the apostle Paul contemporaneously, historically, and even by this present small work are well and truly merited. But, Paul, the self-described "chief of all sinners" was not Christ, but a man, albeit a great one. After becoming the great apostle Paul, did he retain and exhibit any faults, flaws or dare we say it sins (the apostle himself certainly had no hesitation stating it)? Yes.

Commitment, determination, steadfastness, and ambition for truth and for its triumph are marvelous and somewhat rare qualities, and in no man were they found in more abundance that with Paul. Sometimes, each of these characteristics individually and certainly collectively are capable and even prone to mutation into stubbornness, obstinacy, and just plain self-will. So they did at times, with Paul, and as with all its heroes the scriptures are never reticent in directing attention to their shortcomings. It is no denigration of the character of this truly great man to be of an opinion that he was not necessarily an easy companion with whom to work or a man (who like all of us) p0referred his own way. On this Third Missionary Journey, against all caution and advice, the obstinacy of Paul was in full glory of display for the world and future generations to view. His goal, all along the winding and wearying route was to arrive in Jerusalem before the Feast of the Passover, the time when the city would be filled with his fellow countrymen. So important was this to Paul that he decided to omit a visit to the celebrated city of Ephesus, where he and others had labored long, hard, and successfully to build a great church. Instead the elders of the Ephesians met Paul at Miletus where with a great emotional outpouring Paul confessed that he did not know what fate awaited him in Jerusalem, but:

> "Now, behold, I go bound in the spirit unto
> Jerusalem, not knowing the things which shall
> befall me there, Save that the Holy Spirit wit-
> nesseth in every city, saying that bonds and af-
> flictions abide me."

In plainer terms, he knew not what was in store for him in Jerusalem, but that personally it would not be pleasant. Paul, in one of his most emotional outpourings in an outwardly emotional age poured out his heart to them, summarizing his believable sincerity inherent in all his work, but that regardless of all cautions, warnings and the human odds facing him he was still bound for Jerusalem, the city that rejected Christ Himself. Paul and the Ephesians fell upon each other in a catharsis of fear, sorrow, and weeping, but Paul's next moves were still in the direction of Jerusalem.

Men and women, no matter how sincere and strong are their beliefs and feelings can be wrong. We have averred that Paul could be in error, and so could other Christians along the way. Perhaps even a man named Agabus, a Judean prophet who had come to meet Paul while he was staying in Caesarea, could be in error. Agabus, apparently a man of some renown and repute, and with a decided flair for the dramatic:

> "(T)ook Paul's own sash, and bound his hands
> and feet, and said, Thus saith the Holy Spirit,
> So shall the Jews at Jerusalem bind the man that
> owneth this sash, and shall deliver him into the
> hands of the Gentiles."

Paul was the last man to be accused of being dim-witted and a fool and he never once disputed the probability, even the certainty, of dire trouble in Jerusalem.

As error, misjudgment, character flaws and defects were natural components of men, even men of the moral caliber of Agabus, the Ephesian elders, Luke and even of Paul, and none would have denied it. These flaws, imperfections, obstinacies, and sins, though, are not an element in the character of the Creator of the Universe, God Himself, to whom the final word always belongs. Earlier at Tyree, Luke remarked:

> "(F)inding disciples, we tarried there seven days; who said to Paul through the spirit, that he should not go to Jerusalem."

All along the route, the disciples warned Paul. These were not men and women of any flippancy, but rather well versed in the will of God and quite knowledgeable of the world in which they lived. "Yes, yes..." we can hear the apostle saying, "but" and following this preposition was some form of expression "I am going to Jerusalem anyway." A man with the character, knowledge and disposition of Paul was not easily dissuaded from a set course.

Paul's record of service to God and personal sacrifice is so vast, an astounding breadth and depth of physical brutalization, peril, and battles against seemingly impossible odds that a charge of self-glorification and personal aggrandizement cannot justifiably be made against him. From the moment he became a Christian (and really even before) his motives were pure and as he himself had remarked he had served God "... in all good conscience." Maybe, though, this chosen apostle, perhaps even unknown to himself, had begun to view his presence and labors with at least a tinge of indispensability. Why Jerusalem? He was the chosen apostle to the Gentiles, and this city of David seemingly was home to a large, perhaps even a thriving Church. It was a Church and a work which apparently was not bereft of workers and leadership. Likely Jerusalem was either the residence or an important point of demarcation for many of the other apostles, none of whom were lacking in the qualities possessed by Paul. Further, as we have referenced perhaps the most significant figure of leadership in the Jerusalem Church was James, the brother of the Lord. So, was Paul's presence in Jerusalem not only full of danger but was it even necessary? Paul thought yes, but God Himself thought otherwise. Would He abandon Paul in the maelstrom and cacophony of terror and fear that was about to envelop Paul? As always, God had the final word.

CHAPTER FIFTEEN

CHAOS IN JERUSALEM

A merican culture has long been deeply permeated by a saying obviously pilfered from the game of baseball, and simply it is "Three strikes and you are out." Our popular culture
grants more credit to the currently reigning ethic and gives
more credit to itself than it does to God. For many they accuse
God of being so harsh and strictly legal that "one strike and
you are out" is the reigning mantra of the Deity. As with much,
if not most commonly accepted religion's wisdom, both apho-
risms begin to crack and crumble under historical and scriptural scrutiny. The Old Testament itself could almost bear the
nomenclature of God's Book of Patience, when the student sees
time after time, year after year, generation after generation,
God's patience being tested and strained beyond reason by His
own people. This is borne out from the time of Moses's leading
the Israelites from slavery through the days, even the centuries,
of judges, kings, and prophets, with God only in extremis turning from his people. The patience which copiously flowed from
Jesus to His disciples and even His apostles remains both inspirational and comforting. The Savior's teachings were not just
adorned with the stories of forgiveness, but redemption and

forgiveness formed the very core of His message. The forgiving Father of His famous Parable of the Prodigal Son remains a template for patience tried and forgiveness abounding. Paul, even though warned by God and man, remained under the watchful care of Heaven.

Finally, for better or worse, Paul and his party of companions arrived in Jerusalem, where they were happily received, especially by the Church's most prominent leader, James, as well as all the elders. James gave Paul a report on the local Church and with pleasure and likely justifiable pride noted that thousands of Jews had become Christians. (As a parenthetical it is to be noted that save for the Church's beginning on Pentecost this seems to be the only mention of the Church's numerical size in the New Testament). Not only this, James added, but success was being found among the Gentiles, and "... when they heard it they glorified the Lord." It's all good, Paul, however...

> "Thou seest, brother, how many thousands of Jews there are which believe; and they are all zealous of the law. And they are informed of thee, that thou teachest all the Jews which are among the Gentiles to forsake Moses, saying that they ought not to circumcise their children, neither to walk after the customs."

James wanted from Paul, perhaps unadvisedly, a public demonstration that he was still a Jew and bore no malice, ill will or even criticism towards his countrymen. The means was at hand, James believed, for Paul to demonstrate to the Jews that he meant them no harm and that he himself was still a Jew. In plainer terms, James wanted to placate the distrusting Jews by having him prove something for which proof was not needed. It was Paul who had proclaimed that "I am all things to all people," and he throughout his Christian life had proven that he would venture anywhere and do anything to make his disciples.

The Old Law, and especially the customs and traditions which followed Moses, and which had clung to the Law as barnacles on a ship was highly ritualistic, and such was about to be borne out. We have four men, James explained, who have shaven their heads in compliance to some real or invented Mosaical instruction. Join them, James advised, so:

> "Then Paul took the men, and the next day purifying himself with them entered the temple to signify the accomplishment of the days of purification, until that an offering should be offered for every one of them."

In other words, show the Jews that you are still observant to their customs and that you mean them no harm. As compromises so often do and even with the best of intentions it backfired. After the established one week's purification Paul walked into the temple where he was espied by "the Jews which were of Asia," likely from Ephesus; its capital. He was recognized and received a tumultuous indictment from the mob. All of James's carefully laid plans for Paul were met with the Asian Jews seeing him in the temple:

> "Crying out, Men of Israel, help: This is the man, that teacheth all men everywhere against the people, and the law, and this place: and further brought Greeks also into the temple, and hath polluted this holy place."

Just as the enraged street rabble in an old American Western movie the people were galvanized into a mob, and in the twinkling of an eye Paul became to them a detestable criminal and heretic. This ancient lynch mob was primed to ender this "wretch" justice.

At first it was just a few enraged souls who broke into the Temple to apprehend this vilest of criminals. Then more, dozens, hundreds, even thousands more as "... all the city was moved, and the people ran together, and they took Paul." Likely but a few Jews personally recognized the apostle, for it had been many years. The natural weathering of age and his shaven head though did not fully obscure his identity to them. An untold number likely knew of Paul, though to varying degrees of personal awareness; however, with confidence it may be asserted that the bulk of this multitude was swept away by the current emotional tide. None had ceased to be human and responsible for their actions, but now the multitude had congealed into that vilest of beings, a mob. Mobs, mob rule, mobocracy and mob thinking, and emotions all merit serious study, the breadth and intensity of which is beyond this work. It is sufficient, though, that a couple characteristics, which are certainly shared by this Jerusalem mob, are necessary to mention. A mob is a powerful, destructive force, almost a force of nature, such as a tornado. Its span of life may be but momentary, from a few minutes to, in extreme instances, a few hours. Its duration is brief, but most mobs are fueled by a highly lethal mixture of two quite volatile elements, hatred, and ignorance. Both were in abundant quantities that day in Jerusalem, and it looked as if the life of the great apostle Paul, nee Saul of Tarsus, was measurable in minutes. Mobs, though they be frightfully and horridly powerful, like storms, do not act in a vacuum. Powerful though they are, their forward impetus soon dissipates without the aid and temperance of outside forces.

Politically, little or nothing had been altered in Jerusalem for over a generation, certainly dating back to those black days of the mob during Christ's Passion. Rome was still the ultimate earthly power, and this western land's reaction to a breach of the peace was severe deprecation and harsh punishment and reprisal. The peace in the Judean capital had been smashed:

> "And as they went about to kill him, tidings came unto the chief captain of the band, that all Jerusalem was in an uproar."

Should the Jewish mob have beaten Paul to death the Roman repercussions would have been great. The state of the Roman Empire jealously guarded its monopoly upon lawful violence. Its concern for one strange Jewish teacher of a strange other worldly doctrine meant little or nothing to the Roman rulers. The maintenance of the peace, though, remained a sine qua non for the Roman masters. The Roman response was rapid, as the captain:

> "(I)mmediately took soldiers and centurions, and ran down unto them: and when they saw the chief captain and the soldiers, they left beating of Paul."

In the presence of the situation's immediacy the Roman soldiers had saved Paul, but salvation was not Rome's business. The Empire's stock in trade was power, power that was expected to be answered by compliance, obedience, and even subservience.

Now, with this assumedly miscreant Paul safely in the clasp
of the Roman soldiery what their commander most wanted was
order. Still, a cacophony of noise was assaulting his ears, as the
mob cried for various measures of violent depravity upon this
prisoner, so he commanded that his troops take their newly acquired prisoner into the army's fortress. Still, the mob followed
closely, crying "Away with him." Of all people who ever lived
one of the least likely to remain silent, even in these harsh environs, was the apostle Paul, and here he did not disappoint.
Just before the soldiers led Paul into the fortress, in the Greek
language the apostle inquired of the chief captain, "May I speak
unto thee?" We now see what will become increasingly apparent, and this is the ability of Paul, second only to the Master
Himself, to take control of even the most stressful situation
in the direst circumstances. Startled to hear Greek, the lingua
franca of the Roman Empire, in Jerusalem, the captain stopped
short and asked what was really a rhetorical question:

"Canst thou speak Greek?"

Then, the captain demonstrated official Rome's then pre-
vailing attitude toward Jewish religious questions and debates
by asking a strange question:

"Art not thou that Egyptian, which before these
days made an uproar, and led out into the wilder-
ness four thousand men who were murderers?"

The captain, a man of intelligence and authority, had mistaken Paul for an earlier insurrectionist. Paul simply identified
himself and requested permission to speak to the crowd. To
God we leave the choice of the "greatest" moments in the life

of a man or a woman, but here we submit that what followed was probably the most illustrative moment scripturally of the career and character of the mature apostle Paul.

This man has been guilty of nothing more than as a Jew walking into the Temple with four other Jews. He has been forcibly and violently extracted from the holiest place of worship of the Jews, the Temple, shoved, pushed, kicked, spat upon, cuffed about, and humiliatingly dragged through the streets of Jerusalem. This self-appointed posse, be they learned or unlearned, religious or not, of thugs has manhandled him and begun to beat him savagely until the intervention of the Roman army. Then the Romans drag him away, likely not with any care or tenderness, and Paul realizes the nature and severity of the brutality which awaits them at their hands. Finally he is mistaken for an Egyptian terrorist and murderer. Still, he is compelled to speak, but not of complaint or of defense. He beckoned the crowd to listen to his detailed message of his own personal history, lengthy but capable of being summarized under the theme of "Let me tell you what Jesus Christ has done for me." Well Paul merits the recognition and accolades of being perhaps the most singularly focused man in history. His speech, recorded in detail by our historian Luke, personally present that day, recounts his life as a persecutor of Christ, a man without mercy, until the Savior Himself appeared to him on the road to Damascus. He ended with perhaps the most affecting event in the life of Paul, his "... consenting unto the death of Stephen." Chillingly, the speech's effect upon the Jewish crowd was identical to the Jewish audience's reaction to the earlier famous defense by Stephen:

"And they gave audience to (Paul's) word, and
said, Away with such a fellow from this earth; it
is not fit that he should live."

Yet we may rightly ponder the reasons and/or rationale
which these Jews, likely religious observers to a man, had for
canceling Paul and putting him in his grave. For a time they
had listened, probably attentively, to his defense, and Paul to
his lasting credit owned up to his vile role in one of the central
events of extant Jewish history, the martyrdom of Stephen, to
which the apostle admitted to "...consenting to his death." Still,
the Jewish audience, doubtless growing restless and increasingly uncomfortable, gave ear to Paul. It was his final statement,
though, that lit the conflagration of hate and seemingly doomed
Paul:

"And (God) said unto me, Depart, for I will send
thee far hence to the Gentiles."

Gentiles, a word which remained a poisonous opprobrium to
the zealous, orthodox Jews, who even a generation after Christ
trod the earth, could not for a scintilla of a moment consider
that they were no longer God's chosen people, but that equally
salvation was proffered to all men and women, of whatever race
or nation. Luke's account is straightforward and emphatic that
Paul's listeners "gave him audience" until this statement, but
now again the dam had broken, and Romans or not, this scoun-
drel renegade Paul was marked for a quick death, likely similar
to the work of the ancient lynch mob which slew Stephen.

The Roman presence, though, was too strong to be ignored,
and besides Rome did not grow so great by any squeamish aver-
sion to shedding blood. A long-standing cliché is that "history

repeats itself," but little more than a cursory examination will reflect that this is a hit-or-miss proposition. Here, though, the bull's eye of repetition is struck, and with an eeriness and déjà vu reminiscent of Governor Pilate's acquiescence before the Jews:

> "The chief captain commanded him to be brought into the castle, and bade that he should be examined by scourging; that he might know where fore they cried so against him."

The legal theory seemed to be that if you beat a man within hailing distance of his demise you could extract any statement from him that his afflicting torturer so desired. Actually, this savage beating with leather straps the fury of which was emboldened by chips of metal and bone, probably boasted a very high rate of success. Even for powerful, swaggering Romans, though, life has an occasional surprise:

> "As they bound him with straps, Paul said unto the centurion that stood by, Is it lawful for you to scourge a man that is a Roman, and uncondemned?"

A Roman? This unprepossessing, non-descript Jewish religious enthusiast was a Roman? The centurion's cardiovascular system likely suffered a sudden serious moment of distress when he realized that he was about to unlawfully beat a man boasting the status of Roman citizenship. The centurion halted the proceedings and advised the chief captain of the inherent dangers in unlawfully beating a Roman, and so the chief captain, with consternation and amazement came to his bound prisoner and basically asked him how he got to be a Roman. This was a prized honor, not easily obtained for the chief captain said:

> "With a great sum obtained I this freedom, and
> Paul said, but I was free born."

The scourging was off, and it was apparent that the Roman officials and soldiers wanted the Jews to handle this, another of their eternally endless religious disputes among themselves. The chief captain (showing wherein the real earthy power lay) commanded the chief priests and the Sanhedrin to appear and assemble, whereupon he set Paul down before them.

We are required to be reluctant in stating that anything short of Divine prophecy is inevitable, but the scene which now ensures is close. Paul before the Sanhedrin. The actions of the Sanhedrin, assemblies, trials, deeds and more often misdeeds have been shown to be important to both the founding and the history of the Church. From the "trial" of Christ to the repeated early harassment and persecution of the apostles Peter and John to the great message and martyrdom of Stephen the Sanhedrin was fervent in its opposition to Christ. Now, its one-time prodigy, its emerging star and the turncoat of turncoats, Paul stood before them, seemingly helpless and powerless. He began to speak:

> "Men and brethren, I have lived in all good con-
> science before God until this day."

Replicating Caiaphas before Christ, the current high priest, commanded that Paul be struck in the mouth. Nothing had changed with these lords of Judaism. Although the character of Paul had been transformed the determination and courage at his core had not been modified as he returned fire:

> "Then said Paul unto Ananias, God shall smite thee, thou whited wall; for sittest thou to judge me after the law, and commandest me to be smitten contrary to the law?"

The apostle's appearance before the Sanhedrin, which collectively wished to be his death chamber, had gotten off to a rousing start. Paul quickly perceived that as always and before the Council was divided into two warring factions, the Pharisees, and Sadducees Paul's aim above all was to teach Christ, but he was a multi-talented master, who recognized that in so preaching Christ he could divide his accusers, so he began:

> "Men and brethren, I am a Pharisee, the son of a Pharisee: of the hope and resurrection of the dead I am called into question."

This statement struck the primary fault line between Pharisee and Sadducee, the latter which denied the possibility of life after death, and thus he turned, at least momentarily the two sects away from his and upon each other. But not for long. The Pharisaical scribes were convinced of Paul's genuineness, truth, and authenticity and in fact provided a corollary to Gamaliel's statement of years ago (see Chapter Four) when they argued:

> "We find no evil in this man: but if a spirit or an hath spoken to him, let us not fight against God."

The argument became increasingly ferocious and was on the very rim of violence "... lest Paul should have been pulled in pieces by them." The chief captain, fearing above all a Jewish riot, ordered his soldiers to forcibly extract Paul and return him to the military barracks. For a body as august, respected, and magisterial as the Sanhedrin, their sessions with a remarkable consistency ended with tumult and violence.

Paul had survived the day, but the question was ever in the strong, powerful hands of the Romans, would he survive another. As Christ had spoken at its base the world's hatred for the apostles was a hatred for Christ, yet this hatred is often so deep and spreading with a virulent toxicity that men and women are engulfed in its floodtide. So bitter was the hatred of some for Paul that more than forty Jews:

> "...banded together, and bound themselves under
> a curse, saying that they would neither eat nor
> drink till they had killed Paul."

They huddled with the chief priests (past masters of the practice) to form a conspiracy, to persuade the Romans to bring Paul down again so that he might be further questioned, whereupon the opportunity would be fashioned to murder him. The apostle, though, had a young nephew who had likely come to visit him and who overheard the plot being made. He so informed Paul, who then passed the information onto one of the centurions, and presumptively as a prisoner gave the command to take his nephew to the chief captain. The apostle, a natural leader who was accustomed to directing activity was obeyed, and to the chief captain his nephew was taken. Once more, from the gospels forward, the purity of the image of Roman commanders as little more than brute beasts is belied as:

"The chief captain took him by the hand, and
went with him aside privately, and asked him,
What is this that thou has to tell me?"

The young man, worthy as a nephew to Paul, spoke boldly
to the chief captain of the assassination plot and its likely repercussions if successful. With a province of secrecy given the
youth was released, and such was his manner and demeanor
that the chief captain Claudius Lysias instantly believed him.
Quickly he gave the orders for the mobilization of two hundred
infantrymen, two hundred spearmen and seventy cavalrymen,
all mustered and prepared for travel and combat at nine o'clock
at night. They, this large body of almost five hundred, were to
be the escort for one lone prisoner, an aging Jew who was certainly no threat physically to anyone, and with this strange man
Paul in tow they were to safely transport him to the Roman
governor Felix, who lived at the governors in the northern city
of Caesarea.

So many of the endlessly and tirelessly repeated sayings
which become mantras to all cultures and times are just that,
clichés, sayings, and maxims the truth of which is rarely, if
ever, examined. Some, though, are worthy, and the episode
with Paul, the Jews and the Romans is worthy of its citation.
Truth is stranger than fiction. Less than forty-eight hours earlier Paul, a physically uninspiring presence, was being cuffed,
dragged, and beaten through the streets of Jerusalem. His grue-
some death from a savage, animalistic brutality was a certainty
until the organized intervention of the powerful ruling Romans.
Marked for death by a band of Jewish fanatics and encased in
a Roman prison his lifespan was not most properly recorded
in minutes. With an amazing swiftness it all changed as Paul,
albeit yet a prisoner, was being personally escorted by a force

of five hundred Roman legionaries, itself so powerful that it could be challenged only by an opposing army of equal size. Soon the apostle was safely ensconced, though in incarceration, at Caesarea, a center of Roman power and authority. All these amazing events, occurring with a shocking rapidity were not occasioned by any real change of heart in their prime players, the Romans, the Jews, or even Paul himself. For the moment, the extant earthly power structure remained inviolate. Between imprisonment in Jerusalem in preparation for a quick death, legal or illegal, and being a prized prisoner of Rome escorted to safety by five hundred of its soldiers something or someone must have intervened. The answer lies in a moment during Paul's last night of imprisonment in Jerusalem when God stood by Paul and told him:

> "Be of good cheer, Paul: for as thou hast testified
> of Me in Jerusalem, so must thou bear witness of
> me in Rome."

God's ways truly are mysterious, and only He could fuse from the earthly powers of the Jewish hatred, the Sanhedrin, and the Roman Empire, all of whom would willingly have played their parts in Paul's death and transform their actions into necessary and congruous elements in not only Paul's ministry but the spread of the gospel to Rome itself. That is power, real power.

Traveling with Paul and the military entourage was a letter which was written by the chief captain, Claudius Lysias. The letter, produced in detail by Luke, is basically a formal report by one Roman official to a higher Roman official, the governor, an office at one time most infamously occupied by Pontius Pilate. With general, though not impeccable accuracy, he outlined and summarized the Jerusalem events which had given rise and impetus to these proceedings. Interestingly, in the letter Lysias commented:

> "(Paul), I perceived to be accused of questions of their law, but to have nothing laid to his charge worthy or death or of bards."

With that Lysias presented his special prisoner to the important governor who would hear his case. The governor's name was Marcus Antonius Felix.

CHAPTER SIXTEEN

POLITICS, RELIGION AND CHRIST

At least three forces began to employ the predicament into which this itinerant Jewish evangelist found himself to blaze parallel routes to power. This portion of their roads all converged into the northern Judean city with the decidedly non-Hebraic name of Caesarea. This was a city built in the first century before Christ by none other that King Herod the Great to honor Augustus Caesar, effectively the First Citizen of Rome and its long term de facto emperor. It was Judea's major seaport in New Testament days, the Roman administrative center of the nation and the home of its governor, at this moment the previously noted Marcus Antonius Felix. As almost all Roman governors Felix could boast of being well connected into the aristocratic nexus of Roman society and politics. A man who had a total of three wives the most noted of which was a woman who was the granddaughter of Mark Antony and Cleopatra. Felix, as both our limited historical record and the scriptures adequately demonstrate was himself an unscrupulous man, which placed his reputation squarely in the ranks of the world's

225

great historical tradition. But he represented power, the mighty power of Rome, and nothing could be done in Judea without his approval. Rome was the power of stability, and at this juncture in Jewish history seemingly the power of permanence. These disciplined organized conquerors from the west had been there for over a century, since 67 BC, and they had revealed no desire to leave.

The power of the Jewish religion's establishment could never be brushed aside. It had shown a remarkable aptitude in finding a very comfortable niche under the Roman rulers. They imposed their increasingly harsh regime of rules and regulations upon the people, and Rome cared not a jot nor a tittle for their crazed religious beliefs. Just stay peaceable and pay taxes, and all would be fine. A coterie of the Jewish establishment had marched parallel to Paul in his forced journey from Jerusalem to Caesarea. They included Ananias, the high priest, and an esteemed orator named Tertullus, who would serve as a sort of special council and prosecutor of Paul. Tertullus, a man for whom the historical record is sparse, is really of less interest than his retainers, chiefly Ananias, and his colleagues. After too much history, the priesthood was wary of these Christian heralds, from the fishermen Peter and John to Stephen and to them the most dangerous of all, the present prisoner Paul. Their case needed professional representation and so he was retained.

That third power that met in Caesarea was of course, Paul Himself. His journey was long from finished, but surely he would ponder that winding road from point man of the Jewish persecutors to a shackled Roman prisoner preparing to give a defense of his conduct and his Master before the Roman governor. Even an unknowing visitor from the far side of the world would have grasped the power structure and relative strengths of the players.

The trial began with Tertullus, doubtless flowing with the most flattering of ancient oratory as he began uxoriously:

> "Tertullus began to accuse (Paul), saying, Seeing that by thee we enjoy great quietness, and that very worthy deeds are done unto this nation by thy providence.

We accept it always, and in all places, most noble Felix, with all thankfulness."

It matters not whether Tertullus spoke in Greek, Latin or Hebrew, the real language was a tongue forever extant, that of servility and of pandering to power. It is the toady who wants something from his master. To call what follows "court proceedings" is a stretch, for this entire session before Governor Felix is a strange mixture of politics, religion, and baseless accusation. Tertullus laid forth point by point an indictment against Paul, every allegation without substance and often stark lies. His first sentence of indictment begs its entire quotation:

> "For we have found this man a pestilent fellow, and a mover of sedition among all the Jews throughout the world, and a ringleader of the sect of the Nazarenes."

"Pestilence" is a slippery word, easily slithering from the speaker's accusation and almost incapable of precise definition. In fact, Paul is so called this by Tertullus likely as the prosecutor's attempt to conjure in the mind of Felix an initially distasteful image. Without the slightest doubt, though, the most important allegation and the one that piqued the governor's interest was that of Paul's being a "mover of sedition among all the

Jews throughout the world." Felix was in the governor's chair to ruthlessly quash the slightest hint of sedition or even rebellion. Thus, the same lie which commanded Governor Pilate's attention a generation before when Jesus of Nazareth stood before his judgment seat accused of setting aside the authority of Caesar. In the plainest terminology, both with Christ and with Paul this was a lie. Paul, the most prolific of New Testament authors and the most far ranging of the apostles never issued a word on the subject other than still extant admonitions to obey all laws of civil authorities. As for "ringleader of ... the Nazarenes" even two thousand years later we note this not so much as a factual statement but rather as a phrase of derision and contempt.

Tertullus, though, had additional major difficulties of meshing his versions of Paul's "indictable" offenses with actual truth. He felt impelled to bring before Felix, a Roman who cared nothing for Jewish religious squabbles one way or the other, the allegation:

> "(Paul) also has gone about to profane the temple, whom we took, and would have judged according to our law."

Likely at this juncture Felix wondered as to reason of such a "petty" dispute between a people, the Jews, who were in the main repulsive to Roman tastes, was even before him as governor. Tertullus's statement of the temple's profanation, though, was merely a prelude to the allegation that would capture the governor's attention:

"But the chief captain Lysias came upon us, and
with great violence took him away out of our
hands."

Understandably, the prosecution conveniently neglected to
mention that the Jews effectively were rioting and of the violence being inflicted upon Paul. The omission of facts deleteri-
ous to one's argument was hardly an invention of Tertullus and
is common politically and judicially yet today. Still it must be
clarified that any violence which the Roman soldiers may have
inflicted upon the Jewish mob was in the cause of saving the life
of a defenseless man.

It was the omission of the next salient fact in Tertullus's argument whereby the thrust of the story was diverted dishon-
estly in favor of the Jewish accusers:

"(Lysias commended) his accusers to come unto
thee: by examining of whom thyself mayest take
knowledge of all these things, whereof we accuse
him."

In a rough, unhewn manner the statement of Tertullus contains elements of truth. Conveniently dropped, though are the
real reasons why Paul was brought by an outsized force of Roman
soldiers to stand before the governor in Caesarea. In Jerusalem,
amidst the threats which crystallized into a spearpoint of a
planned assassination of the prisoner, the Jewish establishment
had foreclosed any possibility of Paul's being treated fairly or
even safely. In any event the case of Tertullus, undoubtedly a
professional of the first rank was well and smoothly articulated
and received the unanimous and probably rousing support of

the supporting "... Jews (who) assented, saying that these things were so."

How unfortunate, perhaps better described as even piteous, for the Jews and the prosecution that this was not the night of the Savior's Passion when the man who was both prosecutor and judge, the high priest Caiaphas, tore his regal clothing and shouted "... what need of we of further witnesses." This was a Roman governor, a man who cared not a trace for the Jews' endless religious debates and who was accustomed to regularly dealing with political figures who wielded far more clout than did the Jewish high priest. Instead Felix called the accused, Paul, before him and invited him to speak and argue his own case.

In Jerusalem, the cabal of the high priesthood, the leaders of the major sects and scribes basked in the security of the presumed safety of their power and the high station in Jewish society which they had secured for themselves. The farther from Jerusalem they ranged, though, their power weakened and waned, and their influence and intimidation weakened. They were highly intelligent, learned men, adept in speech and in their own particular interpretation of the Law. Remarkably they had balanced themselves for generations upon a tightrope between the Romans and the Jewish populace, and all in all, had done so with remarkable skill and aplomb. Yet, even, though judged by their own standards they had done well, they had made a mistake of enormous proportions. Albeit as an accused prisoner, the Jews' enmity towards Christ had placed perhaps the greatest evangelist in Church history squarely before a Roman governor, who gave Paul his undivided attention. God had not only circumvented the Jews' power but had grasped it and wholly reconfigured it for use in His purposes.

Paul was not a man, even while bound in chains, to miss such an opportunity that had been presented him. This was a man not only in the front rank of evangelists with his special apostolic ability and fervor but also a thinker, religiously, philosophically, and culturally subordinate to no man or woman who ever lived. His personal courage and physical stamina always moved him forward, when other men, good men themselves might hesitate, slow, and stop. This "apostle born out of due season" was many things, but not least among them and especially for one who lacked the formal training, in arguing a case, he was the equal and likely superior to any lawyer who ever practiced.

Calmly, thoroughly, and meticulously Paul commenced to respond to the charges which had been leveled at him by Tertullus. Paul's answer to the initial salvo of charges, that he was a seditionist and had profaned the temple he answered in the form of a general denial and stated without equivocation that they had no proof of these allegations. On the subject of his presumed heresy Paul became more exercised:

> "But I confess unto thee, that after the way which they call heresy, so worship I the God of my fathers, believing all things which are written in the law and in the prophets."

Likely, if not certainly, the Roman Governor Felix had no interest in whether Paul had been a faithful Jew or not. Even with Paul's eloquence at this point in Paul's defense the attention of Felix may have been essentially perfunctory listening to this odd man talk about temples, Jewish laws, and customs, all of little concern to him. As brilliant and eloquent as was Paul and likely, for that matter, Tertullus, to this point these proceedings likely had a pro forma, even stilted manner, to a hardened worldly Roman governor. After protesting his innocence and affirming his lifelong Judaism the apostle broached the subject which always (and still does) in some manner bring a reaction:

> "And have hope toward God, which they them-
> selves also allow, that there shall be a resurrec-
> tion of the dead, both of the just and unjust."

When he spoke of resurrection to the Greek intelligentsia and philosophers at the Acropolis in Athens he was mocked. An entire branch of the Jewish religious hierarchy, the Sadducees from which came the high priests, denied even the possibility of such an extraordinary concept. Paul was talking to a Roman, whose religion, if he had any at all, was an ever-changing mixture of gods, goddesses, and mythologies.

For the moment, though, Paull deferred discussion of the resurrection and focused on demonstrating his own innocence. He briefly returned to his own plight, protesting that he had "... always a conscience void of offense towards God." With specificity he explained why he was even in the Temple on that day of which his Jewish accusers had charged him with its profanation. Life any good lawyer, though, Paul was adroit and to his opponents lethal in being able to identify and define the real point of an argument between two litigants. Lawsuits, allegations, political campaigns, and even religious movements may be attired in gaudy finery, soothing or perhaps even inflammatory speech, and the disputants make argument at the fringes of the issues. Paul, though, came to the crux of the argument which Satan has with Christ and Christianity:

> "Touching the resurrection of the dead I am
> called in question by you this day."

As we note these words and then observe their effect upon Felix we see that Paul's phraseology but even more the substance of his message is what commands our attention now as it did with Governor Felix so long. The gospel message, the great Christian truth is no more and certainly no less than that simply but eloquently first expressed by Mary Magdalene on that early Sunday morning so long past:

"He is risen."

This is the lodestone of truth, the rock of ages, the explanation for all matters and all things. The skeptic then and the atheist and agnostic now, perhaps with even a cynical form of sincerity, inquires of the faithful "how can you believe all that 'nonsense' in the Bible, the miracles, the Divine intervention, the healings and so forth?" To the Christian, though, to Paul and the apostles and to the believer today is more simply expressed. If one believes in the resurrection of Christ all else is possible, even probable, and actually certain. The words are now spoken in different languages and the outer veneer of society has altered, but the central truth remains. It is still so awesome and yes, even "other worldly" that we will observe the strange reaction it provoked from Felix, the substance of which momentarily will be considered.

For the moment, the apostle continued with his argument, with an envious precision of detail describing the events which brought him here before Felix. Luke tells us that Felix now had a more "perfect knowledge" of these events, and it is almost certain that he accepted Paul's version as the real truth. Just as Pilate found no fault in Jesus of Nazareth, neither did Felix with Paul. Nonetheless, Felix sailed to that pleasant port, that safe haven of indecisiveness that all bureaucrats and politicians see as their natural home – delay and deferral of decision. Felix had his evidence, but rather than release Paul on the spot he loftily declared that he would issue his decision when chief captain Lysias arrived with the apparent "real" story. In the meantime Felix placed Paul in a strange kind of limbo, free to come and go and receive visitors but always under the supervision of a watchful Roman centurion. Actions do speak louder than words, and by his actions a high Roman official, Felix, displayed to the world that he knew that Paul was guilty of nothing. Meanwhile, let us return to words.

Back to the "resurrection of the dead." This, among other teachings enthralled Felix, this highly successful player in the high ether of Roman power politics. Temporarily, the governor adjourned Paul's case, but his interest in Paul did not wane. Luke tells us of his marriage to a woman named Drusilla, herself a Jewess, so Felix likely had more than a coldly official interest in Jewish matters. Besides, Paul fascinated him, for such men did not commonly appear in chains before the governor. Intellectual, eloquent, self-sacrificial and speaking, maybe even "babbling" about strange concepts such as the dead coming back to life, Felix wanted to hear still more.

Felix was now accompanied by his wife, and together the two wanted to hear still more from this singularly fascinating teacher. So, with the great power vested in the governor's hands he sent for Paul so that they could hear more "... concerning the faith in Christ." A private audience with Paul, who is obviously given freedom to speak without fear of retribution and/or castigation (not that its existence would have made any difference to Paul) must have been a mentally and spiritually daunting but exhilarating experience. With the official couple Paul "... reasoned of righteousness, temperance and judgment to come." Felix, though, had not climbed to his elevated billet in the Roman power structure by having such principles as righ-teousness and temperance or moderation as his watchwords. Likely, the" judgment to come" was an unwelcome thought to his mind so much that his reaction to Paul's teaching was that "... Felix trembled." He wanted to hear no more for the present and thus brusquely dismissed his prisoner with the admonition:

> "Go thy way for this time; when I have a conve-nient season I will call for you."

So Paul, who had obviously achieved a mental and emotional superiority over his captor left the great governor's presence, at least for the moment.

Every salesperson knows and dreads the phrase "more con-venient time" or any linguistic equivalent. In almost all instanc-es it really means simply no. Strongly, though, Felix had the classic approach avoidance reaction to what Paul was selling. At some level it enthralled him and even frightened him, es-pecially the section on the "judgment to come," for which he trembled. He sent Paul away but called him increasingly. In fair-ness Felix must be credited with at minimum an intellectual interest in Paul's doctrine, but that rested in the shadows of the governor's real interest. For two years Felix kept Paul in Caesarea for reasons known so well to history and to the ever-current state of affairs:

> "He hoped also that money should have been given him of Paul, that he might loose him."

Felix was a politician on the make, his hands extended for a bribe that never came. Thus for two entire years he kept an innocent man in prison "... willing to show the Jews a pleasure, for he left Paul bound." After the conclusion of this couplet of years Felix became irrelevant to the story, as a new governor arrived. His name was Porcius Festus, who himself would soon have an official visitor with a very familiar name, King Herod Agrippa, the second of that title.

CHAPTER SEVENTEEN

JERUSALEM OR ROME

H ome field advantage. It is a phrase which any sports fan, especially an American, understands almost instinctively to his very core. Home, its wonders and comforts, is a vast subject beyond the scope of this work; however, its bearing on the events of this chapter is enormous, not by its presence but by its absence. In all sports, be they baseball, football, basketball or otherwise the home team has an innate advantage, not necessarily by any particular advantage in the rules but rather by an emotional familiarity with the situs of the event. A game is more enjoyable and its outcome slightly more favorable at home. The advantage of home, though, is not confined to the world of sports, entertaining it may be but seriously essential it is not. Even long before the birth and development of our Anglo-American system of jurisprudence lawyers and litigants recognized the value of one court above and; if possible will try to place their case at that locale. It is called "venue shopping," a hunt for the most favorable judges and where necessary, a jury. Two thousand years ago no one understood this home field edge more than the Jewish religious establishment which had literally sworn the death of Paul, now a prisoner for two years in the northern town of Caesarea.

A new Roman governor, Portius Festus, had replaced Felix, an open-handed politician who had sought both the favor of the Jews and a bribe from Paul, neither of which came his way. Now Festus had come and soon went to Jerusalem, the largest and most important city in his jurisdiction. This same Jewish cabal, which had bayed for the blood of Paul two years previous, now desired and petitioned that Paul's upcoming trial would be transferred to their home ground in Jerusalem and its "special" suitability:

> "And desired favor (an advantage) against Paul,
> that he (Festus) would send for him to Jerusalem,
> laying wait in the way to kill him."

Festus, though, a seasoned Roman politico ruled that his trial would be held in Caesarea, to which Festus was about to return. Festus was no naïve waif who had mysteriously found himself to be a Roman governor with Jerusalem in his jurisdiction. Surely he knew of its wild, difficult history and its intimidation of prior Roman officials. Paul had been sent to Caesarea earlier because the chief captain of a large Roman force believed he could not keep order even to the extent of repelling the murder of one prisoner. Most notoriously decades earlier a powerful Roman governor named Pilate had quaked in fear of what the Jews might do if he did not order the crucifixion of Jesus of Nazareth. So Festus must have pondered, who am I to withstand the strength and fury of this bizarrely permanent conspiracy of the Jewish establishment.

Yes, who was Governor Festus? Actually, little is known of him apart from the scriptures and the observations of Josephus,

the most famous of all Jewish historians. Likely he was Roman
to the core, having acquired a high political position and with
an Italian name. He seemed to have neither fondness nor hatred of the Jews and apparently saw them as a difficult political
entity that had to be controlled, and, at times appeased. As we
shall observe, he was certainly no Christian. Josephus, though
opined that he ruled well and wisely. Doubtless this case against
Paul was more than a primer for Festus, and he soon learned of
Jewish determination, even in the winds of unpopularity.

It is often overlooked, but a truncated trial of Paul began
soon after Festus returned from Jerusalem. The Jewish conspirators were ready and the prisoner Paul stood bound before
Governor Festus as the Jews:

> ".. from Jerusalem stood round about, and laid
> many and grievous complaints against Paul,
> which they could not prove."

At this juncture, though, unbeknownst to all the levers of
power rested not with the Jews, the Roman governor or any but
one, the beshackled defendant Paul. Festus, as was his predecessor Felix was a politician:

> "Festus, willing to do the Jews a pleasure, an-
> swered Paul, and said, Wilt thou go up to
> Jerusalem, and there be judged of these things
> before me."

Paul, the great apostle to the Gentiles, the bearer of Christ's
name before kings, was also an uncannily brilliant lawyer, a
profession for which he had not even been educated. Knowing

full well that Jerusalem meant death, but that his Roman citizenship still retained great value he answered Festus:

"I stand at Caesar's judgment seat, where I ought to be judged: to the Jews have I done no wrong, as thou very well know.

> For if I be an offender, or have committed any thing worthy of death, I refuse not to die: but if there be none of these things whereof these accuse me, no man may deliver me unto them. I appeal unto Caesar."

When Paul said "Caesar" it was not in any representative or metaphorical sense, for he meant the emperor in Rome, the presumably most powerful man in the world.

How glorious and intoxicating these words meant to Festus, for he had that prize which all politicians, even the most powerful, covet the opportunity to shift responsibility for a difficult decision to another, or as the modern jargon succinctly describes "to pass the buck." Festus briefly huddled with his councilors and advisors, and with an undoubted and perhaps even an undisguised sense of euphoria announced:

> "Hast thou appealed unto Caesar? Unto Caesar shall thou go?"

The farther from Jerusalem they traveled the more the conspiratorial Jews' power diminished. In Caesarea it had dimmed, but in Rome it would be non-existent.

Sometimes a certain narrative of events will begin to overtake the facts, and while we strive to adhere to the truth it is well to remember the simplicity of the event that over two years earlier had led to this lengthening tether of riots, threats, escapes, journeys, hearings, and trials. It all began when Paul, without fanfare walked into the Jewish Temple, as was the right of any Jew. Now, it seems that events, coincidences, and the very emotions and timing of key events was about to propel him to the center of the world, Rome itself. Yet ... before he began that long journey one more hearing, trial, assembly, or whatever nomenclature we may prefer, was to occur in Caesarea. This was to be the most fascinating and revealing of all, and it began with two visitors of pre-eminent and royal status who had dropped by to pay their respects to Festus. Luke identifies them with their best-known names, King Agrippa and Bernice, who had come to Caesarea to "salute" Festus.

The description of the scene by Luke is so illustrative and cogent that it invites a full quotation:

> "And on the morrow, when Agrippa was come, and Bernice, with great pomp, and was entered into the place of hearing, with the chief captains, and principal men of the city, at Festus's commandment Paul was brought down."

As always Luke the historian is a plentiful provider of facts and expert at their setting. In other words, anybody who was anybody in Caesarea, the great and the good had received the "summons" (more accurately translated as "order") to come to view this strange extra-legal and extra-judicial spectacle of this strange aging otherwise innocuous little Jewish man at its center. Remember we must, however, that in large measure this is a spectacle staged by Governor Festus for his esteemed guests, King Agrippa and Bernice. But exactly who were these guests? The name Agrippa should be familiar to the interested reader, for this young king was Herod Agrippa II, the son of the infamous and ill-fated King Herod Agrippa I, murderer of the apostle James and a self-proclaimed god who had perished in the most wretched manner possible (see Chapter Eight). Within six months of his father's death this Agrippa had secured from the Roman emperor Claudius the tetrarchy of his uncle Philip, and to this the emperor Nero later added other lands. Though not as powerful as either his father or certainly his great-grandfather Herod the Great, he was a powerful man, and he was a Herod. Historians have debated whether Agrippa had one or two wives, and from this phrase it is expectant that the next should be "of which Bernice was one." Actually no. Bernice was the sister of Herod Agrippa II, his consort, and the lover with whom he engaged in a longtime incestuous relationship. Herod Agrippa II was a true Herod.

Whoever or whatever they were, though, the pair entered with "great pomp," the nature and extent of which is left to the mind and imagination of the scholar. When we in the twenty-first century think of pomp, our thoughts are bemused by visions and sounds of trumpets blaring, of regal royal raiment, perhaps even of proud soldiers marching in some variation of lockstep until at last our eyes and ears feast upon the bedazzling figures of our "betters," the royalty and officialdom that direct our lives. The entrance of Agrippa and Bernice doubtless lived up to such splendor, for the ancient Romans were masters at such pomp. We eschew any entrance into the thickets and woods of psychology, yet we opine that the essential, basic purpose of pomp it to further remind the observer of his own minute insignificance compared with the power of his heralded rulers.

Yet there is an undoubted contrast here. The full panoply of Roman royalty and the provincial governor, seated above all, like demigods of challengeable power surveying their realm.

Now brought before them is Paul, the onetime Saul of Tarsus, small, aging, literally in chains with a history of bowing to no man except that whom he encountered on the road to Damascus long ago. Respectful as always, he is not servile. It is Governor Festus who opened the proceedings by explaining to his understanding how this man has come before them in this situation and for what reason. Agrippa began with some simple words to Paul:

"Thou art permitted to speak for thyself."

All will retain their seating and place arrangements throughout the proceedings which followed, but with those words Agrippa unwittingly handed to the prisoner Paul the agenda and the power which followed. The apostle was a man who knew how to employ such power, and the first thing he did was place a spotlight of solar intensity upon one man, King Agrippa himself. Paul's speech and defense was for all to hear, but he made his (defense?) argument to one man alone, King Herod Agrippa II. The defense which followed remains a model for presentation and argument for lawyer and non-lawyer alike. Paul's opening statement was brilliant and exemplary, and perfectly illustrates that to convince a man or woman of anything he or she must first find some common ground, and if it may be done with words of conciliation and praise so much the better:

"I know thee to be an expert in all customs and
questions which are among the Jews: wherefore
I beseech thee to hear me patiently."

It is the rarest of rarities to find a person who does not fancy praise, and Agrippa has already secured it from Paul. All, especially Agrippa, are now listening to Paul, the prisoner who is the most powerful man in the entire assembly.

Paul began with a familiar recitation, his life not just as a Jew but a "Jew's Jew," a Pharisee, of the strictest order of the faith. He recalled the Old Testament promise of redemption which would come through the Jewish people, a redemptory promise, his belief of which has made him the vilest heretic in the eyes of the Jewish hierarchy. Always, and that in its literal sense, would Paul broach the primary message which he always lay before Jews, Gentiles, kings, and commoners:

> "Why should it be thought a thing incredible
> with you, that God should raise the dead?"

With that attention getting thrust, especially to Festus and all the other Gentiles about, Paul plunged a dagger into his own previous life as a type of official angel of death for Christians:

> "And I punished them oft in every synagogue,
> and compelled them to blaspheme; and being ex-
> ceedingly mad against them, I persecuted them
> even unto strange cities."

How strange, even weird this must have sounded to both Festus and Agrippa. Not just the centrality of the resurrection to Paul's beliefs but here stood a defendant who is certainly in danger of death at the hands of the Romans clearly, without duress, proclaiming unhesitatingly his own complicity in the persecution and murder of untold numbers of subjects of Rome. What a strange man he must have seemed.

Paul's message, though, is never himself or the history of death and destruction at his hands. His message focused on the appearance of Christ to him on the famed road to Damascus, his frightened, even terrified, hearing of Jesus and ultimately his obedience. By now Festus likely was shaking his head in disbelief, and despair at how so obviously intelligent a man as Paul could believe such wacky religious "rigamarole" but it was not Festus to whom Paul was aiming his words. His target remained Agrippa.

But who exactly was King Herod Agrippa II? The salient facts of the lives of the three prior Herods of Biblical note are well and fully told in the Bible. Herod the Great, Herod Antipas and Herod Agrippa I have dark stories all told at length in the scriptures, but the Biblical story of this King Agrippa is here before us and only here. The history of the Herods is a multi-volume project, but for our present understanding let us be reminded that they were Edomites, descended from Esau of old, brothers and sisters to the Jews but never fully accepted by "real" Jews, yet many, including in a very stilted pro forma manner, saw themselves as descendants of Moses and worshippers of the one true God. First and foremost, though, they were creatures of politics and remarkably successful at siphoning power from Roman officials, even emperors. Herod Agrippa II was the latest in this line (and, in fact, would prove to be the last of the Herods). Paul's salutation of him as a man familiar with Jewish laws, customs, traditions, and religion was surely true. Especially for purposes of this hearing, he was an appointed official of the Romans, but for the brevity of this moment, at least, he was a Jew.

Paul's words were and are for all to hear, but it should never be forgotten that the entire speech was directed at one man, Agrippa. Enhanced with the powers of the Holy Spirit, natural talents likely the equal of any person who ever lived and at the height of his ability the formidability of the apostle and his arguments must have been awe inspiring. So why, my fellow countryman King Agrippa, am I Paul, an observant Jew all my life in danger of imminent death from the Jewish priesthood and hierarchy? Because, he explained, I obeyed God and His Son, and so taught my fellow Jews and so important to the case at bar, Gentiles as well. It is for this, these events so well and thoroughly foretold by Moses and the prophets that his fellow Jews:

> "For these causes... caught me in the temple, and
> went about to kill me."

All this was bad to the traditional imbedded Jewish hierarchy but what followed thereafter, the logical conclusion to all his teaching, was anathema itself:

> "That Christ should suffer, and that he should
> rise from the dead, and should show light unto
> the people, and to the Gentiles."

The resurrection, always the resurrection, and its mention and teaching still yet elicits the spectrum of reactions it did this day in Caesarea. It was Paul himself who had written to his fellow Christians at Corinth:

> "For we preach Christ crucified, unto the
> Jews a stumbling block, and unto the Greeks
> foolishness."

The author of those words was now in the midst of a scene where both their accuracy and efficacy would be proven. As Paul continued to speak he was loudly interrupted by Festus who exclaimed:

"Paul, thou art beside thyself; much learning doth make thee mad."

Echoes of the laughter and sarcasm from the Greek intelligentsia's similar reaction to Paul's teaching reverberated throughout the assembly. Festus, a noble Roman, was Gentile (i.e. Greek in translation) to the core, and to the extent that he believed in any divinity it would have been the gods and goddesses of the Romans, a hodgepodge of terrifying spectral, even fiendish beings, continually at war with each other and with the humanity over which they supposedly presided. These entities today even in the still studied and often told tales of mythology are coupled with lust, avarice, and death. The religion of which Paul taught proclaimed a Father and a Savior of love, service, and eternal life. It was all too much for Festus to take, and the bitter sarcasm of Festus did not even rise to the level of the attitude of his predecessor Felix, who had been visibly shaken by Paul's teaching and deferred him to a more convenient time. As for Festus, a Gentile, as Paul had written, the whole matter was "foolishness."

Nonetheless, the real target of Paul this day was King Herod Agrippa, the longtime ruler of Jews and by a lengthy family history a member of the Jewish community. The events that followed immediately in the wake of Festus's denial are superlative examples of the skills, both substantive and oratorical, of the apostle and perhaps history's finest example outside of Christ Himself of a captive commanding an audience in a hostile environment. If Christ and His resurrection was "foolishness" to the Gentile Festus did the reaction of the Jewish Agrippa conform to the definition of "stumbling block?" The simple answer is yes. First, though, the exchange of words between Paul and Agrippa, forever famous, should be examined.

Following the interruption Festus's outburst Paul quickly refocused his gaze upon Agrippa. He first brushed aside Festus with the dignity of the following:

> "I am not mad, most noble Festus; but speak
> forth the words of truth and soberness."

Quickly to Agrippa the apostle, still with the binding chains of a prisoner rattling and clanking with every movement, he turned and prisoner or not, assumed full control of the proceedings. Never, for one scintilla of a moment should it be forgotten that Paul was a lowly prisoner, standing before high Roman officials who were literally looking down upon him. All civil authority and power were vested in their hands. When the hearing was over they would retire to exquisitely comfortable lodgings with the best of food prepared for them. Conversely, Paul would return to his cell or room, closely guarded, and watched by soldiers, dine upon whatever his keepers tossed his way that day and then sleep in uncomfortable surroundings. Yet it is Paul who now assumed a mastery of the moment seldom seen anywhere, anytime or on any subject. With an intensity of gaze and purpose more easily imagined than described Paul turned to Herod Agrippa II and in full rhetorical control of the situation spoke:

> "For the king knoweth of these things, before
> whom also I speak freely: for I am persuaded that
> none of these things are hidden from him; for
> this thing was not done in a corner."

With a startling swiftness Paul has seized control of the dialogue and has placed the burden of responding and perhaps even for any contrary view the burden of proof. But Paul, as greatness always does, reached for even more.

How true it remains that the life and teachings of Christ are literally an open book, not "done in a corner" and true Christianity not only welcomes light and transparency, but true Christianity is light. Yet before Agrippa could respond Paul, with divine acumen and his own innate ability and brilliance placed mighty Agrippa in a corner of his own:

> "King Agrippa, believest these the prophets? I know that thou believest."

The brilliance and effectiveness of Paul's statement to Agrippa is practically incalculable. The apostle, a powerless prisoner and a shackled "criminal" is so certain of the true answer to his inquiry that, in modern judicial terms, the criminal defendant has now begun questioning and even cross examining the royal judge.

Effectively Agrippa has been placed into a quandary where he simply must respond to the prisoner. Paul, Festus, his cohort Bernice are waiting and so he does:

> "Then Agrippa said unto Paul, Almost thou persuades me to be a Christian."

Agrippa's simple answer even two thousand years later retains a haunting sadness. For two millennia scholars and commentators have thought and opined upon Agrippa's remark. Was he serious, on the very precipice of becoming a Christian, or was it a mocking sarcasm that came from him? None but Agrippa and God know, yet any study of this is almost compelled to render an opinion or at least an observation.

Let us ponder this scene from a somewhat different perspective. Outwardly, of course, Agrippa was a king and to many, Governor Festus included, Paul was a half-mad lunatic who babbled about the resurrection of the dead. The circumstances may otherwise be described, in spite of all the outward finery and flummery, a one-on-one confrontation between the Truth and its denial. Paul, who was solidly and intensely resolute and single minded and perhaps the greatest religious evangelist who ever lived, and to the Christian believer, a man filled with the Holy Spirit, had narrowed his sights upon one man, King Herod Agrippa II. With each pronouncement, every point and each word Paul was hammering blows of reason and logic into the psyche of Agrippa, an intelligent man. The power of the Word, of Christ, was beginning to overwhelm Agrippa to the point that:

> "... the king rose up, and the governor, and Bernice, and they that sat with them."

Agrippa literally had to leave, for his lifelong belief system, whatever it may have been, was being pounded into pieces by Paul. Agrippa almost succumbed to the power of the Truth. Almost, but lost.

Agrippa confided the obvious to Festus, that Paul was an innocent man, who would have been freed save for his appeal to Caesar. But the powers of Festus, Agrippa and the Jewish hierarchy had reached high tide and were subsiding. The Hand of a greater power, always present, but increasingly more overt, would become more apparent. Paul was off to Rome, the Eternal City, to see the emperor. His path, though, would not be over a yellow brick road.

CHAPTER EIGHTEEN

COLOSSUS ON THE TIBER

These writings have previously asserted that the most famous city in world history is Jerusalem. Boldly, we offer that the second most famous remains Rome. Actually to many historians and scholars it deserves a number one ranking. Regardless, it was the city to which the apostle Paul was about to travel on an arduous sea voyage, which itself became an epic. So much mythology, glamorization and even fantasy has encrusted itself upon the story of Rome for over two millennia that reality compels the observer to form an adequate and accurate view of Rome as it stood in the mid-first century AD. This is not the Rome of modern cinema or even that of the poetic genius William Shakespeare in his great play "Julius Caesar." To what sort of city was the prisoner Paul about to travel?

Long has Rome, located on the western sector of central Italy been deferentially referenced as the "Eternal City." Geographically the city was built on the famed Seven Hills of Rome (actually there were more than seven) which lay east of the Tiber River, a stream of no particular inspiring length, width, or depth, being approximately 250 miles long and meandering through the city in a generally north to south direction.

The passage of two thousand years has in no way diminished the importance of Rome's location to its astonishing growth and success. Almost precisely centered in the world of the Mediterranean Sea, and even more so in Italy itself so many routes from north, south, east, and west and by land or sea led to this amazing metropolis that truly Rome merited the aphorism that "all roads lead to Rome." It was central in locale, thought and certainly central to the power structure of its day. In point of fact, Rome was "the" power among all nations who had even heard of it, and its political and military mastery, while occasionally shown not to be absolute, was preeminent.

These were in the days of the Pax Romana, the Roman Peace, a two centuries long era begun with the reign of Augustus Caesar, emperor at the time of the birth of Jesus of Nazareth, and a man who defined in a multiplicity of ways a claim to being the most successful ruler or head of state in all history. Rome, under Augustus and even maintained by his many corrupt successors of lesser ability, could boast of capable and efficient administration, a workably functional legal system, an international mastery of the world, and by reason of Augustus's instigation a city that "he found brick and turned to marble." Magnificent structures, public buildings, and private palaces, albeit in ruined or partially decayed form remain today as living testimonials to Roman efficiency and accomplishment.

The upper strata of society, as it always does, benefited the most from the Roman genius and aptitude for accomplishment, not just majestic artistry but practical work-a-day accomplishment. More than any city of the ancient world Rome was well served by a series of aqueducts, many of enormous lengths, which brought adequate, even copious, amounts of fresh water for everyday use. The debris and effluvium of a city, an especially difficult problem in all but the most modern environments, was met by an ancient sewage system which was intended to dispose of the offal of antiquity's greatest metropolis. So much of the city must have been close to awe inspiring to the newly minted immigrants, the majority of which came from rough, rural societies. Paul and his companions, Paul to the extent he was allowed freedom of movement, would definitely see all this when they arrived in this colossus on the Tiber. All this was reality, by no means a Potemkin Village (to borrow a nineteenth century Russian term for state fakery), but it was only the shiniest, most glittering facet of the jewel which was Rome. Was this all there was to the Eternal City?

No megalopolis, city, suburb, town, or village is defined solely, or even primarily, by physical structures, topography, terrain or utility and sewage systems. Its real identity and personality will always arise from the nature, character, and actions of its populace, and here we must probe to discover a more complete and accurate view of history's most storied city. It was certainly the most cosmopolitan city in Europe and all of what we would denominate the "Bible lands." Beginning as a small tribal settlement of Italians some eight centuries before our studied setting, throughout these early centuries BC its growth gradually encompassed the bulk of the Italian peninsula until the words Rome and Italy were essentially synonyms. Rome, for centuries a form of an ancient republic had gradually begun to expand by virtue of battlefield conquests and victories and annexations of peoples and nations until as an empire which effectively commenced in the late first century BC it had, with a few later minor accruals, assumed the size and shape for which historical study has offered us. The Roman Empire of Paul's time extended outwardly from Rome in an almost precisely symmetrical pattern, north, south, east, and west.

In its early centuries a visitor would have walked the streets of Rome and seen only Italians and a few Greeks and would have heard and spoken only Latin and Greek. This was changing rapidly, forasmuch as Rome had taken in the world, that same world was taking in Rome. Such a variety of persons of strangely foreign ethnicities and cultures were increasingly moving to Rome. Darker skinned Arab people from northern Africa, along with Egyptians had made their way to the capital. Large numbers of persons from the Eastern Mediterranean, the "levant," had been brought to Rome's environs largely by maritime commercial trade. These included the Syrians, various Palestinian peoples, Phoenicians, Cypriots, and even a sprinkling of Jews (of which more later).

Of course, the Greeks, the progenitors of a noble and classical civilization even older than Rome were plentiful, many in "white collar" positions, the academy and other posts known for intellectual prowess. Often they were not hesitant in expressing their presumed cultural superiority to the Romans. From the far western reaches of the empire, in the Iberian Peninsula, many Spaniards, had come to Rome, and generally these fellow Latins fit well into the Roman cultural scene. Representatives from the northwest in Gaul, that huge provincial territory conquered a century prior by the greatest Roman of all, Julius Caesar. These long haired Gauls, many Celtic in ethnicity, some even with strange red hair, adapted well to the Roman ethos. From the north strange men and women, speaking in an odd and guttural manner, slowly began to drift into Rome. They were from the large number of Germanic tribes, which fanned out, seemingly indefinitely over the plains of northern Europe. These strangely fair skinned persons often had a lighter color of hair, blonde, and sparkling blue eyes, not a common characteristic of an ancient Roman. Altogether, they and scatterings from other lands composed Rome. The Romans, though, still predominated, and their new immigrants made an ancient melting pot were almost all seemed to follow the dictum of "... when in Rome, do as the Romans do."

Race and ethnicity, problematic questions which are raging today as never before, provide only a limited sustenance of quantifiable evidence when discussing the manner in which people lived, a concept today often referenced as "lifestyle." Hollywood cinema, as noted, and other sources of popular entertainment have given us the indelible images of beautiful, stately, marble structures, dignified sober looking men in ancient togas and beautifully elegant women in exquisite dresses. A seed of truth is found in this picture, but it is a seed planted only in the gardens of the prominent and the rich. The average person, man or woman, wore drab, functional clothing suited to physical labor to which most devoted their lives, or such lives as they possessed. If a Roman survived infancy and early childhood, of which a large percentage fell victim, they could plan on the enjoyment of an average life of forty to fifty years.

Evidence and the scraps of history which we possess for the masses reflect that the common Roman ate but two meals a day, with meat a rarity, and based upon a predominant diet of vegetables, olive oil, a bit of wine, customarily with less alcohol than modern wines, or as we still call it today, a "Mediterranean diet." As noted the images of marble halls and beautifully tiled floors immediately appear in our visions when we ponder the lives of the ancient Romans. Those did exist, but, of course, they were reserved for the rich, the crème de la crème. Rome, a gigantic city by ancient measure, was basically a city of stone and especially of wood, the construction materials for almost all housing. Most Romans lived in multi storeyed apartment buildings, the equivalent to modern tenement housing, and susceptible to swift conflagration and destruction by fire, as the Great Fire of 64 AD so tragically demonstrated.

The average Roman dressed, ate, and lived quite simply, for even though as a municipality Rome was a spectacular success, an ancient economy could provide for only so much excess, all of which was siphoned avariciously into the desires of the nobility and the commercial elite. Housing, food, dress, and other factors entice interest, but never have they been the real measure of a person or community. They unveil to us a glimpse of how the city may have appeared and what the inhabitants wore and ate, but the real questions remain. How did the Romans behave, how did they think and what was really important to them? Generally, to posit such questions today is to delve into the realm of what we moderns call sociology. Try as they might, though, write books in numbers which endanger the forests and spend money like water, academics and even theologians usually make matters more complex and complicated than reality suggests. From day to day how did a Roman live, and what were his/her incentives and also the boundaries which limited a Roman's conduct?

The family, in whatever form, is an elemental building block of any society. The Roman family of the first century bore at least a superficial resemblance to what (until but a few years ago) was idealized as a "typical" American or western family. Mother, father, and children – one each of the first two and an indeterminant number of the latter. Like almost all societies until these late modern times, though, the Roman family was of a decided male orientation, as witness their institution of the "paterfamilias." The male head of the family was more than a fatherly patriarch, for he was also the holder of title to all the

family's property, the dictator of its conduct, and in the strict
est sense, especially in Rome's early days held life and death
authority over all its members. Hopefully it was an infusion of
raw power seldom employed by a Roman father.

While the "nuclear" family may have been idealized by
Roman writers and its citizenry its path was not necessarily the
typical route taken by its members. Undoubtedly a city such as
Rome held within its boundaries plentiful numbers of happy
families and spouses who were committed to each other. As
this image is turned, though, we see a society which pioneered
in the concept of "no-fault" divorce, effectively the ability to
terminate a marriage at will. Increasingly, marriage became
cheapened, and the history of the patrician ruling class (admittedly not an absolute measure of any society) increasingly reveals a whirligig of marriage, divorce, affair, adultery, incest,
remarriage ad infinitum to the point where the nomenclature
of the participants becomes hopelessly confused.

The ever viably interesting subjects of marriage, divorce and
remarriage lead the student into the subject matter which almost universally more commanding of most observer's attention – sex. In a work of this nature a guiding principle should
be the avoidance of unnecessarily giving offense, and this is
the path marked for us to follow. Nonetheless, two thousand
years of study of plentiful writings, archaeological evidence et
al. lead to the almost irrefutable conclusion that the Romans of
the first century were obsessed with the relationship between a
man and a woman. Ancient advertisements, signs on commercial establishments, the writings of Rome's foremost authors
to its hack writers reflect not the natural human interest and
fantasy but a deep-seated proclivity to the darkest depths of
the physical. Pornography is present in most, if not all societies, from ancient to modern, east to west, and it would be trite

to state that the Romans "invented" pornography. Invented no, but the came close to a refined perfection of pornography (an oxymoron, if ever there was one). Prostitution was endemic to all societal strata, and a resident or visitor could not walk any street or alley without seeing a commercial, artistic or graffiti representation of a male phallic symbol. Without the slightest reservation we must aver that the ancient Romans were a crude and vulgar people. Regrettable as this is, though, more serious actions grew from these characteristics. Here we must deal with the ancient Roman proclivity to violence, but not violence alone, but rather the entertainment value of violence.

An any modern cinephile knows so well the Romans flocked to their arenas for the enjoyment of gladiatorial games, where well trained warriors fought each other to the death for the crowd's pleasure and amusement. The temptation to compare an ancient gladiatorial spectacle to modern boxing or even certain football games is resisted, but nonetheless suggested. The gladiatorial contests between viciously armed contestants, mostly slaves and/or ex-soldiers were themselves sufficiently brutal, but as time progressed the Romans added other features for the entertainment of the crowd. Chariot races, wild animal shows, often with the slaughter of either the animals or persecuted and condemned prisoners added to the merriment. The Romans sometimes would employ the contests for the demonstration of the corporal punishment of prisoners, including crucifixion of the wretched condemned. The whole production was a sanguinary, brutal savagery, but it was Roman to its core.

Brutality, disgusting, appalling, physical brutality was woven into the moral fabric of ancient Roman life, and it cannot be denied that this marvelously organized and productive people had a deplorable black streak of evil running through its collective heart. No people and no class suffered more than the slaves, whose population in the first century was on the increase. In our view and look backward it is both easy to forget and hard to realize that the percentage of the population that was slave has been calculated variously from one-third to one-half. In the first century the Roman Empire was bloated with conquests, and military defeat for its enemies, whether men, women or children often meant enslavement. A large proportion of those slaves lived in Rome, and effectively with no rights their ownership brutalized both themselves and their masters.

Beautiful, elegant, and ever efficient was ancient Rome, but just as much was it ugly, sordid and a pit of despondency. Did anything soften or mitigate the violence and brutality would be inquired by a reasonable mind, the same mind that would suggest that perhaps the Romans' religion lessened the impact of vulgarity and violence? Even the most post-modern of minds in the twenty-first century, when its thoughts alight on the subject of religion, likely will think of a body of beliefs, rituals, litanies, and practices which in scale from slight to massive have a bearing upon its believer's personal conduct, presumably for the better. Both traditionally and spiritually a disciple of Judaism and certainly of Christ, i.e. a Christian, has an inculcated sincere belief that his religion informs his conduct. In plainer words, the observant Jew of the Mosaical Age and Christians to the present day believe and hopefully practice a religion, a creed, or whatever name is given, that fashions him or her into a better, or more moral person. This dynamic of belief in changed conduct was absent from the religions of the classical civilizations of Greece and particularly Rome.

The Roman religion, heavily borrowed from the Greeks, maintained, as did almost all pagan polytheistic systems, a large panoply of gods and goddesses, the mythology of whom is still studied. These deities were generally exemplary, but of horrid conduct, of lust, brutality, loss of self-control and a general self-centeredness that not only mirrored mortal conduct but magnified it into a type of celestial immorality. Any of the basic virtues possessed by the individual Roman, qualities such as honesty, integrity, loyalty, and the like were more likely the result of a Roman's following natural law rather than his own religion.

No more than modern America produces a so-called "typical American" did Rome of the mid-first century AD offer us a "typical Roman," for humans are too divergent and idiosyncratic to be the grist of easy generalization. Rome was not built by laziness and sloth, though, and Romans had typically valued hard, constructive work. In their midst, though, was a condition that gnawed away at virtues and celebration of work, and that was the growing prominence of slavery, an evil which universally devalues labor. Still, the good solid resident of Rome had much to enjoy and even savor. Since the time of Augustus peace was aplenty, a rare quality in Roman history. Although Rome remained unconquerable militarily, it yet maintained a magnificent army, professional soldiers increasingly recruited from non-Romans and non-Italians. Rome's own citizenry no longer bore the fear and burden of military conscription. Generally daily life was calm and peaceful, with a practical and generally fair and reasonable legal system open to the administration of justice. Certainly the government had its share of corruption, but what government has ever seen its absence.

A Roman could expect a reasonable enjoyment of life, with a reasonable lifespan with reasonable material possessions and perhaps a reasonable expectation of reasonable improvement then death and the darkness of oblivion. Yet was that all life offered? A generation or so before an obscure Jewish teacher, a man who never got anywhere near Rome, identified the Gentile nations, of which Rome was pre-eminent as a world which dwelled in darkness, and that had long rejected the Light:

> "And this is the condemnation, that light is come into the world, and men loved darkness rather than light, because their deeds were evil."

In Rome darkness and power seemed to be malleable elements that had been molded and fashioned into a fearful, dreadful beast, who in these years was personified in one man, Nero Claudius Caesar Augustus Germanicus (AD 37 – AD 68), the fifth emperor of Rome and more commonly called by a name which lives in infamy, simply Nero. He was the "Caesar" to whom Paul had appealed for judgment and before whom he would stand, but who was he?

Nero was the adopted son of the emperor Claudius, who had married Nero's mother, Agrippina the Younger, herself the assassin of her husband Claudius. Nero become emperor at age sixteen, a pudgy, even corpulent youth who always suggested a vague effeminacy in his movements and personality. At first he was under the strict tutelage of two wise tutors, Seneca and Burrus, who effectively ruled the emperor. He broke free from their influence, and the Roman world and history has been furnished a full view of his glory. Nero displayed a self-indulgent almost histrionic passion for the arts and always viewed himself essentially as that, an artist who happened to possess absolute political power. As a youthful emperor, this seriocomic figure would appear suddenly where theater companies were rehearsing their next offerings, insert himself into the rehearsals and always and unsurprisingly be awarded the lead roles in any theatrical production. As a musician Nero considered himself at

the peak of the mountaintop, loving to play the lyre while sing-
ing to the rapturous thunderous applause of his "admirers."

Through the ages into modern times observers have often
played up the emperor Nero as a comic figure, good for a few
laughs, before the scholars returned to serious history. Until
the end of his abbreviated life Nero could portray the role of
oafish buffoon as well as any man or woman who ever held
the deadly sceptre of power in greedy hands. Gradually he had
made bitter enemies of the power classes of Rome, particularly
senators who were even suspected of opposing him. Many were
murdered on the whimsical wishes of Nero, and the hatred of
this ridiculous upstart hardened and deepened among powerful men. So Stygian black was the perverted character of Nero
that he had his own mother, Agrippina, assassinated. Yet, he
remained the all-powerful emperor, the most powerful man
alive, and would so be on his throne when a bound prisoner,
this strange man Paul, from an equally strange ethnicity would
appear before him. To get to faraway Rome Paul had a long, long
journey to make, much of it a sea voyage which Paul and history
would never forget.

CHAPTER NINETEEN

HELP OF THE HELPLESS

For well over two years this aging holy man, likely now in late middle age, has been a prisoner and initially a punching bag for those whose tentacles of power had grasped. At first the Jews had resorted to mob violence in Jerusalem and were in the process of beating him to death when the Romans interceded. They too would have ferociously scourged him save for his Roman citizenship. He had stood before the Great Council, the Sanhedrin, and barely escaping another Jewish assassination plot under cover of darkness and the protection of a large Roman force had been whisked away to the Roman power center of Caesarea. There, with his period of imprisonment unconscionably extended beyond two years two Roman governors and a king had pronounced him innocent. Now, upon his own motion, Paul was to be transported to Rome to stand before Caesar himself. To date, the powers of principalities, mobs, councils, and empires had failed to destroy or even to silence him. Under what power would the apostle now find himself?

The powers of the world, the self consciously real powers now hastily exit the stage which bears the events of the apostle's life. Rome, Jerusalem, priests, emperors, and the like for a

263

time bear no influence upon Paul. To borrow the phraseology of Thomas Jefferson the power, not just the real but the sole power, will be exercised by "Nature and Nature's God" (though President Jefferson's definition of such was somewhat different from the Biblical account). Paul with a few companions was assigned a prominent place as a prisoner for the approximate fifteen-hundred-mile sojourn to Rome, both by land and sea. The Romans, quite accustomed to managing all things would be running the enterprise, which had originally been fomented by the Jewish hierarchy in Jerusalem. All were mere strutting players, though as this was an endeavor managed by God, who exerted the real power.

The voyage began when Paul and "other prisoners" were loaded aboard a ship which would sail northward along the eastern Mediterranean coast. He was under the charge of a Roman centurion named Justus, who continued a Biblical record of substantial length wherein Roman centurions were unfailingly referenced in a favorable light. The ship sailed up the coast and came to the ancient Phoenician city of Sidon, where:

> "Julius courteously entreated Paul, and gave him
> liberty to go unto his friends to refresh himself."

Julius, an Italian, a centurion of Augustus's band" likely had no personal acquaintance with this Jewish evangelist, who was, after all, a prisoner. Why did he extend courtesy even beyond his official capacity and as such evidence kindness? Perhaps the answer is formed by two tributaries of thought, the first being that although a true Roman soldier he possessed an innate spirit of kindness. Also, he as anybody could readily judge a man such as Paul, evidencing the spirit of Christ, and accompanied by the physician and narrator Luke, posed no physical or escape threat.

They sailed from Sidon, and a travelogue of cities and places is provided by Luke, Cicilia, Pamphylia, Cyprus, Myra, and others, when at Myra they in the modern language "changed flights for" ...a ship of Alexandria sailing into Italy." The physical setting of events is often overlooked, and in some cases its understanding is imperative to a full realization of events, as it is here. Alexandria, the major city of Egypt, was its primary port where grain ships sailed, primarily to Rome. Egypt was fundamental to Roman power and prominence, and Egypt was its major granary. For ancient times it would be a large wooden vessel, capable of holding three to four hundred tons of grain. They were generally sturdy but primitive, having but two masts, a mainmast, and a foremast in the bow. This ship, as Luke with his unfailing precision, carried 276 souls, an unspecified number of which were prisoners. Except for its captain, the owner if aboard, and a man of rank such as the centurion, all men slept on deck, exposed to the weather and all elements of nature, both of which were to arise with frighteningly real power.

The ship's voyage continued, the prime sailing season having passed, and the weather was becoming increasingly dangerous, none of which escaped the attention of Paul. One of history's great understatements is to aver that the great apostle Paul was not shy about voicing his opinions. Paul, a landsman, spoke a warning that the property and lives on the ship were imperiled if they continued on course. The owner and captain of this ship, considerably more experienced in nautical matters than this Jewish landlubber saw things differently, and naturally desirous of a financial success wished to sail ahead. With them the ship's arbiter, centurion Justus concurred, and the voyage continued. At first events seemed to confirm the wisdom of going ahead,

266 | JAMES E. KIFER

for the winds and weather softened. The crowded, heavy laden grain ship smoothly passed the great island of Crete. Then, in both a figurative and real sense all darkened.

A "tempestuous wind," named Euroclydon arose, and the ship lost its force, and its momentum became unsustainable. Fearing quicksand, the sails were struck and on the storm's second day they began to lighten the ship, and as the third to even cast out its anchors. In the plainly eloquent words of Luke "... all hope that we should be saved was then taken away." During all these cataclysmic events Paul had not been seen, but finally he appeared in the midst of all. Such greatness of character and steadfast magnificence of purpose Paul claimed in abundance, yet his personality never ceases to remind us that he was only a man for his statement to all was:

> "Sirs, you should have hearkened unto me, and
> not have loosed from Crete, and to have gained
> this harm and loss."

In other words, "I told you so," which has never done well in increasing its speaker's popularity. But Paul was right, and he brought words of salvation, not condemnation. Well could he have now inquired of the 276 souls aboard, where now is the power of the Roman governors, of King Herod Agrippa or even the emperor himself. Where was the dignity and the writ of the Great Council of the Jews, the Sanhedrin, and which of the waves and the winds heeded the call and authority of any man? Had their power vanished, disappeared under the tempest of the seas? Who now exercised real power, a power to master the greedy devouring waves of the sea? Which of the rulers, Roman or Jew, did the sea obey? None of them, and as he well knew neither was it Paul, for he was a prisoner, powerless in his chains. It was Paul, though, who knew that the real source of power remained, and His authority had not been diminished by a single jot or title. Over a generation earlier even more apostles than Paul were crammed into a small fishing boat being bashed about on the Sea of Galilee, when a hitherto sleeping Savior awoke, and the seas were calmed, the saved apostles astonished:

> "And they feared exceedingly, and said one to another, What manner of man is this, that even the wind and the sea obey him?"

Now, Paul, the apostle born out of due season, reappeared and spoke to his fellow shipmates and passengers:

> "And now I exhort you to be of good cheer: for there shall be no loss of any man's life among you, but of the ship. For there stood by me this night the angel of God, whose I am, and whom I serve. Saying, fear not, Paul; thou must be brought before Caesar: and, lo, God hath given thee all them that sail with thee."

All power was in God's hands, and Paul, his chosen apostle and 275 others, would not perish in the maelstrom of the sea, yet the voyage was still fraught with great difficulty.

The storm continued to rage, and as it was wont to do this time of year it was nearing the end of its second week, and the vessel groped for the safety of a landfall. The seamen "sounded" the water for depth and found it to be one hundred twenty and shortly thereafter only ninety feet, but now the hazards of rocks appeared, and the crew began to cast their anchors into the sea. Many of the crew sought rescue by escaping in the vessel's lifeboat, but Paul noticed, so advised centurion Julius, and the lifeboat was cut from its moorings. Still, not a man had been lost. The next morning found the ship approaching land, wherein they saw the mouth of a creek which emptied into the sea.

At this point in the narrative Luke, the physician and historian par excellence, added to his laurels the title of a gifted maritime chronicler. In terms and language which likely would impress the most grizzled navy veteran and old salt he describes the ship's foundering upon the rocks. The ship was dead, hoisted between land and water, an immovable and useless behemoth, and a likely tomb for any who remained on board. It is at moments such as these that the true measure of men and women, both good and bad, is laid bare for all to see. The soldiers, still possessed of their weapons and likely keenly aware that they might be held responsible for the escape of any prisoners, no matter how dire the circumstances, proposed murdering all the prisoners. The ever dutiful and admirable centurion, though, who had obviously developed a personal admiration for Paul, ordered that neither Paul nor any of the prisoners be harmed.

Julius ordered all men who could swim to make for land, while the:

> "... rest, some on boards and some on broken pieces of the ship... escaped all safe to land."

In a scene which could serve as a template for many a cinematic production slowly the entirety of the ship's human cargo of souls drifted onto the beach and the haven of land. They had come ashore on the island of Melita (its more modern variant being Malta), still part of the Roman Empire and a small plot of land which has played an outsized role in history even into modern times. It was quite cold and rainy, but the "barbarous people showed us no little kindness." They were safe, among friends, and the ordeal of the sea was over, so what now could possibly go wrong?

The remedy for cold and dampness is a roaring fire, and so Paul busied himself gathering sticks and laid them on the fire, whereupon:

> "... there came a viper out of the heat, and fastened on his hand."

The Maltese, well meaning but as many ancients deeply superstitious immediately surmised that as they viewed the poisonous serpent literally hang on Paul's hand, that undoubtedly he was a murderer, about to meet the fate of a just punishment. Amazingly, though, Paul shook off the reptile into the fire. How quickly the Maltese observers changed their minds about this strange but unharmed prisoner, snake bitten but still healthy:

> "They changed their minds, and said that he was a god."

Paul was never an idler, even as a prisoner, and while the troop stayed on the island and he and Luke were for three days the houseguest of Malta's governor, a man named Publius. The governor's father was suffering from a fever, possibly malaria, and dysentery, and Paul healed the man. This healing, as it always did, opened the channels for more, and by the time the voyage to Rome resumed Paul had become an honored and beloved figure among the Maltese people.

Three more months elapsed, and the large party continued its voyage, departing on another ship from Alexandria for a journey northward to Syracuse in Sicily and finally to the Italian peninsula just south of Rome. Several hundred miles of an arduous journey, both by sea and land remained, but this is a good juncture in the story for a bit of a synopsis. By now, both his enemies and even friendly observers would be compelled to admit that Paul, this apostle of Christ, was not an easy man to kill. Let us remember that this long, long journey began in Jerusalem when the Romans stopped a Jewish mob from beating him to death. It was spurred northward by a Jewish cabal who sought Paul's blood. Two Roman governors, Festus and Felix, as well as King Herod Agrippa all recognized his innocence, but each had political motives for retaining him in prison. On the other hand it is not unfair to aver that none of these three men would have shed tears if the death of Paul had somehow advanced their own careers.

Paul's sea voyage to this point has served well as a primer for those who hate the water and are reluctant to travel by sea (both characteristic of the ancient Jews). Chained as a prisoner in an overcrowded vessel designed to carry grain, thrown in with prisoners, the bulk of whom were likely hardened criminals, and then subjected to the worst the sea has to offer, a shipwreck. Land was no Garden of Eden, though, except for the presence of a venomous serpent, whose bite he shook off. Many, many powerful persons (and likely Satan, perhaps returning to his serpentine form) wished to kill Paul. Yet, none could summon the power to consummate the deed. On the contrary in his relatively brief stay in Malta he and Luke were "... honored with many honors." But... Paul remained a prisoner.

The remainder of the journey to Rome apparently was uneventful, except for a group of Christians who came out to greet them at The Three Taverns, a major juncture on the famed Appian Way which itself led to Rome.

Finally, his journey was complete. Its destination, Rome is easy to affix and proclaim, but Paul's point of departure not so clear. No argument, though, misses the true significance of Paul's journey to Rome if it avers that it actually began on that dusty road to Damascus so long ago. Then, though, by his own and the world's estimation was a powerful man, armed with death warrants for Christians, and a free man. Now, he was an aging apostle, beaten by the vicissitude of life, the violence of the enemies of Christ and the undying hatred of the Jews. He would not, though, be thrown into a dungeon, and actually those with whom he dealt heated him with as much respect and dignity as possible:

> "The centurion delivered the prisoners to the captain of the guard: but Paul was suffered to dwell by himself with a soldier that kept him."

Most certainly Paul was receiving special treatment, but, all the Romans who had to deal with the fanatical Jewish thrusting this man and problem upon them for over three years always and with remarkable dispatch recognized the innocence of Paul. Patently, this man was no criminal and nothing of his person or demeanor suggested violence. For now the Romans continued to treat him as almost an honored guest, yet he remained a prisoner. The Roman Army, these mighty world conquerors, was unaware, the populace as a whole, the good and the wretched both, and certainly not the great Emperor Nero know a very salient fact. When this much used and abused prisoner crossed the municipal boundaries of Rome, the great city's power structure began to shift. In this one man, an old prisoner from faraway and little-known Judea came to the city, in his person and character infused with the Spirit of Christ, the Rome of the Caesars would be forever altered.

Rome had a sizeable Jewish community, and while they enjoyed no insular popularity in this great cosmopolitan metropolis, they were, as they have always been, successful and influential. Paul waited but three days to call together the chief of the Jews, and in modern parlance they gathered so that Paul could brief them on the situation. After a thorough and factual review Paul paused in his speaking (always a likely difficulty for the great apostle), and the Jews likely surprised him with their response:

> "We neither received letters out of Judea concerning thee, neither any of the brethren that came showed or spoke any harm of thee."

All left but soon returned, for Paul, be it Jew or Gentile, Rome or Judea, the Arctic or the Equator, free or imprisoned he never relented in his duties as God's chosen apostle. The Jewish leaders came again and Paul:

> "... expounded and testified the Kingdom of God, persuading them concerning Jesus, both out of the law and out of the prophets, from morning till evening."

As ever and always some believed and some not, but overall Paul again was frustrated with the results of his evangelistic efforts among his fellow Jews. He thought and spoke of the ancient prophet Isaiah's disgust and disappointment in his fellow Israelites who:

"Hearing, ye shall hear, and shall not understand;
and seeing ye shall see, and not perceive."

Paul's lamentation for the intransigence of his fellow Jews continued, as did his evangelistic work. For two more years he remained Caesar's prisoner, but one of unusual circumstance for he was permitted to live in his own private house.

This strange cult of Christianity had come a long way since that early Sunday morning in Jerusalem some years ago when its founder astonished one of His closest disciples, Mary Magdalene, with the single word of "Mary." In spite of all efforts, legal, illegal, oratorical, and violent, it could not be suppressed. Now, its foremost spokesman, its one-time greatest enemy was about to come face to face with the Roman emperor, Nero, the presumably most powerful man alive, and we have no reason to doubt that Paul continued in the same manner as Luke concluded his great work of Acts:

"Preaching the Kingdom of God, and teaching those things which concern the Lord Jesus Christ, with all confidence, no man forbidding him."

DEATH AND LIFE

Almost everything dies. This simple three-word declaration is so plain that momentarily we will defer its main extended discussion. With the final two-word phrase the world is, has and always will be in agreement, said, cynical, morose agreement. Only a few understand the necessity of the sentence's initial word of "Almost." Its meaning will be deferred to the ending of this, our work's final chapter.

Death is depressing and so in the main will be this chapter. Still, the major figures in our story have life remaining, interesting, fascinating important life. Although Luke concluded his great historical tome of Acts with the apostle Paul's residing in a strange world of house arrest and comfort, most assuredly the great evangelist finally had his proverbial day in court before Nero. With a nod to the possibility of the negative Paul likely had an appearance before Nero himself. Neither Biblical nor current historical account irrefutably confirm this, but the latter part of Acts is replete with references of Paul's going to Rome to "appear before Caesar." Further, by this point he was likely of such fame, notoriety, curiosity, and influence that even a childish dullard such as Nero would have been eager to confront him. In any event at some point in time Paul was released from his strange house arrest.

So what now became of the great Paul? The consensus opinion (which, of course, does not necessarily denote the correct opinion) offers that Paul may have journeyed so far west as Spain, where Luke has told us he had originally planned to travel, and then recrossed the Mediterranean Sea to the eastern provinces, the scenes of his original mission efforts. Many assertions are well made and the result of both scholarship and speculation, but hereafter when discussing Paul often we are not speaking from a dais of certainty. Yet there are certainties, many certainties. Paul, to both friend and foe, cannot be conceived as idle or slothful. He was a man to whom thought, and activity were as automatic as breathing. Even while in Rome, a man under guarded arrest, he was able to teach and make Christians of some unusual material, even including those of "Caesar's household," i.e. part of the staff that served Nero. The time frame is now the early A.D. 60's, and the growth of the Church is dynamic, but perhaps a bit different than before. More Greek and other Gentile names begin to appear in correspondence, and the Church is taking upon itself a decidedly more Gentile tone and complexion. A generation after his selection on the road to Damascus, God was quite aptly pleased with Paul as the chosen apostle to the Gentiles.

Before Paul's story is fully told his path once more would have to intersect with the emperor Nero, whose final years demand observation elucidation. This pudgy little man of enormous power, still only in his twenties, continued a rapid dissipation and degeneration.

The evening of July 18, A.D. 64, was hot and humid in Rome, when at the great stadium of the Circus Maximus a fire crackled to life. Starting in some flammable construction materials the conflagration soon become a monster unlike anything anyone had ever seen. Its spread was rapid, and within six days ten of the fourteen administrative districts were burned to the ground, totally destroyed. The remaining four were severely damaged, and soon the catastrophe, which had taken tens of thousands of lives, was known simply by the title that remains today, the Great Fire of Rome. Few now believe that Emperor Nero in any manner instigated the fire. He was not present in Rome at the time but appears to have prompt in directing efforts to combat the blaze. Nero, though, was a politician, the preeminent one in a city that was one of history's great hives of political activity. By this time Nero had fallen precipitously out of favor with the city's ruling class, his profligate spending, high taxation, and debauched lifestyle adding fuel to his own fire. He still retained some favor with the poorer classes, and this grotesque plumpery of a man sought to make a political comeback. Just as plants require water, problem beset politicians require scapegoats. The emperor's was ready made. Someone must be responsible for the horrible catastrophe that had befallen the city, and the finger of blame easily fell upon a strange, new religious sect, the Christians. To the Romans it was a strange cult whose birth was in the still weirder land of Judea, where natives had been eaten up by religious commitment. This new cult, composed of converted Jews and Romans of the lowest rungs of the plebian class and slaves bore the blame for the fire. Thus, Nero became the first Gentile persecutor of the Church, and the tales of barbarous grotesqueries ordered by him remain current. For our observational purposes, though, we note that he had its most famous teacher, Paul, imprisoned for the second time.

Outside the walls of the prison which held Paul, emperor Nero now came into his own sadistic self. Our primary source is the great Roman historian Tacitus, certainly no friend to

Christianity, but who nonetheless chronicled that Christians were strapped to poles and beams, hoisted above the ground, doused with oil to literally become flaming torches which served as macabre streetlights. The Romans' insatiable appetite for the games of the circus become enriched by the introduction of the "Christians and the Lions," a tableau which yet lingers in the modern conscience. Human flesh was ripped from bones and devoured by half-starved beasts of prey, all for the amusement of the mob of spectators.

Mainly, though, these men and women were like most Christians of all ages, known only by their family, friends and by God and Christ. The story of the early church is told in large measure through the travels and travails of one man, the apostle born out of due season, Paul. What of the other twelve, the men who spent three years in the company of the Savior? Admittedly, both the Biblical and historical records for many are sketchy, traditional, and conjectural. Nonetheless, herein is offered somewhat of a consensus of opinion.

First it was James, the son of Zebedee and brother to John, who within a decade of the Church's founding was the victim of the murdering King Herod Agrippa I in his soon to be squelched rise to Power. The intervention of God stayed Herod's blood-soaked hand as he sought next to slay James's fishing partner and the most prominent of the twelve Peter, who lived a long and incredibly fruitful life. Yet Peter died as Christ had once foretold, crucified by the Romans, likely during the persecutions instigated by Nero. One of the first great evangelists was Peter's younger brother Andrew, whose death, a believable tradition informs us, was upon an x-shaped cross in Greece, a symbol now known as the Cross of St. Andrew and an integral part of the national flag of the United Kingdom. One James was not enough for Jesus, and so He included in His twelve apostles

James, the son of Alpheus, of whom little is recorded outside his listing in the gospels. Traditionally, though, it has long been taught that he was martyred while teaching in Egypt. One of the true outliers among the apostles was Matthew, a despised publican, and the author of the eponymous gospel. Several schools of thought compete for historical recognition, but the most common belief was that he was martyred in Italy in the A.D. 70's. Upon the suicide of the traitor Judas Iscariot a new apostle was selected, a man named Matthias, perhaps the most obscure of the twelve. Tradition, though, speaks of his death by stoning in Judea.

Nathanael (or at times Bartholomew) was the early skeptic of anything which came from Nazareth. Not particularly prominent in historical records he may have ranged as far afield than any other apostle, having gone to India, where he was martyred either by crucifixion or drowning. An apostle who was not hesitant to ask questions of Christ non-Biblical accounts indicate that his later apostolic efforts were concentrated in Phrygia, Syria, and Greece. He was killed likely by crucifixion, in the Greek city of Hierapolis. After his selection by Christ the New Testament remains silent on Simon the Zealot, and the historical records are not plentiful. He is identified as having preached in both Iberia and Gaul (modern Spain, Portugal, and France), and if, the Roman Catholic traditional teaching is true he may have died the worst death of any of the apostles, being sawn in half. Thaddeus (also known as Jude) was the author of one of the Bible's shortest books, and he is believed to have died in Syria in A.D. 65 at the hands of an axman. Thomas, whose very name is quite unfairly linked to doubt, traveled to India, was quite successful, but died by being impaled on spears.

So long before while all these men were young did they re-cline in that upper room in Jerusalem and enraptured listen to the foreboding words of their Master:

> "The time cometh that whosoever killeth you
> will think that he doeth God service."

To the powerful executing authorities each man was worthy of death and had to die for the good of God, or the gods, for Rome, the Law of Moses or whatever. Those who kill gener-ally make at least an attempt for justification by enswathing the bloody act in the garb of nobility or the public interest. One remained, though, the man who in his early days had inflicted much suffering upon the disciples but now was at the end of a long journey where he himself suffered as much as any person who ever lived. One day he was awakened, bound, and taken from a filthy dungeon cell, and this frail man in his sixties was summarily and likely without ceremony beheaded. No record of Paul's words in these last moments exists, but this was a man who understood what death was to a Christian when earlier he had penned:

> "To live is Christ, to die is gain."

It is now time to account for the one man who was respon-sible for so much death, Nero himself. Following the Great Fire any popularity he may have gained from killing Christians (and even this is doubtful) was dissipated and he continued a person-al and political decline. He forced his longtime advisor Seneca to commit suicide. When his wife Poppaea died in AD 65, ei-ther from childbirth or Nero's own murdering hand, Nero went into a lengthened period of melodramatic mourning. He went so far in the year 67 to "marry" a young boy named Sporus, who resembled the deceased Poppaea and had him castrated in an attempt to make him a woman, the emperor apparently being an early enthusiast of the LGBTQ agenda.

Romans, though, were accustomed to the bizarre personal lives of their rulers, and this alone was unlikely to bring down an emperor. Nero's tax policies had become so onerous that powerful people began to rebel, and assassination conspiracies were plentiful. Finally, Nero knew that it was death for him to remain in Rome and left for the port of Ostia in anticipation of a journey to the eastern provinces. The Senate had declared him a public enemy, and his foes finally ran him to ground ion a small villa outside Rome. All his companions advised him to commit suicide, but this porcine pervert, at whose hand so many had been killed, was too cowardly to so act. A servant then drove the knife home. Even as he gasped his last breaths he remained a buffoon, uttering his final words:

"Oh, what an artist dies in me."

Sic transit gloria.

It was now the year 68, to historians the year of the Four Emperors. In succession to Nero came three non-entities known as Galba, Otho, Vitellius, all abject failures at playing the Roman power game, for all were assassinated. Rome would survive all this, for in so many ways ancient Rome was and to this day remains great. The Empire would settle for it was still within the Pax Romana, the Roman Peace, where no foreign power posed a serious threat to the rulers on the Tiber. The maddened almost rabid scramble for the emperor's throne would be calmed somewhat, and whatever their character Rome for decades would begin to flourish under the leadership of a series of stable emperors, mostly extending through the second century AD. To other far greater and more learned scholarship we defer to a scholastic treasure of major works written on the Roman Empire, volumes that chronicle all conceivable tides of movements and the activities of the great and the good of ancient time. As does every listening thing, though, Rome would be in a continual state of change. For centuries its parameters and influence remained great, but internally it was and did become a different power. Rome was always Rome, but it would become less that Italian city on the Tiber and more of a multi-national and multi-ethnic conglomerate spread from east to west and north to south far-flung boundaries.

For our interests, though, Rome maintained a certain sporadic behavior, a greatly inconsistent behavior in regard to its attitudes towards the Church and Christianity. For over two centuries persecution was real, but it was sporadic and often localized. The depth, intensity and locale of persecution would often depend upon the identity of the emperor, the governor or local politicians at a given place and time. Yet untold numbers of disciples were harassed, tortured, and perished at the whims of Rome, so much that in the final pages of the New Testament God referenced Rome as:

> "The mother of harlots and abominations of the earth. And I saw the woman drunken with the blood of the saints, and with the blood of the martyrs of Jesus: and when I saw her, I wondered with great admiration."

The number of Christians who suffered and died at the hands of Rome is known but to God, but known to us is that in 325 A.D. Emperor Constantine, albeit clothed in his personal understanding of the faith, accepted Christianity. Old Rome itself, mighty Rome, and for all its faults, flaws, and grotesqueries a legitimate point of admiration even today, began to die. The rise, glory, decline and death of Rome has long maintained its own academic discipline and study. Opinions, theories, assertions, and the like are as the sand of the seashore, innumerable. The date of A.D. 476 was long asserted as the terminus of the Roman Empire (at least in the West), for this was the date when the last Roman emperor, a young man named Romulus Augustulus, was deposed by a German king, Odoacer. Except for the handful of individuals directly involved in this overthrow, though, it is unlikely few even noticed. The Rome of antiquity, the mighty Rome of the Bible with Augustus, Pilate, Nero, and others had already died. Ordinary persons, communities and certainly nations had long since ceased to fear the tread of Roman armies and the sting of Roman power. The same first century Biblical account which bespoke of Rome as the "great harlot", but a few verses later described her "... great is fallen, is fallen..." Rome had a type of earthly glory and grandeur, but it was buried long ago. The power, real at one time, had ceased, and it went to the grave with the corpse of a mighty civilization.

Centuries passed before Rome faded from the terrestrial scene, and the Empire itself was the instrument of death for so many. No conquest, no campaign, and no battle in which its legionaries fought, though equaled the First Jewish War of 66-70 A.D. Military campaigns, strategies and tactics are not the meaning of this work, and so we find Roman armies under a general, later an emperor named Titus, in 70 A.D. surrounding and besieging the city of Jerusalem. No military clash in history has ever been the subject of more foretelling than this. We elide over Old Testament prophecies and even apostolic comments but rather focus our gaze on the predictions made by

Christ Himself only days before His crucifixion. His story of
the prophecy of Jerusalem's destruction, made in the late 20's
A.D., is too lengthy for a full quotation but the more salient
declarations foreshadow horrible death and destruction at the
hands of the Romans. Addressing His fellow Jews the Savior
spoke darkly:

> "Then shall be great tribulation, since as was not
> since the beginning of the world to this time, nor
> ever shall be. And except those days should be
> shortened, there should no flesh be saved, but
> for the elects sake those days shall be shortened."

The Jewish people, by virtue of heritage and character never
made an easy people to push around, and finally in 66 A.D. the
small nation had exploded in rebellion. The Jews were not easily reconquered, but eventually the Romans pushed them back
to Jerusalem, to which they laid siege. Starvation became common and to the Jews whom the Romans captured no quarter
was shown. Thousands were crucified before the city's walls,
and the still living Jews saw a preview of what awaited them.
The Romans finally broke through, and the death and destruction rendered has tested the creative pens of many authors. For
millennia it has been a figurative cliché that the "streets ran
red with blood." In Jerusalem it was no figure of speech, for the
streets flowed with the life's blood of the people. Depending
upon the source and the historian tens of thousands to hundreds of thousands perished. Survivors were ill-treated, women
defiled, and they and children sold into the abominable abyss of
ancient slavery. The male survivors who were deemed worthy
were conscripted to the short brutal life of gladiators. The remainder were unceremoniously slaughtered.

Even in the agony of carrying the cross on the Via Dolorosa on that Friday, Christ spoke to the women who were weeping at His dilemma:

> "Daughters of Jerusalem, weep not for Me, but weep for yourselves, and for your children.For behold, the days are coming, in the which that they shall say, Blessed are the barren, and the wombs that never bore, and the paps which never gave suck."

That day came, and Jerusalem was destroyed, and it was dead. Yes, a city was rebuilt and exists today, but the Old Jerusalem of the Testaments had perished. Among other talents when necessary the Roman soldiery could destroy more thoroughly than any army that ever marched. Ancient buildings, monuments, all gone, as well as even the Great Temple, of which Christ had spoken:

> "There shall not be left here one stone upon another, that shall not be thrown down."

Even more importantly, though, were the human casualties. The old Levitical priesthood begun with Aaron, the brother of Moses, was dead. It had been held and the power of the chief priesthood relished by men such as Annas, Caiaphas, and Ananias, all of whom were dead. With the destruction of Jerusalem came the historical vaporization of a family whose tentacles clung to the Jewish people for ever a century, the Herods. Herod the Great, Herod Antipas and Herod Agrippa were all dead, and soon would be Herod Agrippa II, the last of the family with any historical cachet.

At the outset of the Church's birth the Church and Christ's greatest earthly persecutors were those of the Jewish establishment, but their power was no longer real. For centuries the Jewish people would struggle just to survive.

Island of Light and Life

All of this world's lives end in the tragedy of death, and the brief story of Christ's Church in its early years is strong confirmation. The first century Anno Domini (A.D. – the "year of out Lord") was rolling to its conclusion, and we indulge in a review of brevity. The players in the Gospels, Mary and Joseph, the apostles, the early Christians and probably most, if not all of the second generation of disciples has passed from this world. By 90 A.D. not only they but the villains of our story lay dead and buried. No more did the Jewish priesthood, the scribes, Sadducees, and Pharisees persecute and torment the early Christians. The Herods were now settling into the ignominy of historical toxicity. The majestic Roman rulers, from the great Augustus to the evil and opprobrious Caligula and Nero had long since bled their last. From the old days of the founding of the Church of Christ Himself on Pentecost nobody seemed to remain. Death, Satan's great gift to the world had claimed all.

All but one. Readers with a meticulous eye may have noted that earlier in this chapter when an inventory of the fates of the initial twelve apostles was offered, only eleven were noted. As late as circa 90 A.D. one remained, an aged exile on the tiny island of Patmos in the eastern Mediterranean Sea. When he first appeared in the gospels he was a headstrong robust young fisherman, who with his older brother James had been called the Sons of Thunder by Christ Himself. No man ever lived who saw more of the great events of life than did this apostle John, now a frail aged man, a persecuted exile on the Isle of Patmos. The Romans had placed him there, forgotten by all, and what remained of life was to wither and like everyone else, die. Even in its final act life can be replete with surprises, and this man, the "beloved disciple," the apostle who was personally closest to Jesus was to witness its greatest Revelation, for now John was summoned to write the Book of Revelation, the most complex and enigmatic of all scripture, and far beyond the scope of this work.

To John, though, it was light and life which was revealed. One of the revelations confirmed to him was that this world, this "terrestrial orb" is just that temporal, i.e. temporary, not in any manner built to last beyond its intended purpose. Just as all the Romans, the Jews, the pagans, and the Christians of the first century world have lone since perished so will we and all that we see, hear and touch. Yet it was Christ who said that.

"He is not the God of the dead, but of the living."

It was Jesus, touched by the immense sorrow and grief of his friends Martha and Mary who reached the heights of heaven, of beauty and of promise with:

"I am the resurrection and the life: he that be-lieveth in me, though he were dead, yet shall he live. And whosoever liveth and believeth on me shall never die."

It was the great apostle Paul, who nearing the end, identified his alternatives as:

"To live is Christ. To die is gain."

Beautifully and earlier he had expressed in triumphant mockery of the fear of death:

> "O death, where is thy sting? O grave, where is thy victory?"

Finally, as he was closing his book in a few words which sprang from his emotional core John implored:

> "Even so, come (quickly), Lord Jesus."

Still, it is appropriate that the only man who consistently claimed that He was Life, itself but yet both suffered and conquered death should provide the most salient wording on the subject. Towards the end of this life and ministry Christ assured His disciples of His permanence:

> "Heaven and earth shall pass away, but My words shall not pass away."

So, in the end just how powerful was Christ and was there any permanence in His work? On the coasts of Caesarea Philippi, standing amidst His apostles and surrounded by stone sculptures of pagan idols He spoke:

> "Upon this rock (His being the son of the Living God) I will build my Church; and the gates of hell shall not prevail against it."

That is power, real power.

www.ingramcontent.com/pod-product-compliance
Lightning Source LLC
LaVergne TN
LVHW051457080426
835509LV00017B/1787